raising the Sum of Two thousand Pounds Sterling, to be disposed of as now about to order.

It has been an op... ...Es.
from his Ancestors, is under some kind of obligation to transmit the s...
to their Posterity: This obligation does not lie on me, who never inher...
a Shilling from any Ancestor or Relation. I shall however, if it is n...
diminished by some accident before my Death, leave a considerable
Estate among my Descendants and Relations: The above observation...
made merely as some apology to my Family, for my making Bequests th...
do not appear to have any immediate relation to their advantage.

I was born in Boston, New England, and owe my first
instructions in Literature, to the free Grammar Schools established t...
I have therefore already considered those Schools in my Will. But I am
under obligations to the State of the Massachusetts, for having unask...
appointed me formerly their Agent in England with a handsome Salar...
which continued some Years; and altho I accidentally lost, in their servi...
by transmitting Governor Hutchinson's Letters, much more than the am...
of what they gave me, I do not think that ought in the least to deminis...
my Gratitude.

I have considered that among Artisans good Apprentic...
are most likely to make good Citizens; and having myself been bred to a
manual Art Printing, in my native Town, and afterwards assisted t...
...ness in Philadelphia by kind S... of Money from two S...
there which was the foundation of my Fortune, and of all the utility in
that may be ascribed to me, I wish to be useful even after my Death, i...
possible, in forming and advancing other young men that may be ser...
able to their Country in both those Towns.

To this End I devote Two thousand Pounds Sterling, whi...
give, one thousand thereof to the Inhabitants of the Town of Boston, in ...
...chusetts, and the other thousand to the Inhabitants of the City of Phil...
...phia, in Trust to and for the Uses, Intents and Purposes herein aft...
mentioned and declared.

The said Sum of One thousand Pounds Sterling, if accept...
by the Inhabitants of the Town of Boston, shall be managed under
direction of the Select Men united with the Ministers of the oldest
episcopalian, Congregational and Presbyterian Churches in that To...
who are to let out the same upon Interest at five per Cent per Annu...
to such young married Artificers, under the Age of twenty five Ye...
as have served an Apprenticeship in the said Town, and faithfully
fulfilled the Duties required in their Indentures, so as to obtain a
moral Character from at least two respectable Citizens, who are t...
to become their Sureties in a Bond with the Applicants for the Rep...
of th... ...ies so... ...th Interest according to the Terms herei...

BENJAMIN FRANKLIN'S LAST BET

The Favorite Founder's

Divisive Death,

Enduring Afterlife,

and

Blueprint for

American Prosperity

Also by Michael Meyer

The Last Days of Old Beijing

In Manchuria

The Road to Sleeping Dragon

BENJAMIN FRANKLIN'S LAST BET

Michael Meyer

MARINER BOOKS

Boston   New York

Endpapers taken from Benjamin Franklin's Will and Codicil, June 23, 1789.
Courtesy of the American Philosophical Society.

HarperCollins books may be purchased for educational, business, or sales promotional use.
For information, please email the Special Markets Department at SPsales@harpercollins.com.

FIRST EDITION

Library of Congress Cataloging-in-Publication Data
has been applied for.
ISBN 978-1-328-56889-2

Designed by The Cosmic Lion

22 23 24 25 LSC 10 9 8 7 6 5 4 3 2 1

For Adam Hochschild
and
Georges Borchardt

If you wou'd not be forgotten
As soon as you are dead and rotten,
Either write things worth reading,
Or do things worth the writing.

– Poor Richard's Almanack

The meaning of life is that it ends.

– Franz Kafka

Contents

Act III
REBIRTH, 1904 and Beyond

Introduction

All About
the Benjamins

I took a wide route to this story, one that its subject might have appreciated. Benjamin Franklin was long fascinated by China, especially its inventions, silk production, and agriculture. In 1770, while living in London, he excitedly mailed a packet of bean seeds to a botanist friend back in Philadelphia. Franklin's letter included an "account of the universal use of a cheese made of them, in China, which so excited my curiosity." This was North America's first recorded description of the food that Franklin spelled as "Tau-fu."

Packets of Chinese rice and tree seeds followed. After filling a front page of his *Pennsylvania Gazette* with the sayings of Confucius, Franklin once scored the margins of a traveler's account of visiting the Middle Kingdom with his own calculations of the journey's time and costs.

Visiting China proved to be a bridge too far for him, but I made the journey in 1995, as one of its first Peace Corps volunteers. I knew far less about the place on arrival than Franklin would have. But I ended up staying in China for over a decade, and writing a trilogy of books about life in its overlooked corners.

After I moved back to the United States, a fellow Midwesterner I had met in China, working for then vice president Joe Biden, added my name to the guest list for a lunch welcoming the Chinese leader Hu Jintao on his 2011 state visit. I picked my first suit off a Herald Square clearance rack and boarded the train south to Washington, D.C.

When seen from the C Street sidewalk, the U.S. State Department building does, as a critic frowned at its unveiling, look as nondescript as a chewing gum factory. To me, the edifice also appeared incongruously familiar. Its unadorned limestone façade and rectangular rigidity would not look out of place in Soviet Moscow or Mao-era Beijing.

Inside, however, the State Department's plush Diplomatic Reception Rooms belie the building's exterior austerity. Picture herringbone wood floors the color of fresh honey, Chippendale sofas, brass andirons, Paul Revere silver, and the type of heavy curtains that catch fire in old movies. The luncheon guests did not wear name tags, because everyone seemed to know one another. Even the Chinese officials looked relaxed, which was a first. Barbra Streisand chatted with Colin Powell. Yo-Yo Ma cradled his cello upon a dais.

Feeling self-conscious, I sidled out of the chandeliered dining hall and stepped into an adjoining room, empty of people. *Without coincidence,* as the Chinese saying holds, *there would be no story.* As I leaned, exhaling, on a polished writing table, an unseen voice snapped: "Please don't touch that."

A young, uniformed Marine guard stepped forward from the wainscoting.

"Sorry," I said, straightening, attempting to hide my embarrassment. "Is it old?"

"That's the table where Benjamin Franklin signed the Treaty of Paris."

I had forgotten that he had done this, let alone what the agreement had settled. The Marine told me that the State Dining Room was named for Franklin, known as the father of the Foreign Service. Franklin was the first American expatriate, the Marine continued. He crossed the Atlantic eight times, and between 1757 and 1785, he spent only three years on American soil. I had been carrying a bit of him on my own travels. Embossed on my blue passport cover was the motto

E pluribus unum—"Out of many, one"—which Franklin had helped select for the Great Seal.

The Marine pointed to the room's porcelain sculpture of Franklin and Louis XVI signing the 1778 Treaty of Alliance, which brought crucial French support for American independence. The figurine depicts the twenty-four-year-old king in courtly attire, facing the seventy-two-year-old commoner wearing a beaver-fur-collared robe. The Marine then directed my attention to an oil portrait that shows Franklin dressed in the same simple clothes. In Paris, Franklin played up his Americanness, refusing to powder his shoulder-length hair. Sweating through a cheap, ill-fitting suit, I admiringly added "business casual" to Franklin's long list of inventions.

The lights flickered, calling guests to lunch, and I reluctantly left the erudite Marine. Sitting in the ballroom's farthest seat at the farthest table from the dignitaries, I suddenly felt stupid. I knew far more about Chinese dynasties than the basic foundations of my own country. In China, one constantly hears residents boast of their civilization's "five thousand years of history," even if their compatriots have spent nearly as many years smashing its heritage to pieces. There is a profundity in what remains. The dilapidated Beijing courtyard where I had lived predated the American Revolution, and had the plumbing to match. Its neighborhood's dense tangle of alleyways was more than twice as old as the United States itself. History was not in a textbook, but palpable and present. Touching Franklin's table at the State Department delivered that same jolt.

If I had previously thought of Franklin at all, I saw a kite. Then his wizened face, smirking on the hundred-dollar bill, and speaking only in gnomic quips like some American Yoda. But, as Poor Richard charitably put it, "the Wise and Brave dares own that he was wrong."

Back in my room after lunch, I opened my laptop. Where to begin with Benjamin Franklin? I started with the table. Formerly it had lodged at the Hôtel d'York, where Franklin and the American delegation had met the British representative to sign the treaty that recognized America's independence, ending the Revolutionary War. The hotel is gone, but a plaque marks the site, located directly across the Seine from the Louvre. The address, 56 rue Jacob, is now, fittingly, home to a university's Center for International Studies.

One link led to another. I spent the night clicking Franklin, not suspecting that this was the start of a decade-long trail that would wind through Boston and Philadelphia archives, the Library of Congress (whose central entrance is topped with Franklin's bust), his former London town house, and his ancestral Northamptonshire village, nestled amidst fields of beans. To begin with Franklin is to pull on a kite string that keeps pooling at your feet. The man contained multitudes.

Benjamin Franklin invented bifocals, the lightning rod, and a musical instrument called the glass armonica. (Mozart composed a piece for it.) He proved that lightning is electricity, and coined the words *electrician, battery, conductor, positive/negative charge,* and *electric shock.* He founded Pennsylvania's first library and fire department, and co-founded its first hospital and college. (All remain open.) He perfected the odometer and the rocking chair. He designed a better catheter and a more efficient stove. He drew the first American political cartoon: a sliced-up snake captioned JOIN, OR DIE. He explained the northern lights and mapped the Gulf Stream. He also invented swim fins. For his own prowess in the water, Franklin was posthumously inducted into the International Swimming Hall of Fame. He once astounded a party by leaping from a boat and swimming three miles from Chelsea to Blackfriars against the strong tidal current of the river Thames.

As Poor Richard, he spun aphorisms that went viral centuries before this was a thing, including "Fish & Visitors stink in 3 days" and "Three may keep a Secret if two of them are dead."

Not all of his sayings were gems; think of the last time you heard someone utter "Men and Melons are hard to know" or "She that paints her face, thinks of her Tail." Others have been updated, even if unknowingly. It's a short walk from "He who multiplies riches, mul-

The earliest known portrait of Franklin, c. 1746, depicting him in the year he turned forty.

tiplies cares" to "Mo Money Mo Problems," a song by the Notorious B.I.G., who also dubbed hundred-dollar bills "Benjamins."

Some of Poor Richard's most quoted sayings, such as "God helps those who help themselves," actually originated elsewhere. Franklin plucked that one from a vine that ran back to Sophocles in ancient Greece. But then Franklin was an inveterate borrower, starting with his first published essay at the age of sixteen and continuing to his last will and testament, written in his eighty-fourth year.

The line between Franklin fact and Franklin fiction blurred even during his lifetime. Franklin himself hid behind pen names that included Silence Dogood, Martha Careful, and—my favorite—Caelia Shortface. From London in 1774, Franklin wrote a letter of introduction for "an ingenious, worthy young" Englishman looking for work, perhaps as a surveyor. After the immigrant arrived in Philadelphia and published a pamphlet that ignited the movement for American independence, many people, including Thomas Jefferson, suspected that *Common Sense*'s "Thomas Paine" was just another Franklin pseudonym.

Franklin's autobiography is often credited as the first American memoir. Davy Crockett supposedly carried it to his death at the Alamo. Dale Carnegie modeled *How to Win Friends and Influence People* on it. Elon Musk—a fellow electrical visionary—tabbed it as his favorite book. Yet for a man known for his plainspokenness, Franklin could be cagey about his personal life. In his memoir, he characterized his visits to prostitutes as "Intrigues with low Women that fell my Way, which were attended with some Expense and great Inconvenience." He also never publicly revealed who had mothered his firstborn child.

To a modern reader, the autobiography's most glaring omission is that Benjamin Franklin once owned slaves. While he is often described as being a man ahead of his time, such praise elides the fact that Franklin was also a man very much of his time. As a young entrepreneur, Franklin profited from slavery, printing in his weekly *Pennsylvania Gazette* advertisements selling enslaved men and women, or seeking those who had escaped. He earned income, too, from slavery's opponents, publishing in 1729 two of the colonies' first abolitionist tracts, as well as the 1737 book *All Slave-Keepers That Keep the Innocent in Bondage, Apostates,* which excoriated the trade as being "the Mother of all Sins."

Yet during his rise to business and scientific success, Franklin and his family intermittently owned at least six "servants," as he euphemistically called them: King, George, John, Peter and his wife, Jemima, and a boy—their son, perhaps—named Othello. While Franklin's hagiographers have often tucked this uncomfortable truth into the recesses of back chapters, or expurgated it completely, at the time it was no secret.

Because Franklin did not finish his autobiography—the depicted events end in 1757, the year he turned fifty-one—he also failed to recount his conversion to the abolitionist cause. Although influenced by campaigners in Philadelphia and London before the Revolution (during which, Franklin wrote, "a King of England is endeavouring to make Slaves of Freemen!"), the war's aftermath laid bare the hypocrisy of championing American liberty but keeping silent on the fate of its population that remained chained.

In 1787, four years after Franklin signed the Treaty of Paris and one month before the start of the Constitutional Convention, the eighty-one-year-old was elected president of the Pennsylvania Society for Promoting the Abolition of Slavery. In 1790, two months before he died, Franklin submitted the first petition to Congress demanding the end of the barbarous slave trade, as well as "the Improvement of the Conditions of the African Race" in the United States.

His signed appeal challenged the Constitution that Franklin had helped to create. Although it was doomed from the start, Franklin's plea added a final footnote to his legacy, one that he perhaps hoped would set him apart from his fellow founders over time.

Franklin was sensitive to how the public perceived him. "In order to secure my Credit and Character as a Tradesman," he recalled of his beginnings, "I took care not only to be in *Reality* Industrious and frugal, but to avoid all *Appearances* of the Contrary. I drest plainly; I was seen at no Places of idle Diversion . . . and to show that I was not above my Business, I sometimes brought home the Paper I purchas'd at the Stores, thro' the Streets on a Wheelbarrow." After rising to become one of America's best-known writers, Franklin once admitted, "I have frequently heard one or other of my Adages repeated, and I own that to encourage the Practice of remembering and repeating those wise Sentences, I have sometimes *quoted myself* with great Gravity."

Even as his middle-aged science experiments made Franklin America's first transatlantic celebrity, he could be reticent about sharing his mistakes. "Do not make it more Publick," he wrote to his older brother after nearly electrocuting himself ("the crack as loud as a pistol shot") while attempting to cook a turkey with electricity, "for I am Ashamed to have been guilty of so Notorious a Blunder."

Eighteen months later, in 1752, Franklin hoisted a kite into a fulminous sky. Oddly, he never wrote a first-person account of his most famous experiment, which proved that lightning was electricity. His detached description appeared four months later in his *Pennsylvania Gazette,* where in a short paragraph Franklin explained his feat. Step one: Build a kite from a handkerchief. "Silk," he wrote, "is fitter to bear the Wet and Wind of a Thunder Gust without tearing." Step two: Attach a foot-long wire to the frame, and a key to the string. Step three: Welcome a storm. "As soon as any of the Thunder Clouds come over the Kite," Franklin related, "the pointed Wire will draw the Electric Fire from them, and the Kite, with all the Twine, will be electrified, and the loose Filaments of the Twine will stand out every Way, and be attracted by an approaching Finger."

Anyone, he added, could do it. And yet, before him, no one ever had.

In mythology, Prometheus was punished for conducting fire down from heaven. But Franklin was rewarded with honorary degrees and became a living folk hero. "I Sopose you See our Newspapers," his sister Jane wrote from his birthplace of Boston, "where you See how fond our People are to Say Something of Dr Franklin I beleve mostly to do him Honour but some chuse to Embelish the Languge to there own fancy."

After Franklin's death, the parade of his biographers—from the crusading Christian capitalist Parson Weems to the socialist civil rights campaigner W. E. B. Du Bois—painted his portrait from a perspective that illuminated their own times. Virginia Woolf once observed that there are some stories that have to be retold by each generation. As we will see, every generation seems to discover Franklin for themselves.

· · ·

It is true that, if not for Benjamin Franklin's edit of Thomas Jefferson's preamble, the Declaration of Independence would have proclaimed that we hold these truths to be "sacred and undeniable." After John Hancock boldly added his large signature to the document in 1776, legend holds that he turned to his fellow signatories and announced: "We must be unanimous. There must be no pulling different ways; we must all hang together."

"Yes," Franklin purportedly replied. "We must, indeed, all hang together, or most assuredly we shall all hang separately."

Eleven years later, at the Constitutional Convention's conclusion, Franklin is said to have been stopped outside the belfried brick building known today as Independence Hall. A Philadelphian named Eliza Powell supposedly asked the eighty-one-year-old, "Well, doctor, what we got, a republic or a monarchy?"

"A republic," Franklin replied, "if you can keep it."

He was so frail then that prisoners from the Walnut Street Jail often carried him in a sedan chair to the sessions, held less than two blocks from his home. Two years later, Franklin wrote to a friend in France that although the Constitution had "an appearance that promises permanency . . . in this world nothing can be said to be certain, except death and taxes." Less remembered is that this witticism came as he faced his own inevitability. "My health continues much as it has been for some time," Franklin's letter continued, "except that I grow thinner and weaker, so that I cannot expect to hold out much longer."

He died five months later, maligned in his final days by the republic he helped to build. There would be no state funeral, and the nation that grieved most would not be his own.

History has, of course, reversed this cold shoulder. Franklin's face remains—as he boasted to his daughter more than two centuries ago—as recognizable as the moon's. In fact, one of its large impact craters is named for him, as are schools, bridges, stadiums, streets, parks, a zoo, this typeface, a genus of flowering tree, one of the world's tallest giant sequoias, and mountains—in Alaska and New Hampshire—that bookend the United States. According to the U.S. Postal

Service, Franklin is America's most common place-name. The first of these thirty-one towns, platted in Massachusetts, wrote to Franklin in 1785, asking for money to purchase a church bell. Instead, the seventy-nine-year-old sent them 116 books, "Sense being preferable to Sound." That same year, he sat for a French portraitist, whose rendering is engraved on American currency.

What could there possibly be left to say about Benjamin Franklin? He appears to be self-evident, as elemental to history as water is to earth. Over the centuries, bookshelves have progressively sagged with titles recounting his remarkable life. Here, for a change, is the untold story of his inspiring afterlife.

On the same day my clumsy handprint inadvertently summoned his ghost to the table, I stumbled upon Franklin's last will and testament. Initially, only one line on my laptop's screen captured my attention: "My timepiece, that stands in my library," Franklin directed, "I give to my grandson William Temple Franklin. I give him also my Chinese gong."

Try as I might, I never did find that gong. Instead, I found this tale, one barely hinted at by the end of his doorstop biographies, which conclude when the founder is laid to rest. Poor Richard warned that "Bad Commentators spoil the best of books," and so I say this with all respect for the many authors who have followed Franklin before me: writing a biography of water might well require tracking down fewer sources. (My more than eight hundred citations, along with a time line, appear in the back pages.) But even after the cemetery gates—and those other book covers—are shut, there remains one last bit of narrative string to pull. It holds a charge, still, pulsing from his past down to our present.

In his will, as in his life, the forefather of American philanthropy gave generously. And much like the adages of his many alter egos, Franklin's gifts came with lessons attached. To his fractured family, he left inheritances that publicized his core beliefs: loyalty and patriotism, racial and gender equality, education and public service. But before signing away the last of his fortune, Franklin drew up an imaginative scheme.

At a time when the demise of the United States seemed more likely than its success—when the banking system was fledgling and the dollar so unstable that it had yet to be made the official currency—Franklin placed a final bet on the "rising generation" of young tradesmen.

To his hometowns of Boston and Philadelphia, he gifted twin funds to jump-start what we now call blue-collar careers. The money was to be continually doled out in low-interest loans across two hundred years. On the bicentennial of his death, the accounts—fattened by centuries of earning compound interest—could be cashed out and spent on civic improvements.

Franklin believed that skilled workers formed the foundation of American democracy. They provided crucial services while interacting daily with people of all classes, creeds, and colors. Essentially, they kept the pulse of a community's street-level public and economic life and laid the groundwork (literally) of a healthy society. "Good apprentices," Franklin wrote in his will, "are most likely to make good citizens."

What happened to Franklin's fortune and his hopeful wager on the working class? Surprisingly, given the swings in the nation's fortunes between the eighteenth and twentieth centuries, his bet paid off, although not in the manner, or with the results, that he had predicted. But like the lessons from his life, Franklin's death has much to teach us still.

"The slightest events in the life of a famous man," eulogized one of his Parisian friends, "become the most interesting, when they give birth to a new way of thinking that all of a sudden changes the direction of his will."

Where to begin with Benjamin Franklin? This story starts at his end.

Act I

DEATH

1789–1791

"My earnest desire to be useful"

Philadelphians who picked up the *Pennsylvania Gazette* on April 21, 1790, learned that in the national capital of New York City, Congress was debating whether counterfeiters should be hanged. Another article reported that a sloop had run into a heavy gale off Nantucket, and "T. Edwards a seaman was lost overboard." Below this came good news from "the Indian country." Native chiefs had received the Cherokee agent Bennet Ballew's explanation of the new federal Constitution "with great alacrity." Ballew would soon be shot down by a Creek named Mad Dog, but on the *Gazette*'s crowded front page, he lived still, "hoping to bring about the glorious work of civilization."

Yet how many readers on that spring day even noticed these stories? For there, placed dead center on the broadsheet, black-bordered and as long and leaden as a casket, lay this news:

> On Saturday night last departed this life, in the 85th year of his age, Dr. BENJAMIN FRANKLIN, of this City. His Remains will be interred THIS AFTERNOON, at four o'clock, in Christ-Church burial-ground.

No obituary followed, which was common in this slower era of worsted hose and whickering cart horses. Printers set type by hand, so breaking stories — Franklin had died four days earlier — tended to run short. But then, did any American need to be reminded of Franklin's achievements? The rival *Federal Gazette*'s eight-line story on his passing admitted, "It is impossible for a newspaper to increase his fame." The *Massachusetts Centinal*'s five lines said that the world was too well acquainted with Franklin's virtues and services "to need any attempt of ours at a recital."

Though longer, the *Pennsylvania Gazette*'s notice also omitted Franklin's biography, including the fact that after purchasing the paper at the age of twenty-three, he had made it colonial America's most read publication. Instead, the *Gazette* printed his physician's account of Franklin's last days, spent surrounded by family and friends, and an air of *"Jeux D'esprit"* that burst when the abscess on his lung finally erupted. This empyema, the doctor related, "discharged a great quantity of matter," after which Franklin's "organs of respiration became gradually oppressed. A calm, lethargic state succeeded, and on the 17th about 11 o'clock at night, he quietly expired, closing a long and useful life of 84 years and 3 months."

Franklin's last words were not reported then, nor did the article reveal who was beside him in his final moments, or — just as tellingly — who was not. Those details would emerge in the coming weeks, with the publication of Franklin's will. The *Gazette* story ended with a reminder that this had been the third time Franklin had contracted pleurisy, an inflammation of the tissue separating the lungs from the chest wall that makes breathing sound and feel like two pieces of sandpaper rubbing together. The first occurrence of the extremely painful condition had nearly suffocated him at age nineteen.

History had been bent by Franklin's recovery then. The *Gazette*'s death notice gave no indication of how his legacy would continue to inspire and inflame people on both sides of the Atlantic.

Despite his scabrous lungs, Franklin ended up living more than twice as long as the average American at the time. As a barrel-chested young printer, strengthened by pushing those wheelbarrows of paper and carrying heavy trays of type, Franklin was an early fitness guru. He dabbled in vegetarianism and argued that exercise was most effective through intensity, not duration, making him an early proponent of aerobic training. As a Boston teen, Franklin trained himself to survive a shipwreck by swimming miles-long circuits in the ocean with a book-filled suitcase strapped to his back.

While working in a London printshop, an eighteen-year-old Franklin recorded the effects of lead poisoning. The affliction could be prevented, he theorized, by wearing gloves when handling the metallic letters and washing one's hands before eating. To his co-workers' incredulity, Franklin never got sick. They also couldn't believe that this upstart refused to drink pints of ale with them throughout the day, instead favoring nonalcoholic refreshments. The men, innocent as to why a sober Franklin outworked them, teasingly called him "the Water-American."

In middle age, Franklin favored taking cold-air "baths," for which he stripped naked and sat in front of an open window. "I rise early almost every morning," he explained to a friend, "and sit in my chamber, without any clothes whatever, half an hour or an hour, according to the season, either reading or writing. This practice is not in the least painful, but on the contrary, agreeable." He did not record what his neighbors thought of their view.

A century before Louis Pasteur's germ theory, Franklin held that the common cold was spread by contagion. His remedy was ventilation and air circulation, as he expounded during a fractious night in bed with John Adams. In 1776, the pair traveled to Staten Island to parley with the British in an attempt to end the Revolutionary War. The inn had but one vacancy, a small room with a tiny window. Adams shut it because, as he recorded in his diary, "I was afraid of the evening air."

"Come," Franklin replied, "open the window and come to bed. I believe you are not acquainted with my theory of colds."

Adams was forty then and deferred to his seventy-year-old elder. He dryly recorded that Franklin "began a harangue upon air and cold and respiration and perspiration with which I was so much amused that I soon fell asleep, and left him and his philosophy together."

Neither man caught a cold that night. Adams, however, became infected by an enmity that flared and festered during their posting as American ministers to France, where for nine years Franklin shone as the caressed favorite of court and commoners alike. Adams resented Franklin's charm offensive, which, in order to secure French support for the Revolutionary War, saw the elderly widower flirting, attending late-running soirées, and conducting science experiments with Parisian peers. Only months before the signing of the Treaty of Paris, James Madison reported to Thomas Jefferson, "Congress yesterday received from Mr. Adams several letters not remarkable for any thing unless it be a display of his vanity, his prejudice against the French Court & his venom against Doctr. Franklin."

Seven years later, as Franklin lay dying in his Philadelphia bed, Adams — then serving as the United States' first vice president — peevishly fumed to a friend, "The History of our Revolution will be one continued Lye from one End to the other. The Essence of the whole will be that Dr Franklins electrical Rod, Smote the Earth and out Spring General Washington. That Franklin electrified him with his Rod — and thence forward these two conducted all the Policy Negotiations Legislation and War."

Yet Adams was also self-aware enough to consider how this gripe would be read by posterity. "If this Letter should be preserved," he continued, "and read a hundred Years hence the Reader will say 'the Envy of this J.A. could not bear to think of the Truth'! But this my Friend, to be Serious, is the Fate of all Ages and Nations . . . No Nation can adore more than one Man at a time."

Upon his death thirteen days later, Benjamin Franklin was not that man.

• • •

Ten months earlier, in June 1789, an ailing Franklin, tucked in at Franklin Court — his self-designed two-story home in Philadelphia, set steps away from today's Independence Hall — suddenly remembered his promise to add a final beneficiary to his last will and testament.

Franklin's waking moments then were scored by the pain caused by a stone passing with excruciating slowness from his kidney to his bladder, along with other maladies — not least of which was eighteenth-century medicine. To relieve the stone, he drank a vile and dangerous tonic made of water, quicklime, and soap lye.

Franklin was tended by his only daughter, Sarah — called Sally — and her son Benjamin Franklin Bache, known as Benny. Franklin had trained his namesake in the tools of his trade and proudly wrote to his former Parisian neighbors that the nineteen-year-old had started working on his own in Franklin's former printshop.

Benny's work ethic stood in contrast with that of Franklin's other grandson William Temple Franklin, called Temple. Franklin nonetheless adored this twenty-nine-year-old, the sole offspring of his only surviving son, William. After years of dissolution, Temple was attempting life as a gentleman farmer on his father's former lands, located across the Delaware River in New Jersey. This square of heirs — children William and Sally, grandsons Temple and Benny — was due to receive the bulk of Franklin's sizable estate, consisting of property, manuscripts, diplomatic gifts, scientific and printing equipment, sundry banknotes, and a tract of land in Canada.

Each gift would come wrapped, metaphorically, in a moral, one that Franklin knew would be reported in the press. In his will, he also left money to the Pennsylvania legislature "to be employed for making the river Schuylkill navigable." Beyond improving Philadelphia's watery western border, the bequest barely concealed an undercurrent of rectitude. Franklin instructed that the money would equal the uncollected salary "due to me as President of the State," as the governorship was then called.

At the Constitutional Convention the year before, Franklin had argued that elected officials should not be paid. "There are two Passions which have a powerful Influence in the Affairs of Men," he told delegates. "These are *Ambition* and *Avarice;* the Love of Power, and the Love of Money." If an office became a "Place of Profit," Franklin warned, it would only attract "the Bold and the Violent, the Men of strong Passions and [in]defatigable Activity in their selfish Pursuits. These will thrust themselves to your Government and be your Rulers."

James Madison—who had proposed that congressional salaries be pegged to the average price of wheat—wrote in his notes that Franklin's idea "was treated with great respect, but rather for the author of it, than from any apparent conviction of its expedience or practicability."

Yet, for three years starting in 1785, when he was appointed as Pennsylvania governor for consecutive one-year terms, Franklin put his money where his mouth was, refusing to be paid. When term limits ended his tenure, Franklin's ledger showed that the state still owed him "£2250 paper money." Converting historic currency into its modern equivalent is an inexact science, but at the time, £1 sterling equaled $4.44. Franklin's foresworn wages, then, totaled approximately $10,000, or, when accounting for inflation, around $300,000 at the time of this writing—but with a purchasing power of millions.

Franklin could afford to forgo a salary. His success as a printer had allowed him to experience, he wrote, "the Truth of the Observation, 'that after getting the first hundred pound, it is more easy to get the second': Money itself being of a prolific nature."

Yet he had previously profited handsomely from public service. After the British appointed Franklin postmaster of Philadelphia in 1737, he overturned his predecessor's rivalrous ban on the *Pennsylvania Gazette* from traveling freely in the mails, as favored publications could do. The result was a rise in his paper's circulation and revenue. After Franklin was promoted to joint postmaster general of the American colonies in 1753, he increased delivery speed by ordering carriers to ride at night, and, in an age when citizens usually fetched their mail at the post office, he introduced home delivery.

Carriers trod a well-worn path to Franklin's front door. He was a voluminous correspondent at a time when writing a letter meant inking a quill and scratching it across fibrous paper commonly made not from wood pulp, but from old sails, hempen ropes, and rags. His surviving letters number nearly eight thousand. Panning this river of words reveals the many aspects of his character, and also the genesis of his parting gifts.

In October 1788, three months after signing his last will and testament, the eighty-two-year-old Franklin wrote to a friend, "I am diligently employed in writing the History of my Life." As with his will, he intended his autobiography to teach. He hoped that the book would benefit "the young reader, by showing him from my example, and my success in emerging from poverty, and acquiring some degree of wealth, power, and reputation, the advantages of certain modes of conduct which I observed."

Among the lessons was one gleaned from his work as a tradesman and small business owner, where a broken promise, missed deadline, or late payment could lead to ruin. "I grew convinc'd," Franklin wrote, "that *Truth, Sincerity and Integrity* in Dealings between Man and Man were of the utmost Importance to the Felicity of Life."

Yet when writing the manuscript, he could be as circumspect as a self-preserving politician. To a friend, he admitted omitting "all facts and transactions that may not have a tendency to benefit . . . and the errors which were prejudicial to me."

But it is these small facts that provide a glimpse of the man behind his righteous mask. In his memoir, Franklin recounted visiting his father's ancestral East Midlands village. There, in Ecton, he discovered that he was "the youngest Son of the youngest Son for 5 Generations back." Only in a private letter did Franklin candidly continue, "Whereby I find that had there originally been any Estate in the Family none could have stood a worse Chance for it."

The same section of the autobiography relates Franklin's visit to the parish churchyard to pay respects at the family graves. Only in a private letter to his wife did Franklin reveal that his relatives' tombstones "were so covered with moss that we could not read the letters," until

Peter, the slave who "behaves very well to me," knelt and "scoured them clean."

In the same year that Franklin worked on his memoir, he also wrote to the governors of northern states, urging them to forbid their shipyards to build boats for slave trading, "a practice which is so evidently repugnant to the political principles and form of government lately adopted by the Citizens of the United States." One recipient, the governor of New Hampshire, later helped shelter Oney Judge, a woman who, after being born into slavery at Mount Vernon, escaped from George Washington's President's House in Philadelphia.

Franklin never rose to that level of action. The men and women he held in bondage appear to have died before him, or run away, unpursued. While in an earlier version of his will, written in 1757, Franklin had ordered the release of the slaves Peter and Jemima upon his death, his final will and testament mentioned a different name. In it, Franklin directed the cancellation of the large debt owed to him by his son-in-law—calculated to the shilling at £2,172.5—on the condition that he "immediately after my decease manumit and set free his negro man Bob."

Only from the grave would Franklin legally emancipate his first slave. It would not be one he had owned.

My Constitution is much broken," Franklin admitted to a friend in May 1789, "but I am still among the living." In another letter written on the same day at Franklin Court, he reflected, "My Friends drop off one after another, when my Age and Infirmities prevent my making new ones . . . so that the longer I live I must expect to be more wretched."

Franklin was mostly bedbound in this, the last year of his life. An invoice from his druggist shows recurring orders of castor oil, peppermint water, smelling salts, and the brandy-based laxative named Daffy's Elixir. He was also billed for "large syringes," "ivory pipes," "opium pills," and a recurring dosage of laudanum purchased once, and then twice, monthly. The opiate ameliorated the kidney stone's scraping crawl, but brought a side effect: "It has taken away my Appetite," Franklin wrote, "and so impeded my Digestion that I am become totally emaciated and little remains of me but a Skeleton covered with a Skin."

And yet, in June 1789, two months after George Washington's presidential swearing-in, and just as Franklin's own exit seemed near, the frail eighty-three-year-old placed a bet on the endurance of his class and country. If successful, his wager would also write the blueprint for their continued prosperity.

"It having long been a fixed political opinion of mine," Franklin added in the codicil to his will, "that in a democratical state there ought to be no offices of profit, for the reasons I had given in an article of my drawing in our constitution, it was my intention when I accepted the office of President [of Pennsylvania], to devote the appointed salary to some public uses."

Realizing that the money he had earmarked to make the Schuylkill River navigable would "do but little towards accomplishing such a work," Franklin now revoked that bequest, "having entertained another idea, that I hope may be more extensively useful."

Before revealing his scheme, Franklin braced his four primary heirs for the news that this sizable gift would not be coming to them. "It has been an opinion," he wrote, "that he who receives an estate from his ancestors is under some kind of obligation to transmit the same to their posterity. This obligation does not lie on me, who never inherited a shilling from any ancestor or relation. I shall, however, if it is not diminished by some accident before my death, leave a considerable estate among my descendants and relations. The above observation is made merely as some apology to my family for making bequests that do not appear to have any immediate relation to their advantage."

He owed his education to his birthplace of Boston, Franklin continued, and his career to Philadelphia. "Having myself been bred to a manual art, printing, in my native town," he wrote, "and afterwards assisted to set up my business in Philadelphia by kind loans of money from two friends there, which was the foundation of my fortune, and of all the utility in life that may be ascribed to me, I wish to be useful even after my death, if possible, in forming and advancing other young men, that may be serviceable to their country in both these towns."

Franklin announced that he was leaving each city £1,000. The money was to be lent in small amounts to young skilled workers to stake their own businesses. The men were to repay the loans over ten years, at a below-market annual interest rate of 5 percent. Although the term would not be coined for another two centuries, Franklin's ethical lending scheme can be seen as a forerunner of microfinance.

To ensure his funds benefited only tradesmen, Franklin forbade his principal to be spent on overhead. "As it is presumed that there will always be found virtuous and benevolent citizens," he wrote, "willing to bestow a part of their time in doing good to the rising generation," he expected—and challenged—sympathetic men to step forward and manage the loans without pay.

Franklin understood how a seemingly small amount of seeding could multiply into a forest of green. The secret was patience: even a low rate of return, when compounded annually, would create a windfall. (Warren Buffett, a modern adherent of this strategy, calls it the Methuselah Technique.) If "this plan is executed," Franklin explained in his will, "and proceeds as projected without interruption for one hundred years," then each city's £1,000 would exponentially increase to £131,000.

"I would have the managers of the donation," Franklin directed, "then lay out, at their discretion, one hundred thousand pounds in public works, which may be judged of most general utility to the inhabitants, such as fortifications, bridges, aqueducts, public buildings, baths, pavements, or whatever may make living in the town more convenient to its people, and render it more agreeable to strangers."

The remaining £31,000 was to be continually loaned to skilled tradesmen, at interest, for yet another century. "At the end of this second term," Franklin calculated, "if no unfortunate accident has prevented the operation," each fund's balance would soar to a final sum of £4,061,000. Franklin ordered this mountain of money divided among Philadelphia, Boston, and their respective states, "not presuming to carry my views farther."

It was an audaciously optimistic idea from a man known for level-headed pragmatism. "Blessed is he that expects nothing," Poor Richard once observed, "for he shall never be disappointed."

And yet, as he lay dying, Franklin expected (1) civic-minded book-keepers to step forward to (2) administer, without compensation, (3) ten-year loans to tradesmen (4) for two centuries. Provided that (5) every borrower repaid their debt in full, the principal's balance would snowball and could be spent in a manner that (6) the public democratically decided would benefit the common good.

What could go wrong? Furthermore, the man who once advised young tradesmen, "Remember that Time is Money," ordered that his loan scheme "begin to operate within one year after my decease." Poor Richard warned that "Sloth, like Rust, consumes faster than Labour wears, while the used key is always bright," but it is also true that grand designs take time to build. At the time that Franklin completed his will, only eleven states had ratified the Constitution. Earlier that foul-weathered spring, only eight of the twenty-two senators had managed to make it to the capital to open the new Senate.

"Considering the accidents to which all human affairs and projects are subject in such a length of time," Franklin admitted in his will's conclusion, "I have, perhaps, too much flattered myself with a vain fancy that these dispositions, if carried into execution, will be continued without interruption and have the effects proposed. I hope, however, that if the two cities should not think fit to undertake the execution, they will, at least, accept the offer of these donations as a mark of my good will, a token of my gratitude, and a testimony of my earnest desire to be useful to them after my departure."

Did he sense that his end was near? "As to the Pain I suffer," Franklin wrote to his sister Jane one week later, "about which you make yourself so unhappy, it is, when compar'd with the long life I have enjoy'd of

Health and Ease, but a Trifle. And it is right that we should meet with something to wean us from this world to make us willing when call'd to leave it: otherwise the Parting would indeed be grievous."

The pair had outlived their fifteen other siblings. Franklin sent more letters to Jane than to anyone else in his life. In the first that survives, dated 1727, he confided, "You know you were ever my peculiar favourite." Over a half century later, as the winter of 1789 blanketed Philadelphia, Franklin found himself craving a taste of his hometown, which he had last visited, as deputy postmaster, twenty-six years earlier. "I have lately wished to regale on Cod's Tongues and Sounds," he wrote to Jane, "and if you could now and then send me a small Keg of them, containing about two Quarts, they would be very acceptable and pleasing to your affectionate Brother."

His strength ebbed and flowed. On the day after Christmas, Franklin felt well enough to produce a long letter to the lexicographer Noah Webster, in which he curmudgeonly complained about the new trend to use the nouns *notice, advocate,* and *progress* as verbs. Franklin could be wrong, and not all of his schemes proved revolutionary. Webster that year published Franklin's proposed new alphabet, which omitted the letters *c, j, q, w, x,* and *y.*

As the calendar turned to 1790, Jane sent birthday greetings on January 17: "This Day my Dear Brother compleats his 84th year." Ever charming, she added that she was six years younger, "but to Apearance in Every wons sight as much older." A keg of cod bits was on its way. "I have Tasted them and think them very Good."

He had four months to live.

In February, Franklin performed his last act of public service, submitting to the First Congress his signed petition calling for the abolishment of slavery. A slave-owning South Carolina senator stormed the floor to denounce Franklin for stepping on states' rights. At the Constitutional Convention, the senator later recounted, he had witnessed Franklin "consent to the Federal Compact. Here he was in clearest Violation of it." Presided over by Vice President John Adams, the Senate rejected Franklin's appeal outright.

The House of Representatives, however, voted to send his petition to a select committee, over the objections of dissenters, including Georgia congressman James Jackson, who warned that Franklin's defiance would "blow the trumpet of civil war."

When the House reconvened in March, the committee reported that a constitutional clause forbade the federal government to end slavery before 1808, a year that marked the passage of one generation after the compact's ratification. Now it was northern politicians who turned on Franklin. "The firmness of his mind has been suspected," observed one. "Even great men have their senile moments," commented another.

Jackson, whose booming voice often carried through the capitol's floorboards, stood again to shout his disbelief that *Benjamin Franklin! Author of* The Way to Wealth*! Would harm prosperous slaveholders! The Bible sanctioned slavery! Without it, who would work the hot plantations!*

The bedbound Franklin responded to these hysterics in ink. His final published article, like his first, was a hoax. At age sixteen in Boston, Franklin had poked fun at sanctimonious Puritans in the guise of a middle-aged widow named Silence Dogood. Sixty-eight years later in Philadelphia, Franklin called out slave owners' self-righteousness under the cover of an historian called Historicus.

"Reading last night in your excellent paper the speech of Mr. Jackson in Congress," he wrote to the *Federal Gazette,* "against meddling with the affair of slavery, or attempting to mend the condition of slaves, it put me in mind of a similar one made about one hundred years since . . . Mr. Jackson does not quote it; perhaps he has not seen it."

No one had; what followed was pure fiction. To demonstrate the hypocrisy of slavery's churchgoing defenders, Franklin related the story of an Algerian divan that had rejected a petition to release the realm's Christian slaves. "Who, in this hot climate, are to cultivate our lands?" asked the councilors. "Who is to indemnify their masters for the loss? And if we set our slaves free, what is to be done with them?" After a lengthy debate, the men resolved, "The doctrine that plundering and enslaving the Christians is unjust, is at best *problematical;* but that it is the interest of this state to continue the practice, is clear; therefore let the petition be rejected."

Since, Franklin concluded, "like motives are apt to produce in the minds of men like opinions and resolutions," Congress was kin to this barbarity. The eighty-four-year-old signed off from public life by speaking truth to power, just as he had begun.

Two weeks later, Franklin composed his last private letter, to Thomas Jefferson, America's first secretary of state. Jefferson had asked if Franklin could remember which map he had used during the negotiations of the Treaty of Paris. British settlers, Jefferson suspected, were illegally crossing the St. Croix River into present-day Maine.

"Tho' at the time he was in the greatest Agonies," Franklin's twenty-year-old grandson Benny recounted, "in more Pain than I ever saw him — it was with great Difficulty that he could breathe — yet he dictated a Letter of a Folio Page and an half, upon Business that required every Exertion of his Memory & Judgment, without once requiring me to read back what I had written, or enveigling me to correct more than one small Error; and yet he has been but little in the Habit of dictating. The letter was as good a one as he ever wrote."

Franklin said he was "perfectly clear in the Remembrance," and sent Jefferson the map that showed the agreed-upon border, where it remains fixed today.

The following week, a racking cough impaired Franklin's labored breathing. He ran a high fever. Yet, a friend reported, "his conversation with his family upon the subject of his dissolution was free and cheerful. He rose from his bed, and begged that it be made up for him so that he might die 'in a decent manner.'"

Franklin's daughter, Sally, said that she hoped he would recover and live many more years. "I hope not," Franklin replied.

"From that day," Benny recorded, "he grew worse & worse, and took but little food. In the Morning of the 17th of April he refused all sustenance, by Shaking his Head . . . before he spoke for the last time." After someone suggested shifting himself in bed so that he could breathe easier, Franklin, sharp to the end, retorted, "A dying man can do nothing *easy.*"

"Whenever I approached his Bed," Benny wrote, "he held out his hand & having given him mine he would take it & hold it for some time; this shows that he was not insensible. He did not change his Position that Day. And at a quarter before eleven at Night, his Breathing was quicker & Pulse more feeble, [Temple] and myself being in the Room. This alarmed us, and occasioned my calling my Father, who having had no sleep for 56 hours had retired into the next Room; But he came too late, my Grand Father gave a Sigh, breathed a few seconds & died without Pain."

In Boston, his sister Jane received a letter from Benny's father that began, "My duty calls upon me to make you acquainted with an event which I know will be a sore affliction to your affectionate Breast . . . Nature was at last worn out."

"He while living was to me every enjoyment," Jane reflected. "Every line from him was a pleasure." Presciently, she saw that her brother's death did not mean that his account was closed. "Hardly a newspaper comes out in this town without honorable mention of him," she noted, "and indeed it is a fund that cannot be exhausted."

Benny, stoic in grief, wrote to his fiancée, "I think there is something remarkable in his End. His mental Faculties unimpaired or but little impaired, at his age—his Resolution unshaken—His Principles fixed even in Death—show a man of a superior cast."

Next he hinted at his grandfather's parting gifts. "His Will is a great Man's Will. It is of a piece with his Life."

Benny was unaware, then, what little time he had left to use his inheritance, let alone the more than two-hundred-year journey that Franklin's legacy was about to begin. "It would be necessary to enter into Particulars too long for a letter, to convince you of this," Benny concluded. "You can take my Word for it perhaps."

2

The Foundation
of His Fortune

The ships crowding Philadelphia's harbor lowered their flags to half-mast. Even the British vessels dipped the King's Colours in deference to Benjamin Franklin. "It is recommended to the Citizens who propose to attend the Funeral of Dr. FRANKLIN," the *Pennsylvania Gazette* reported, "to meet at the State-house THIS AFTERNOON, at three o'clock, to form themselves in their proper order."

History does not record where they all stood. An estimated 20,000 mourners—in a town of 28,000—formed the largest crowd ever gathered to that point in what was then America's largest city.

The bells of every church tolled at three o'clock that Wednesday afternoon of April 21, 1790. As the somber din faded away, the sharp report of minute guns pierced the air.

Exiting Franklin Court's Market Street archway, the procession, led by all eighty "Clergy of the city, including the Ministers of the Hebrew congregation," solemnly paced to the Christ Church Burial Ground, approximately one long block away. Two years earlier, Franklin had helped save Philadelphia's synagogue from default, just as he had donated to the building funds for each of the city's sects.

As an apostle of religious freedom and tolerance of all faiths, Franklin would not have approved a sectarian funeral. He had not been a regular churchgoer, despite subscribing to a family pew at the Episcopalian Christ Church, two blocks east down Market Street. It had been his wife Deborah's parish. In the early 1750s, Franklin managed two lotteries to raise funds to build the two-hundred-foot steeple that had made it America's tallest building. Ever the pragmatist, he had hoped to use the steeple to attract lightning. But its construction had yet to begin when his kinetic mind flashed upon the idea of using a kite to connect to the heavens.

If we take him at his word, Franklin was never asked, in public or private, about his faith. Like many leading Enlightenment thinkers, Franklin considered himself a deist. He believed in a benevolent creator, but not organized religion, corrupted by centuries of dogma. As an adherent of rationality and common sense, he also embodied the Age of Reason. After a ship carrying him to London narrowly avoided running ashore on the deadly rocks of Scilly, Franklin wrote to Deborah that, once safely docked, the passengers went to church to give thanks for their deliverance. "Were I a Roman Catholic," he reflected, "perhaps I should on this occasion vow to build a chapel to some saint; but as I am not, if I were to vow at all, it should be to build a *lighthouse*."

In the month preceding his death, a minister asked Franklin about his faith. "It is the first time I have been questioned upon it," Franklin replied (unbelievably). "Here is my Creed: I believe in one God, Creator of the Universe. That He governs it by his Providence. That he ought to be worshipped. That the most acceptable Service we can render to him, is doing Good to his other Children. That the Soul of Man is immortal, and will be treated with Justice in another Life respecting its Conduct in this. These I take to be the fundamental Principles of all sound Religion, and I regard them as you do, in whatever Sect I meet with them."

As a young printer making his mark in Philadelphia, however, one preacher had managed to entice Franklin to attend church. The itinerant Irish Presbyterian Samuel Hemphill also activated Franklin's life-long dedication to philanthropy. "His Sermons pleas[ed] me," Franklin wrote in his autobiography, "as they had little of the dogmatical kind, but inculcated strongly the Practice of Virtue, or what in the religious Stile are called Good Works."

In 1735, after the synod charged Hemphill with heterodoxy, Franklin defended him in his *Pennsylvania Gazette.* He cited the book of James, which taught "that Faith without Virtue is useless." Jesus himself, Franklin wrote, instructed that "'tis the Doing or not Doing all the Good that lies in our Power, that will render us the Heirs of Happiness or Misery." Or, as Poor Richard put it, "Serving God is Doing Good to Man, but Praying is thought an easier Service, and therefore more generally chosen."

In the end, it was not heresy that exiled the minister, but plagiarism. "I stuck by him however," Franklin remembered, "as I rather approv'd his giving us good Sermons compos'd by others, than bad ones of his own Manufacture." Franklin, after all, had cadged his first pen name, "Silence Dogood," from the titles of the Boston Puritan Cotton Mather's sermon on grief, "Silentiarius," and his book *Bonifacius, or Essays to Do Good.*

After the minister Hemphill's expulsion from Philadelphia, the next edition of *Poor Richard's Almanack* included the maxim "Don't throw stones at your neighbors, if your own windows are glass." Franklin did not note that the Welsh poet George Herbert had said it before him. Only more than two decades later, at the conclusion of his almanac's final edition, did Franklin slyly show his hand. After Poor Richard watches an orator hold a crowd's attention by quoting his best-known sayings, he confesses, "The frequent Mention he made of me must have tired any one else, but my Vanity was wonderfully delighted with it, though I was conscious that not a tenth Part of the Wisdom was my own which he ascribed to me, but rather the *Gleanings* I had made of the Sense of all Ages and Nations."

● ● ●

Franklin never credited the source that inspired his final bequest. The idea for his two-hundred-year loan scheme actually had been seeded by another man's joke. Five years before his death, Franklin received in his Paris mail a satiric essay, written in French, titled *"Testament de M. Fortuné Ricard,"* or the Last Will and Testament of Fortunate Richard. The pages related the tale of a plainspoken teacher who found himself in possession of a vast fortune, and then struck upon a novel way to dispose of it.

The story begins when Richard is a young boy and his grandfather reveals to him the magic of compound interest. The elder has deposited 24 livres (£4) in Richard's name into a savings account that pays 5 percent interest annually. He promises that after one hundred years, the untouched money will multiply 131 times. Richard cannot believe it, but his grandfather assures him that all he has to do is exercise patience. "My child, . . . remember that with economy and calculation, nothing is impossible for a man."

Seven decades pass. The grandfather's guarantee indeed comes true. Richard, realizing that the money will continue to accumulate after his death, decides to use his unexpected fortune to weave a social safety net in the waning days of ancien régime France.

Richard directs that his money be paid out in five bequests at intervals of one hundred years. His first batch of money is to be spent on reforming corrupt churches that prey upon the poor. The following sum, to be released two hundred years after Richard's death, would reward young artists.

It is the next bequest that appears to have set Franklin's mental wheels in motion. At the close of the third century, Richard orders that a portion of the money—then having compounded to 226 million livres (£10 million)—fund "500 patriotic banks for lending money without interest." The loans were to exclusively assist the poor by helping them start their own small businesses. An additional slice of the cash would be used to build museums of art and natural history, and (in homage to Franklin) public libraries.

After four hundred years, Richard's mountain of cash—could any

vault even hold it?—would build one hundred new towns, freeing the
working class from their tubercular slums.

Finally, at the half-millennium mark, Richard's interest-swollen 4
trillion livres (£1.76 trillion) was to pay off, as a gesture of neighborly
gratitude, England's national debt; create a European bank to prevent
war among its nations; start a national pension scheme; provide every
newborn child with three years of basic income to assist parents with
their care; build free hospitals; support women-owned businesses, so
as to ensure they received equal pay for equal work; and, finally, beau-
tify cities and improve their transportation, including making rivers
navigable.

Franklin forwarded the essay to a friend in London, who suspected
its true provenance. "It is full of humor and sense," the man replied,
"which either come from you we suppose, or has been imitated from
you."

Franklin sent his assurances that "the *Testament* is not mine; nor
do I certainly know the Author, tho' I had a Present sent me of four
[copies], and thence suppose it to be some Friend. I think it on many
Accounts a good Thing, and that it may be useful. Projects that may
be absurd in a Man to undertake for himself, or even for his Children,
(Men and Families being Creatures of so short Duration) may nevertheless be wise in States."

The satire's true author was Charles-Joseph Mathon de la Cour, a
forty-six-year-old mathematician from Lyon who admired Franklin's
philanthropy. Mathon had used his own money to found a science
and language school, and, after the monarchy had refused his appeal,
a shelter for orphaned children.

In 1785, Franklin's friend Richard Price, a mathematician and non-
conformist London preacher who appreciated Fortunate Richard's calculated morality, translated the essay into English. "I am glad that he
has printed a Translation of the *Testament*," Franklin wrote. "It may
do Good."

In fact, the work sank without a trace. Price had rushed the essay into print by sticking it, incongruously, at the end of his sober pamphlet *Observations on the Importance of the American Revolution and the Means of Rendering It a Benefit to the World.* Only Franklin's death would resurrect Mathon's idea.

Franklin never met his muse. In the first of their three surviving letters, Mathon admitted to admiring his icon from afar. "During the last years of my stay in Paris," he wrote in French, "my heart often pulsated with joy when I found the opportunity to join my applause with that which France seemed to grant you as soon as you were seen."

That Franklin "deigned to receive" his jocular essay "with kindness" gave him the most "ardent gratitude."

Franklin responded in French, with praise for the *Testament.* "Reading it gave me much pleasure, and esteem for its author. I regret that I have no other prize to give you."

After he returned to Philadelphia for good that autumn, Franklin did award Mathon a trophy of sorts. "It is right to be sowing good seed," he wrote to him, switching to English, "whenever we have an opportunity, since some of it may be productive. An instance of this you should be acquainted with, as it may afford you pleasure. The reading of *Fortuné Richard's Testament,* has put it into the head and heart of a citizen to leave two thousand pounds sterling to two American cities, who are to lend it in small sums at five per cent to young beginners in business; and the accumulation, after an hundred years, to be laid out in public works of benefit to those cities. With great esteem, I have the honour to be, Sir, your most obedient and most humble Servant, B. Franklin."

Did Mathon ever learn that Franklin followed through, turning a satiric idea into a genuine gift that would assist the working class and improve Boston and Philadelphia? Unfortunately, no further correspondence between the men survives. Nor did Mathon live much longer than his elder. In 1793, the first year of the Reign of Terror, French revolutionaries captured him in Lyon. His full name—de la Cour, "of the Court"—could not have helped his defense. Only three years after

Franklin's death, the fifty-five-year-old Charles-Joseph Mathon de la Cour would himself perish, on the guillotine.

Franklin trusted Philadelphia's city officers—who, to return to the scene of his funeral, silently followed his coffin as it exited his Market Street home—to manage his loan scheme's money. He ordered an additional layer of oversight for his birthplace's gift. "The said sum of one thousand pounds sterling," Franklin wrote in his will, "if accepted by the inhabitants of the town of Boston, shall be managed under the direction of the selectmen, united with the ministers of the oldest Episcopalian, Congregational, and Presbyterian churches in that town."

Franklin's rationale was pragmatic, not religious. Boston was then unincorporated, and its parishes played a prominent role in civic affairs. He had erred in this instruction, however, by assuming that the town shared Philadelphia's ecumenical diversity. No Presbyterian church yet existed in Boston.

Proceeding slowly from Franklin Court, his casket was borne by "citizens," the *Pennsylvania Gazette* reported, naming none. Pacing behind them were representatives of the state government, its legislature, and the judges of Pennsylvania's supreme court. Next came the mayor and other city officials, Philadelphia's printers and apprentices, and the members of the American Philosophical Society, the College of Physicians, and the College of Philadelphia. Franklin had founded or belonged to each institution.

"The order and silence which prevailed, during the procession," the *Gazette* related, "deeply envinced the heartfelt sense entertained by all classes of citizens, of the unparalleled virtues, talents and services of the deceased."

It had been an unseasonably "open" winter, with boys bathing in Philadelphia's rivers even in January. We can picture the city's hawthorn trees in bloom, their branches bowing with white blossoms as Franklin's funeral procession passed by.

The cortege ended in the northwest corner of the Christ Church Burial Ground, at the grave of Franklin's wife, Deborah Read Franklin. Following a series of strokes, she had preceded him here sixteen years before. She was thought to have been sixty-six in 1774, but no birth date had been chiseled into her stone because none had ever been recorded.

Franklin's biographers have typically consigned Deborah to a walk-on role in the blockbuster production that was his life. In the first act, she typically storms onstage looking "sturdy" and "rather plain," while her husband, in contrast, possesses "husky good looks and genial charm." She proceeds to behave "loud," "untaught, and sometimes turbulent." Deborah, the audience learns, had ensnared Franklin with "the prospect of comfort and domesticity." But soon she reveals herself to be a sexless harridan, disinterested in his science and statecraft. Instead, she sits at home, spinning in her shift of tow.

This depiction diminishes not only Deborah's own story but also the crucial role she played in Franklin's, including his afterlife. The beginning of their lifelong partnership in part explains Franklin's stipulation that applicants to his loan scheme be married and "under the age of twenty-five years." Franklin wed Deborah, though not in a church, when he was twenty-four.

Furthermore, she played a key part in his "self-made" success. In 1735, in his fifth year of marriage, Franklin wrote in his *Pennsylvania Gazette:* "A Man does not act contrary to his Interest by Marrying; for I and Thousands more know very well that we could never thrive till we were married; and have done well ever since; What we get, the Women save; a Man being fixt in Life minds his Business better and more steadily; and he that cannot thrive married, could never have throve better single; for the Idleness and Negligence of Men is more frequently fatal to Families, than the Extravagance of Women." Deborah's labors helped enable Franklin to retire, at age forty-two, with a "sufficient tho' moderate Fortune," freeing him to spend the second half of his life energetically engaged in science and diplomacy. And yet, his lengthening shadow obscured her own abilities.

Though denied formal schooling, Deborah was a skilled entrepreneur and accountant. Her surviving ledgers show her recording sales and payments in multiple currencies at the Franklins' printshop, which was stocked with not only stationery, ink, and sealing wax but also sundry items arriving at Philadelphia's busy wharf, including chocolate, coffee, stockings, and barrels of mackerel.

In 1733, Franklin granted power of attorney to Deborah, instead of to one of his many male associates. It was an atypical action in an era when coverture laws assigned married women the same rights as dependent children. Franklin had to strike out the preprinted form's usual noun, so the paper instead read, "I *Benjamin Franklin of the City of Philadelphia in Pennsylvania, Printer . . .* make and appoint my trusty and loving ~~Friend~~ *Wife Deborah Franklin* to be my true and lawful Attorney."

He could count on her always. "I discovered that she always knew what I did not know," Franklin wrote in a letter after her death, "and if something escaped me, I was sure that it was precisely that which she had seized." Earlier in their union, writing as Poor Richard, the usually restrained Franklin published a romantic ballad in her honor. "Now twelve Years my Wife," he mooned, "still the Joy of my Life, Blest Day that I made her my own."

In verse, Franklin described Deborah as "easy, engaging and Free," and "as tender as tender can be." The feelings he made public under his own name were more reserved, and helped shape her portrayal by historians, most of whom were men. In his autobiography, Franklin depicted their marriage more as an alliance than a romance. "She proved a good and faithful Helpmate," he wrote, "and assisted me much by attending the Shop." Only one line in the entire book hints at their intimacy: "We throve together, and have ever mutually endeavored to make each other happy."

It is worth remembering that Franklin structured his memoir as a letter to his firstborn child; the book begins "Dear Son." Perhaps it was parental discretion that prevented Franklin from penning Deborah a valentine. He was also writing as a sixty-five-year-old, four decades removed from their courtship, and with an ocean between them.

We cannot hear Deborah's side of the story; she left no diary behind. Her voice only reaches us, faintly, in a few dozen letters to her husband that survive. In them, her claims of being "so verey poor a writer," are disproved by the lines of a lively, engaged correspondent who shares Franklin's sense of humor. One teasing exchange can stand for many. In 1758, when he was fifty-two, Franklin sent Deborah a "large fine Jugg for Beer" from London. "I fell in Love with it at first Sight," he wrote her, "for I thought it look'd like a fat jolly Dame, clean and tidy, with a neat blue and white Calico Gown on, good natur'd and lovely, and put me in mind of—Somebody."

According to Franklin, Deborah had been one of the first Philadelphians to lay eyes upon him. It was not love at first sight. In his autobiography, Franklin recounted his ignominious arrival in the city in 1723, when he was "near 300 miles from home, a Boy of but 17, without the least Recommendation to or Knowledge of any Person in the Place, and with very little Money in my Pocket." From the wharf, Franklin had wandered up Market Street, "as far as Fourth-street, passing by the Door of Mr. Read, my future Wife's Father; when she, standing at the Door, saw me, and thought I made, as I certainly did, a most awkward, ridiculous Appearance."

At last ashore after a drenched, off-course journey from Boston, the famished Franklin had asked a Second Street baker for "Bisket," the unleavened, biscotto-like snack common in the northern colonies. They did not make it in Philadelphia. Nor did the baker understand what his bedraggled customer meant by a "three-penny loaf." A flustered Franklin asked for 3 pence worth of any bread. "He gave me accordingly three great Puffy Rolls. I was surpriz'd at the Quantity, but took it, and having no room in my Pockets, walk'd off with a Roll under each Arm, and eating the other."

The rolls were boule-size, and so from the doorway of her parents' shop, Deborah saw a tall young man lumbering toward her laden with loaves. He also bulged like a scarecrow. "I was dirty from my Journey," Franklin wrote. "My Pockets were stuff'd out with Shirts and Stockings, and I knew no Soul nor where to look for Lodging." After walking a circuit of ten square blocks — thus seeing most of the town — and giving his remaining two rolls to a needful woman and child who were continuing their journey from the wharf, Franklin eventually returned to the doorway where Deborah had stood watching him. Her parents accepted him as a boarder above their dry goods store.

Although the pair formed an attraction, Deborah's mother, worried about the economic prospects of a printer, an occupation "generally thought a poor one," stalled her daughter's betrothal. In the meantime, the industrious Franklin caught the eye of the Pennsylvania governor, who dispatched the eighteen-year-old to London to purchase Philadelphia's first proper printing press. After sailing seven weeks across the Atlantic, Franklin watched, with increasing dismay, as the mail sack was emptied onto the deck and the governor's promised letter of credit did not appear among the wax-sealed correspondence. The young Franklin was marooned, with "no Credit to give."

He worked to earn his return passage by teaching swimming lessons in the Thames and working in a printing house near Smithfield, London's main cattle market, whose smells were all but visible. (Even a century later, in *Great Expectations,* a wide-eyed Pip found that "the shameful place, being all asmear with filth and fat and blood and foam, seemed to stick to me.") Franklin stayed eighteen months, sending only one letter to Deborah, who read his absence as an abandonment.

Instead, she married a man named John Rogers, only to leave him after learning that he had likely abandoned a wife and child in England. Pennsylvania law sentenced bigamists to thirty-nine lashes for both parties, followed by life imprisonment with hard labor. Rogers left town and vanished in the West Indies, where he was rumored to have been killed in a brawl.

On Franklin's return to Philadelphia in 1726, he and Deborah renewed their affections, this time with her mother's encouragement. Because she could not obtain a divorce, there would be no church wedding; theirs was a common-law union. "I took her to Wife, September 1st, 1730," Franklin wrote, recording the date the pair had taken up residence together in the space that doubled as their printshop. While they initially feared arrest under the colony's anti-adultery and unwed-fornication statutes, "none of the Inconveniences happened that we had apprehended."

In his memoir, Franklin coyly failed to mention that a third person moved with them into 139 Market Street: his infant son. The true identity of William's birth mother remains unknown; she likely was a prostitute. If Deborah had borne the boy—concealing her pregnancy to shield the couple from a prying constable—then the Franklins were meticulous in not leaving any clues. Regardless, Deborah raised William as her son, and William called her nothing but mother.

Two years later, the zine-size *Poor Richard's Almanack*—featuring a caricature of Deborah as Richard's harpy wife, Bridget—began its profitable run, selling up to ten thousand copies of its twenty-odd pages each year. In 1732, Deborah delivered a son, Francis, whom they called Franky, followed in 1743 by a daughter, Sarah, known as Sally.

Success followed success. A hint that the Franklins did not live as ascetically as Poor Richard can be found in the notice Franklin placed in his *Pennsylvania Gazette* in 1750:

> Whereas on Saturday night last, the house of Benjamin Franklin, of this city, printer, was broken open, and the following things feloniously taken away, viz. a double necklace of gold beads, a woman's long scarlet cloak, almost new, with a double cape, a woman's gown, of printed cotton, of the sort called brocade print, very remarkable, . . . a pair of woman's stays, covered with white tabby before, and dove-colour'd tabby be-

hind, and sundry other goods. Whoever discovers the thief or
thieves, either in this or any of the neighbouring provinces, so
that they may be brought to justice, shall receive Ten Pounds
reward; and for recovering any of the goods, a reward in proportion to their value, paid by Benjamin Franklin.

That year's *Almanack* saw Poor Richard caution: "Many a Man
thinks he is buying Pleasure, when he is really selling himself a Slave
to it."

The couple invested their business profits in property, purchasing
houses leased to Franklin's relatives in Boston and several vacant lots
and homes in the growing Philadelphia. In his penultimate will—
written in 1757 as Franklin set sail for the second time to England, to
represent Pennsylvania's interests before the Crown—Franklin left to
Deborah not the customary "widow's third," but rather the bulk of his
estate. She had earned it.

Deborah alone managed their property portfolio then, collecting
rents and contracting repairs. The established narrative is that when
Franklin shoved off for England, he left Deborah behind. This telling
presents her as an unworldly homebody, without considering that her
deathly fear of the ocean, seeded on the storm-tossed voyage when
as a child she immigrated with her family from England, may have
compelled her to stay ashore. (What Franklin terms her "invincible
aversion to crossing the Seas" was not irrational; it was on this trip
that his ship nearly foundered on the rocks of Scilly.) Furthermore,
had she gone to London, Deborah would have been consigned to
play the thankless role, familiar to many expatriates, of the trailing
spouse. Instead of displaying timidity and weakness, Deborah's decision to remain at home—enlivened by family, friends, church, and
business—could also be read as a personal declaration of independence.

Deborah did, however, share her husband's half-measured mind
on slavery at that time. In 1758, she commissioned as a gift to him
a painting—now hanging in the National Portrait Gallery—of the

radical Philadelphia abolitionist Benjamin Lay. Two decades earlier, "the Quaker Comet" had written one of North America's first tracts condemning the slave trade, which Franklin published. In London, Franklin led a philanthropic group that established a free school to educate enslaved Philadelphians. In a 1759 letter, Deborah said she was enrolling Othello there. Yet the boy remained bound to her, even as his likely father, Peter, served Benjamin abroad. If the Franklins remembered that Lay's activism had once extended to kidnapping a slave owner's child so the man could feel the horror and pain of separation, their surviving letters do not reveal it. Othello died of illness the next year.

After the death of her mother in 1762, Deborah used her inheritance to provide for her family, especially her absent spouse. On the Market Street plot that once held her parents' shop, she oversaw construction of the handsome brick house at Franklin Court. "What Room have you chose to sleep in?" Franklin wrote to her from London in 1765. "I wish you would give me a particular Account of every Room, who and what is in it, 'twould make me seem a little at home."

Four months earlier, Franklin hinted that his stay in England would be prolonged by a shift in the political winds. "Very busy about a Bill," he confided to Deborah, "brought in to authorize Quartering Troops on private Houses in America which we hope to get laid aside."

After Parliament issued the Stamp Act, inflaming American grievances, Deborah—who, after being denied formal schooling, spelled phonetically—wrote to Franklin, "I love to hear from you . . . I donte undertake to say aney thing a bought the dis[order] in this porte of the world but to me it semes we air verey wicked and so is the pepel in London and other plases on your sid the watter I pray god mend us all."

She had buried the lede: a mob of Philadelphians, angered by what they perceived as Franklin's docility before Parliament, had besieged Franklin Court. Her unconventional spelling belies her intelligence but not her bravery: "I was for 9 day keep in one Contineued hurrey by pepel to removef and Salley was porswaided to go to burlinton for

The only surviving portrait of Deborah Franklin.

saiftey." Deborah had summoned her brother to bring his gun, and together they converted the parlor "into a Magazin." She refused to leave their home, blockading herself upstairs until the fervor subsided. "I sed when I was advised to remove that I was verey shuer you had dun nothing to hurte aney bodey . . . If aney one Came to disturbe me I wold show a proper resentement and I shold be very much afrunted with aney bodey."

Franklin clearly admired her. His reply to her account of facing down the mob begins not with his usual "My dear Child," but with the more intimate "Dear Debby." "I honour much the Spirit and Courage you show'd," Franklin wrote, "and the prudent Preparations you made in that [Time] of Danger . . . I am, my dear Girl, Your ever loving Husband."

Many of the couple's letters have been lost, so we can only speculate about what Franklin may have written that occasioned Deborah that autumn to reply, "I have bin so happey as to reseve severel of your dear letters with in these few days and . . . am I plesed to read over and over a gen I Cole it a *husbands Love letter.*"

The next year, Deborah received Franklin's news that "I am just now made very happy by a Vote of the Commons for the Repeal of the Stamp Act." In a follow-up letter, he told her, "As the Stamp Act is at length repeal'd, I am willing you should have a new Gown . . . Had the Trade between the two Countries totally ceas'd, it was a Comfort to me to recollect that I had once been cloth'd from Head to Foot in Woollen and Linnen of my Wife's Manufacture, that I never was prouder of any Dress in my Life." In addition to other presents, he included "a few Beans, a new Sort for your Garden," as well as a box of cheeses. "Perhaps a Bit of them may be left when I come home."

He was her "affectionate husband"; she was his "Afeckshonet wife."

As his absence lengthened, however, and the calendar turned from 1766 to 1767 to 1768, the couple's communication lagged and overlapped as ships carrying their letters made the long crossing to the Atlantic's opposite shore. Franklin's elegant cursive handwriting slanted forward, making his lines—filled with billowing *b*'s, *k*'s, *h*'s, and *f*'s —look like a fleet being blown, full-sailed, across the page. He usually signed his letters to most people "B. Franklin," a signature that can stand as another complete sentence, an imperative: *Be Franklin.* When his writing brims with curiosity, empathy, and humor, it reads like an invitation. But not in his late-in-life correspondence with Deborah.

As 1769 began, Franklin promised his wife that he intended to return that summer. "We are, as you observe, blest with a great Share of Health considering our Years now 63. Yet I would not have you think that I fancy I shall grow young again. I know that Men of my Bulk often fail suddenly."

Unbeknownst to him, Deborah had that winter suffered the first in a series of debilitating strokes. The following autumn, after he complained of not receiving letters from her, Deborah wrote honestly about her pain; the time for deference was gone. She admitted feeling so "distresed att your staying so much longer that I loste all my resey lushon and the verey dismall winter bouth Salley and my self live so verey lonley that I had got in so verey low a Staite and got into so unhapey a way that I Cold not sleep a long time."

A few lines later, she recounted being bled by a doctor, going sleepless for several months, growing emaciated, and losing her memory. She also appears to describe another stroke: "I fell down and cold not get up agen indead it was not aney sicknes but two much disquiit of mind but I had taken up a resey lushon never to make aney Complainte to you or give you aney disquiet to you."

In another note sent that year, Deborah related that their children had spotted the Great Comet, visible to the naked eye, and supposed that Franklin had glimpsed it, too. "I have not seen it," she added (sadly). But she did witness, at Christ Church, their daughter Sally's firstborn child, "baptised by the Name of Benj Franklin."

With the arrival of little Benjamin Franklin Bache—Benny, the grandson who would hold Franklin's hand on his deathbed—the couple's correspondence frosted over completely.

The poles of Franklin's world reversed in that year of 1770. First, the lifelong loyal British subject absorbed the news that months of festering discontent had finally exploded in what was being called the Boston Massacre. Harassed by a mob, redcoats had shot and killed five men on King Street, mere footsteps from where a pubescent Franklin had served as an apprentice in his brother's printshop. (A young lawyer named John Adams was defending the soldiers.) In Philadelphia, meanwhile, the walls of the new home that Franklin had yet to lay eyes on resounded with the cries of his namesake grandson. And, he discovered via Deborah's intermittent updates, his addled wife seemed to confuse the newborn with their own younger son, Franky, who had died at the age of four.

The Franklins had treasured the child, who had displayed such curiosity and intelligence that they had hired a tutor to begin his schooling when he was two. Two years later, when an outbreak of smallpox swept across Philadelphia, Franklin wanted the boy to be inoculated, but the procedure had to wait until Franky first recovered from a bout of dysentery.

This was a sea change for Franklin. Fifteen years earlier, during Boston's 1721 epidemic, a teenage Franklin had fiercely lobbied in his brother's newspaper against the Reverend Cotton Mather's inoculation campaign. Mather had learned of "transplantation" from the enslaved man he called Onesimus, who had received a small dose of the disease in West Africa. Sounding like an exasperated public health official addressing the "anti-vaxxers" of today, Mather said of Franklin and his supporters: "The People rave, they rail, they blaspheme, they talk not only like Ideots but like Franticks."

Among Benjamin Franklin's more admirable traits was his ability to publicly admit when he was wrong. After his young son contracted smallpox, Franklin quickly dispelled rumors that the preventative had killed him. In the *Pennsylvania Gazette,* he shared the painful news of his and Deborah's loss, while assuring readers that he believed "Inoculation was a safe and beneficial Practice."

Now, thirty-four years later, Deborah was posting to London a stream of letters calling their grandson Benny "our child" and "your son." In one note, she told Franklin that the boy looked just like their cherished Franky.

The toddler saw the resemblance, too. Deborah said that when she would show Franky's portrait to Benny "and tell him he is his littel unkill he will pat it and kiss it and Clape his hand to it." This more accurately proved Benny's resemblance to his grandfather. Franklin had commissioned the painting after Franky's death and, lacking any other images of his son, had posed for it himself.

"All who have seen my Grandson," Franklin later confided to his sister Jane, "agree with you in their Accounts of his being an uncommonly fine Boy, which brings often afresh to my Mind the Idea of my Son Franky, tho' now dead 36 Years, whom I have seldom since

Portrait of Francis (Franky) Franklin, modeled on his father's face.

seen equal'd in every thing, and whom to this Day I cannot think of without a Sigh."

His grief would not dull with time. Nearly two decades later, a Parisian friend recorded the indelible image of an elderly Franklin walking in the Bois de Boulogne, with tears flowing from his eyes as he described Franky. "Don't be surprised," Franklin said, "at the pain I still feel from such an old loss. I still imagine that this son would have been the best of my children."

After Benny's arrival and Deborah's comparison of the child to

Franky, Franklin's letters to his wife grew increasingly perfunctory. During this period, he began writing his memoir, which mentions her only in passing.

Franklin also worked under great strain in London then, fretting about money—his salary was often delayed or not paid at all—and balancing allegiances to the colonies and the Crown. In 1771, Franklin warned Americans that newly proposed taxes would be the seeds that sowed "a total disunion of the two countries."

Two years later, Chinese tea leaves steeped in Boston Harbor. To temper royal retribution, Franklin offered to pay the British East India Company out of his own pocket until its claims for the 342 ruined crates could be resolved. Yet he also leaked letters in which the Massachusetts colonial governor revealed plans to curtail American freedoms. Accused of sedition, the sixty-eight-year-old Franklin was summoned by the Privy Council to the octagonal room that had once been Henry VIII's cockpit, to be baited, humiliated, and stripped of his influential postmaster post. Five months later, in response to the Boston Tea Party, Parliament passed the punitive laws that the colonists called the Intolerable Acts. Franklin's conversion to a rebel was complete.

Deborah became an afterthought. In July 1774, he finally wrote to her to say, "I have had no Line from you by several late Opportunities: I flatter myself it is owing not to Indisposition, but to the Opinion of my having left England, which indeed I hope soon to do." They had not seen each other for a decade.

Their son William replied six months later, writing from Franklin Court. "Honoured Father," began his letter dated on Christmas Eve. "I came here on Thursday last to attend the Funeral of my poor old Mother who died the Monday Noon preceeding . . . Her Death was no more than might be reasonably expected after the paralytic Stroke she received some Time ago, which greatly affected her Memory and Understanding. She told me . . . that she never expected to see you unless you returned this Winter, for that she was sure she should not live till next Summer. I heartily wish you had happened to have come over in the Fall, as I think her Disappointment in that respect preyed a good deal on her Spirits."

After returning to Philadelphia from his wartime sojourn in Paris, in 1788 Franklin received a portrait of himself, painted by a French friend. "Our English Enemies," Franklin replied, "when they were in Possession of this City and of my House, made a Prisoner of my Portrait, and carried it off with them, leaving that of its Companion, my Wife, by itself, a kind of Widow: You have replac'd the Husband; and the Lady seems to smile, as well pleased."

She had been dead fourteen years. Franklin hung his new portrait next to Deborah's, in the home she had built for them, but one they never shared.

In 1728, the twenty-two-year-old printer jokingly composed his own epitaph. It read:

> The Body
> of
> B. Franklin, Printer;
> (Like the Cover of an old Book
> Its Contents torn out
> And stript of its Lettering and Gilding)
> Lies here, Food for Worms.
> But the Work shall not be lost:
> For it will, (as he believed) appear once more,
> In a new and more elegant Edition,
> Revised and corrected,
> By the Author.

When it came to his actual tombstone, Franklin was more succinct. He did not request an elaborate tomb, or a memorial recounting his role in the founding of the United States. In his last will and testament, Franklin stipulated only, "I wish to be buried by the side of my wife."

Their grave was to be plain and simple, as they had affected to appear in life. Franklin wanted to lie beneath a flat marble slab, "six feet long, four feet wide, plain, with only a small molding round the upper edge." If the printer knew that these dimensions would make it look like he would forever rest under a sheet of newsprint, he did not let on.

His selected mason—a man named Chambers, for he still knew the city's tradesmen—chiseled onto the stone the design that Franklin had sketched in his will, linking his name to his wife's, so it read:

BENJAMIN
AND *FRANKLIN.*
DEBORAH

No epitaph could capture Franklin's myriad achievements, and so he listed but one: Deborah.

On April 21, 1790, pallbearers lowered Franklin's body beside her and their son. For the first time since his death, Franky lay beside both parents. As a measure of how precious they counted their time with him, the boy's small headstone said that he had lived for "4 years 1 month and 4 days" and was "the delight of all that knew him."

Twenty thousand mourners turned their backs and filed away, leaving the trio to rest together in peace. But the battle over Benjamin Franklin's legacy was about to begin.

3

Franklin's Inheritors

Benjamin Franklin was, at the time, the most famous American to have died, and also the first of the country's founders to pass. His Philadelphia funeral procession paid tribute to all he had done for the city. The U.S. government, in contrast, dithered over how to mark Franklin's death, and even whether to mourn him at all.

News of his Saturday night passing did not reach the national capital of New York City until Wednesday. On that day of Franklin's burial, Secretary of State Thomas Jefferson proposed to President George Washington that the executive branch should wear "badges of mourning" in the form of a black crepe armband. Since Franklin had not died on the battlefield or in office, Washington starchily declined the suggestion, Jefferson recorded, "because he said he should not know where to draw the line, if he once began that ceremony."

Jefferson suspected another reason behind the president's dispassion for their mutual friend Franklin: John Adams. "Mr. Adams was then Vice-President," Jefferson recounted, "and I thought General Washington had his eye on him, whom he certainly did not love. I told him the world had drawn so broad a line between himself and Dr. Franklin, on the one side, and the residue of mankind, on the other, that we might wear mourning for them. He thought it best, however, to avoid it."

In his diary, Adams marked Franklin's death by adding a triumphant coda to his description of the night the pair had shared that room at the inn in 1776. Franklin "fell a Sacrifice at last," Adams harumphed, "to his own Theory; having caught the violent Cold, which finally choaked him, by sitting for some hours at a Window, with the cool Air blowing upon him." (Later, Adams would seethe, "Secrecy! Cunning! Silence! Washington! Franklin! Jefferson! Eternal Silence! impenetrable Secrecy! deep cunning! these are the talents and Virtues, which are tryumphant in these days." Imagine this man on Twitter.)

James Madison, then serving as a Virginia congressman, proposed that members of Congress don armbands for one month to commemorate Franklin. Although the House had yet to honor a private citizen this way, Franklin's various exertions of "native genius," Madison argued, "have been precious to science, to freedom, and to his country." The motion passed unanimously.

In the upper house, where John Adams presided, a similar proposal was shouted down before it could be seconded. Predictably, the loudest dissent came from southerners still incensed by Franklin's petition to abolish slavery. But they were joined by northerners, too, reproving Franklin's kinship with France.

Jefferson reported the Senate's censure to the American ambassador in Paris. "You will see," he wrote at the end of April 1790, "in the newspapers which accompany this, the details of Dr. Franklin's death. The House of Representatives resolved to wear mourning, and do it. The Senate neither resolved it nor do it."

In his final years, Franklin had seen how quickly a legacy could be erased, how easily history could be rewritten for political gain. Already his detractors were downplaying the nine years Franklin had spent in Paris forging the Franco-American alliance that had proved crucial to winning independence. At the war's outbreak, the Continental Army had been inexperienced. From Paris, Franklin had sent a letter introducing Washington to "an Officer famous throughout Europe for his

Bravery and Conduct." Casimir Pulaski would become known as the father of the U.S. cavalry, and one of only eight people awarded honorary American citizenship. Another, the Marquis de Lafayette, also sailed into the Revolution bearing a letter from Franklin.

In an intimation of the partisan divisiveness that marked Franklin's reputation after his death, Lafayette in 1781 warned him: "You Have Ennemies at Philadelphia Both Within and Without doors." Franklin brushed it off. "You mention my having enemies," he replied. "The English are in a fair way of gaining still more enemies; they play a desperate game. Fortune may favour them as it sometimes does a drunken dicer."

As the war waged on, American forces remained poorly equipped and often threadbare. "Many People have been very much alarmed lately," Franklin's daughter, Sally, wrote to him from Philadelphia at the start of 1781, "by the Soldiers of the Pensilvania line leaving their Officers and Marching towards this City to demand their Cloathing and pay from Congress, they have been without both for a long time, and frequently without provisions." The British, she said, were enticing the rebels to switch sides, and receive their salaries in full.

As a result of Franklin's entreaties, Louis XVI sent money, munitions, and then men. That autumn, twenty-nine French ships and eight thousand troops fought alongside a roughly equal number of American soldiers at Yorktown, forcing the British to surrender and effectively ending the war. In his will, Franklin's sole bequest to George Washington was a reminder of this shared victory. "My fine crab-tree walking stick," Franklin wrote, "with a gold head curiously wrought in the form of the cap of liberty, I give to my friend, and the friend of mankind, General Washington. If it were a Sceptre, he has merited it, and would become it." The walking stick had been given to Franklin by a French countess whose two sons had fought with Washington at Yorktown. Today the gift, standing alone in its own display case, is among the first items visitors see when entering the Smithsonian's National Museum of American History.

The colonies were free; France was all but broke. In the end, it spent as much as Britain fighting America's Revolution. As Franklin and other framers drafted the U.S. Constitution, France diverted 43 percent of its national budget to service its war debt. Louis XVI confessed that he never thought about the American Revolution without regret.

Although at the start of his will Franklin identified himself—after "printer"—as the "late Minister Plenipotentiary from the United States of America to the Court of France," he, too, felt a sting of resentment from that time. On his return to Philadelphia in 1785, Franklin had been dismayed to learn that Congress would not reward him for their shared success, as it had the other American diplomats. As late as the winter of 1788, Franklin had expressed hope for the gift of "a Grant of some small Tract of Land in [the] Western Country, which might have been of Use and some Honour to my Posterity." After none was forthcoming, Franklin remained optimistic that Congress "will do something of the kind for me, whenever they shall be pleased to take my Services into Consideration."

Instead, Congress stiffed him, going so far as to refuse to pay amounts still due to his French wine merchants and grocers. The indignities piled up. After Franklin had been sacked as colonial postmaster in the run-up to the war, the British nonetheless honored the tradition that allowed former holders of the office to receive and send letters for free. "But in America," Franklin grumbled, "I have ever since had the Postage demanded of me, which since my Return from France has amounted to above £50 much of it occasion'd by my having acted as Minister there." The first U.S. postmaster now had to pay for his voluminous mail himself, just like everyone else.

In July 1789, nine months before Franklin died, he received a letter from an erstwhile Parisian neighbor, who exclaimed, "How I miss you in our beautiful moment!" Revolutionaries, he reported, had stormed the Bastille prison, a hated symbol of the king's unchecked power. "If only you had remained in France! You would have had for the second time witnessed the spectacle of an incredible revolution." The nation had "shaken off the yoke" of priests, nobles, and the king. "We will probably have an excellent constitution; our representatives almost unanimously agree with your opinions. Our happiness adds still to your glory."

France's first National Assembly consisted of a single legislature, which Franklin held to be the best design of government, since it provided equal representation among all regions, regardless of size or revenue. Franklin's fellow Constitutional Convention delegates had not been swayed by his arguments. In the same year that the Bastille fell, Franklin again felt rebuked, after Pennsylvania moved to replace its unicameral state legislature with a bicameral one. At the start of his will, he proudly identified himself—after printer, and minister to France—as "President of the State of Pennsylvania." Altering the legislature that he had helped draw up, he wrote in a note, revealed "a Disposition among some of our People to commence an Aristocracy, by giving the Rich a Predominancy in Government." The names of the two chambers irked him, too, since one proudly called itself the "UPPER House," while the other was "degraded" as "the LOWER."

Franklin's thinking had won him no new fans in the U.S. Senate. After he died, the disparaging whispers grew louder. Hadn't the old man passed the war as a pampered *bon papa*, mincing from fête to fête on gout-swollen feet? Didn't he behave scandalously, saucily flirting with libertine women, including one who enjoyed playing chess with him as she soaked in a bath? Never mind that his accusers—John Adams and his wife, Abigail, foremost among them—could not prove that these dalliances had been consummated. From the beginning of American politics, the mere hint of sex was enough to birth a scandal. Lurid minds could fill in the details. The truth here was less salacious. Chief among Franklin's supposed Paris paramours was a sixty-six-year-old known for her intelligence, lively salon, and clowder of eighteen silk-beribboned cats. Madame Helvétius was not an ingenue, but a

witty widowed cat lady who fervently supported American independence, and chose to remain unattached herself.

In April 1790, Pennsylvania senator William Maclay arrived in the
Senate on the day the news of Franklin's death reached New York, fully
expecting to "drape arms for a month." In his diary, Maclay admitted
that he was "never much of an admirer of Franklin. He had every fault
of vanity and ambition." Listening to his peers refuse to mourn the
man, however, "was really insulting. I could hardly find it in my heart
to paint the devil so black."

Many of Franklin's most strident northern detractors would form
the Federalists, the country's first political party. Its members favored
closer ties with Britain, a strong central government, and checks on
direct democracy. Even before Franklin's last will and testament's egali-
tarian bequests were made public, his aristocratic attackers twinned his
name with working-class rabble.

It is tempting to draw a connection between his peers' conduct and
Franklin's addition of the loan scheme to his will. There is something
unknowable in every person's life, let alone one who lived so long ago.
But perhaps Franklin's ill treatment reminded him that Charles-Joseph Mathon's Fortunate Richard had reproached France's leaders with
barbed bequests. Franklin's two-hundred-year wager on the working
class can also be read as a bet against the factional elites that he feared
would otherwise rule the republic.

Whatever its intent, Franklin's last will and testament ensured that
his legacy would not be so easily muted. Within a fortnight of his
death, the tradesman made headlines again.

To the town of Boston, the place of his nativity," the *Massachusetts
Central* reported in May 1790, "he has left a liberal and well judged
token of his remembrance; to the city of Philadelphia, his second place
of birth, he has left the same. But time alone can unfold to his coun-

try and his fellow-men, the numerous treasures of wisdom, which his patriotism and philanthropy have bequeathed them."

The newspaper did not report that Franklin intended his gift to be unwrapped across two centuries. The details of his final codicil had yet to be publicized; first the cities had to agree to accept their £1,000. Franklin had cannily attached a contingency to his bequest, in the event that either would blanche at the prospect of administering his loan scheme. "If one of them," he wrote in his will, "accepts the money with the conditions, and the other refuses, my will then is, that both Sums be given to the inhabitants of the city accepting the whole, to be applied to the same purposes."

Franklin played into his hometowns' rivalry. At his death, the port of Philadelphia was America's pluralistic center of commerce, publishing, and politics. Boston, in contrast, was a largely Puritan, hierarchal town, best known for its churches and academies.

"Boston was our Bristol," noted one historian, "Philadelphia our London." After the British capital, Philadelphia was the world's second-largest English-speaking city. New York was just beginning its ascent. In 1790, its residents, and the federal government, largely clustered at the southern tip of Manhattan. Broadway was still a cattle trail.

Pennsylvania's state constitution, largely penned by Franklin in 1776, was considered America's most democratic; Massachusetts's, mostly written by John Adams, was its inverse.

Adams had been unimpressed by Franklin's adopted home. "Phyladelphia with all its Trade, and Wealth, and Regularity is not Boston," he recorded on his first visit, in 1774. "The Morals of our People are much better; their Manners are more polite and agreeable—they are purer English. Our Language is better, our Persons are handsomer; our Spirit is greater, our Laws are wiser, our Religion is superior, our Education is better. We exceed them in every Thing, but in a Markett, and in charitable public foundations."

Had Franklin branded his philanthropy as an aggrandizing self-advertisement, Adams might have realized that most of Philadelphia's public foundations had been started by his nemesis. Uniquely for his time, and ours, Franklin refused to name his charitable works after himself.

The mingy, absentee feudal governance of the Penns (whose colony appended their surname to the Latin *sylva,* or "woods") had left a vacuum that Franklin's industrious altruism readily filled. In a few square blocks, Adams *could* have walked past signboards for the Franklin Academy, Franklin Hospital, Franklin Library, Franklin Fire Brigade, Franklin Insurance Company, and Franklin Battery, home to the Franklin Militia. The sweepers scooping up horse droppings from Philadelphia's crushed-gravel streets *could* have dumped their loads into carts labeled FRANKLIN STREET CLEANERS. Furthermore, at a printshop Adams *could* have purchased copies of the *Franklin Gazette* and *Poor Benjamin's Almanack.*

If Adams countered that Franklin's famous stove bore his name, he would learn that its users, not its inventor, called it that. Nor had Franklin profited from the stove's design. In his memoir, he recalled that Pennsylvania's governor had offered him "a Patent for the sole Vending of them for a Term of Years; but I declin'd it from a Principle which has ever weigh'd with me on such Occasions, viz. *That as we enjoy great Advantages from the Inventions of others, we should be glad of an Opportunity to serve others by any Invention of ours; and this we should do freely and generously.*"

While the first federal patent act was not passed until 1790, under colonial law Franklin could have applied for the exclusive commercial use of his many inventions. He believed, however, that technology should be shared for the common good. Today he is considered a forefather of the open source movement.

A habitual tinkerer, Franklin made the well-vented, efficient stove to better warm Deborah and Sally's hearth, and pump the choking woodsmoke outside. He crafted the lightning rod to protect his own house, and then published the design so it could be replicated widely.

In 2016, the Maryland State House was saved by the twenty-eight-foot rod, built to Franklin's specifications, that had guarded its dome for over two centuries.

Franklin came up with bifocals so that, while traveling, he could shift his gaze between a close-at-hand book and the far-off scenery without switching glasses. He invented a now-ubiquitous medical device to help his older brother John, who suffered from a bladder stone. "Reflecting yesterday on your Desire to have a flexible catheter," Franklin wrote to him in 1752, "a Thought struck into my Mind how one might possibly be made . . . I went immediately to the Silversmith's, and gave Directions for making one, (sitting by 'till it was finish'd), that it might be ready for this Post." (Spare a thought for John, perhaps puckering as he read the next line.) "But now it is done I have some Apprehensions that it may be too large to be easy."

In 1756, one of the last full years he would spend in America for the next three decades, Franklin's Philadelphia taxable property was assessed at a total of £60. That made the fifty-year-old well-off, but in a city of thirteen thousand, some two hundred residents were richer on paper. Franklin paid the city a levy of 1.6 percent, totaling £1. Other Philadelphians in that bracket worked as coopers, hatters, distillers, butchers, potters, shoemakers, and tavern keepers. But unlike those tradesmen, Franklin received a steady stream of income — untaxed then — without breaking a sweat. To independent entrepreneurs he leased printshops stretching from upper New England to the West Indies, creating the first commercial franchise chain in America. While Franklin's assets grew across the next three decades — he did, after all, die in a house that had a name — the £2,000 he left to support Boston's and Philadelphia's tradesmen still comprised a sizable proportion of his estate.

Nine days after Franklin's death, his friend, the astronomer David Rittenhouse, inventoried Franklin Court. Although Franklin's will would not be contested — at least not until the centennial of his passing — and inheritances were not taxed, in the margin Rittenhouse added his estimate of each item's worth.

The most valuable was a diamond-encircled portrait of Louis XVI, valued by Rittenhouse at £1,750. Franklin's second-highest asset, worth £1,000, was his "printing office and letter foundry." It was a steep drop-off to third place: Franklin's 4,267-volume library, calculated to be worth a little over £184. Rittenhouse's three-page inventory included the telescope Franklin left to him (£43), the harpsichord Franklin had sent to Sally from London (£25), scientific equipment ("French wayweiser," £5), sundry furniture ("6 old chairs," £3), and his Chinese gong (also £3). Rittenhouse catalogued everything, from Franklin's forty-six honorary medals down to his andirons (£1).

If not for the king's diamonds and his own printing press, the £2,000 that Franklin entrusted to Boston and Philadelphia could have purchased the entire contents of his house — three times over.

Rittenhouse did not tabulate Franklin's entire real estate portfolio, but only three mortgages he had underwritten, totaling £7,877. In addition to the governor's salary owed to him by Pennsylvania, Franklin held £1,800 in bank stock, £500 in "State Paper," and £3,051 in loan certificates. If any money was on deposit in faraway banks in Paris and London, Rittenhouse did not include it. He did record the balance of Franklin's Philadelphia account: £136, 19 shillings, and 3 pence.

Poor Richard said, "A fat Kitchen makes a lean Will." In the house itself, Franklin had left behind coins that totaled a little over £2.

"Life, like a dramatic Piece," he once mused to a friend, "should not only be conducted with Regularity, but methinks it should finish handsomely. Being now in the last Act, I begin to cast about for something fit to end with."

A well-written will can disperse not only a lifetime of accumulated wealth but also earned wisdom. Franklin's parting words read like the missing chapters of his memoir, and his bequests were more than just tangible assets. Each one imparted a lesson to his beneficiaries — friends, family, and especially the republic he had helped found.

· · ·

Franklin was right to expect that the document would be made public. "I hear my Dear Brothers will is Printed," his sister Jane wrote to his daughter, Sally, in 1790. "I wish you would send me won of them."

The actual will can be seen in Philadelphia, at the American Philosophical Society. It's thrilling to handle the document's twelve pages —since bound in red leather, giving it the heft of an oversize menu at a pricey restaurant—not least because of the precariousness of the red wax blot, still clinging to the parchment, that punctuates Franklin's billowing signature.

"The Public Curiosity was greatly excited to know [the will's] Contents," Franklin's grandson Benny wrote to his fiancée two weeks after attending the Philadelphia funeral. The bequests "have much surprised some of _my_ good Friends & well wishers . . . Dr. F has left more than I expected."

Benny, the infant whom Deborah had once adored, now looked like a twenty-one-year-old facsimile of a young "Dr. F." To this beloved grandson Franklin left all his "types and printing materials." According to the estate inventory, the press was worth only half of what Franklin had devoted to his loan scheme. But to Benny, its true value was incalculable. His inheritance, he wrote, "is chiefly in Tools that [my] Industry are to put in Motion."

Franklin had raised Benny in his image, starting when he brought the boy at the age of seven along with him to Paris. A neighbor recalled watching the elderly Franklin teach Benny to swim in the early morning, "crossing the Seine with him from one side to the other." Benny told a visitor that his grandfather was "very different from other old persons, for they were fretful and complaining and dissatisfied, and he is laughing and cheerful like a young person."

Although Benny's tutors taught him how to dance, draw, and fence, Franklin wanted him to master practical skills. He oversaw his penmanship lessons, and soon Benny's ballooning signature replicated Franklin's. In the year that Benny turned fourteen, he wrote home to Philadelphia, "I learn to Print and send you a Copy of my first Printing."

The grandfather was teaching the grandson his treasured trade.

"He is a very sensible and a very good Lad, and I love him much," Franklin told Benny's parents. "I had Thoughts of . . . fitting him for Public Business, thinking he might be of Service hereafter to his Country; but being now convinc'd that *Service is no Inheritance,* as the Proverb says, I have determin'd to give him a Trade that he may have something to depend on, and not be oblig'd to ask Favours or Offices of any body."

After Franklin's death, Benny would make use of his inheritance to defend his grandfather against Federalists who slandered his legacy. These enemies, whose ranks included John Adams, would nickname the boy "Lightning Rod Junior."

Franklin's other grandson Temple had also accompanied him to Paris. The Franklin trio lodged in a mansion owned by a merchant sympathetic to American independence. The boys had roamed its orangery and, from the manicured emerald lawns that sloped to the Seine's Right Bank, watched demonstrations of a new invention called a hot-air balloon. (Upon hearing a man scoff, "What good is it?" Franklin reportedly retorted, "What good is a newborn baby?") Temple would later be credited as the recipient of the first airmailed letter, sent by balloon across the English Channel from his exiled father, William, in London.

For the Franklins, the War of Independence was also a civil war. Franklin had intended his heir apparent to be his firstborn son, William. As a teen, "Billy" had traveled the colonies at his father's side and assisted in his scientific experiments. It was likely William's hand that held the storm-lashed kite string when his father, as one account evocatively put it, "presented his knuckle to the key, and (let the reader judge of the exquisite pleasure he must have felt at that moment) perceived a very evident electric spark."

Another current ran through them. When he accompanied his father on his 1757 trip to London, the illegitimate William himself fathered an illegitimate son. Temple, who never knew his mother, was named for the city's Middle Temple, one of the Inns of Court where William was studying law.

In 1761, Franklin took his son to the coronation of George III. "I was enable to see the whole Ceremony," William wrote to his sister, Sally, "and to walk in the Procession quite into [Westminster] Abbey." Little did William suspect that he had paced the fault line that would sever father from son.

Upon returning to America, William — through Franklin's connections — was appointed the royal governor of New Jersey. In 1774, after the British had censured Franklin and stripped him of his posts, he had warned William that he should also expect to be sacked. It was not a job worth keeping, Franklin pointedly noted, "since it has not afforded you sufficient to prevent your running every year behind hand with me." William's debt notwithstanding, Franklin advised him to wait to be fired, since in politics, "one may make something of an Injury, nothing of a resignation."

William sided with the Crown. Franklin, stunned and unemployed in London, demanded repayment. William broke his two-month silence only to report Deborah's death. In that sad letter, he encouraged his father to return home, "to a Country where the People revere you, and are inclined to pay a Deference of Opinions." The deadlocked Second Continental Congress had suffered from Franklin's absence, "as they imagined had you been there you would have framed some Plan for an Accommodation of Differences."

Militiamen arrested William in 1776. As his father edited the Declaration of Independence in Philadelphia, the loyalist rotted in a spartan Connecticut jail cell assigned to prisoners condemned to die. "I suffer so much in being thus buried alive," he wrote, "that I should deem it a favor to be immediately taken out and shot." Two years of malnourished confinement took most of his teeth and hair. George Washington denied William's parole request so he could say goodbye to his bedridden wife, who died, alone, from an ailing heart.

Two years earlier, Franklin had angrily promised William that he would make Temple, then under his supervision, into a "Free Man," independent of political patronage, since "Posts and Places are precarious Dependencies." But a decade later in France, Franklin the diplomat thrust the teenage Temple into a world of courtly favor, making him his personal secretary. If the exiled William could have seen Benjamin West's painting of the signing of the Treaty of Paris, he would have spotted his father seated at that familiar table, flanked on the left

A half-painted Temple appears to the right of his grandfather. The British representatives refused to sit for Benjamin West, who left the portrait unfinished.

by John Jay and John Adams, and on the right by Henry Laurens and
—in a sort of eighteenth-century photobomb—Temple. William had
lost both wars.

He also lost his inheritance. While Franklin's previous two wills
had left William a substantial slice of his estate, in his final version he
closed their account. Listing William as his first bequest—where readers could not help but take notice of his wounding words—Franklin
pronounced: "To my Son William Franklin late Governor of the Jer-
seys, I give and devise all the lands I hold or have a right to, in the
province of Nova Scotia. I also give to him all my books and papers,
which he has in his possession, and all debts standing against him on
my account books. The part he acted against me in the late war, which
is of public notoriety, will account for my leaving him no more of an
estate he endeavoured to deprive me of."

On paper, the land—twenty thousand acres granted by the Crown
to Franklin in 1767—appeared to hold significant value. But William
would have known that this thirty-square-mile plot was barren, often
frozen, and, at the time, completely worthless. (Today it is the site of the
Halifax airport and the village of Enfield, population 4,469.) Moreover,
all of William's books and papers—indeed, everything he had owned
—had been burned or destroyed in the war. Franklin likely knew this.
Canceling his son's debt added further insult. William thought it had
been settled when he had signed over to Temple his last remaining
American asset, some six hundred acres of New Jersey farmland.

Benny, writing to his fiancée after his grandfather's passing, tabulated the value of each of Franklin's four main heirs' inheritance. Next
to William's name he inked "0000."

The will deprived William even further. Franklin replaced his son
with his son-in-law, leaving his musical instruments, a gold watch,
cash bonds, and the bulk of his Philadelphia real estate—including
the two-acre Northern Liberties pasture where William had boarded
his childhood pony, and where he and his father had likely flown the
kite—to Sally's husband, Richard Bache. William cursed the man as
"that fortune-hunter."

Unrepentant, William lived on a £500 royal pension in a rented flat near Trafalgar Square, on the dead-end Suffolk Street. (At its entrance today, a statue depicts his king, George III, rearing up on a horse, and also going nowhere.) "The Revolution in America and the Shameful Injustice of my Father's Will," William wrote to a friend, "have in a manner dissolved all my Connexions in that Part of the World of a private as well as publick Nature." But Franklin's will would pull William back into his father's orbit yet.

If Franklin's bequest to his apprentice Benny promoted the tools of a trade that had helped forge American democracy, then his posthumous censure of William delivered a lesson in loyalty, to both family and flag.

Franklin's gifts to his daughter, Sally, meanwhile, set an example that was rare in an inequitable era of coverture laws. After leaving her the bulk of his real estate—including Franklin Court and its household items—to own together with her husband, Franklin also gave Sally a portfolio of bank shares to hold independently, "as her private pocket money" for her "sole and separate use." Perhaps to forestall any disquiet at Franklin Court due to dented pride, Franklin added, "This provision for my daughter is not made out of any disrespect I have for her husband."

His progressive paternalism did not, however, extend to giving Sally carte blanche with his most valuable bequest, which he also passed solely into her hands. This gift came with a lesson attached, meant for all Americans.

"The King of France's Picture set with Four hundred and eight Diamonds," Franklin continued in his will, "I give to my daughter."

As her father had prepared to depart from Paris in 1785, Louis XVI had told Temple, "I want Mr. Franklin to be treated well." While diplomats often received tokens of appreciation from their hosts, his gemstone-ringed portrait broke the mold. Temple estimated that the gift, ringed with diamonds "of a beautiful water," was worth five times the value of the gold snuff boxes given to the other American ministers. Such a souvenir would have been useless to Franklin, who, ever watchful of his scarred lungs and health, "never snuffed, chewed, or smoked," and was certain that "tobacco would, in a few years, go out of use."

Under the Articles of Confederation—drafted in part by Franklin—American officeholders were banned from receiving "any present, emolument, office, or title of any kind whatever, from any King, Prince, or foreign State." But given Louis's crucial support for American independence, Franklin decorously accepted his gift. On his return to Philadelphia, Franklin declared the present to Congress, which allowed him to keep it, and soon after added to the Constitution what became known as the Emoluments Clause.

No American officeholder could accept an unapproved gift from abroad, but Sally was bound only by her father's request, written into his will after handing her the king's carats, "that she would not form any of those diamonds into ornaments either for herself or daughters, and thereby introduce or countenance the expensive, vain, and useless fashion of wearing jewels in this country; and those immediately connected with the picture may be preserved with the same." Franklin had made his point, but he also had failed to suggest what a Philadelphia mother of seven—including a son named for Louis—might do with such an extravagant bauble.

Franklin's gift to his grandson Temple was weighted with more explicit instructions and expectations. In Paris, Temple had earned a reputation as a fop, and so in his will Franklin stipulated that the thirty-one-year-old's large, £3,500 debt to him would be canceled only "upon the day of his marriage." Perhaps a spouse could improve Temple, as Deborah had Franklin. In addition to that elusive Chinese gong, he also left Temple a potentially lucrative treasure chest: "All my manuscripts and papers."

Franklin may well have reconsidered the gift had he known Thomas Jefferson's privately stated measure of Temple's ability, which he rated as "good enough for common uses but not great enough for uncommon ones." But after Franklin had failed to secure a government post for Temple, then watched his grandson fail in law studies and at farming, Franklin bet that this bequest would provide for him for life. In leaving his papers to Temple, Franklin also had selected his personally groomed editor, an ally whose work, he hoped, would cement both of their reputations for posterity.

Temple vowed to start the project immediately, booking passage to London and Paris to retrieve the manuscripts left there. But his old political habits died hard. First he informed John Adams of his forthcoming trip, adding, "If during my stay in Europe I can in anyway be useful to your Excellency, I beg you will command me freely, & be assur'd that I shall at all times be happy to prove to you my Gratitude."

Adams brushed off this toadying. Instead, the vice president presciently advised the easily distracted Temple to publish his grandfather's papers as quickly as possible. "A certain ardor of curiosity," he warned, "wears off in such cases commonly in time."

But Franklin's will, designed to keep him in the public eye, would prove Adams wrong. Twenty years later, Adams would still be stewing over Franklin's reminder to its readers that he had diverted his gubernatorial salary to fund his loan scheme for tradesmen.

"No sentiment more weak and superficial was ever avowed," Adams wrote to a newspaper, referring to Franklin's insistence that elected officials should not be paid, "than one that he procured to be inserted in the first constitution of Pennsylvania, and for which he had such a fondness as to insert it in his will . . . unless he meant by one satyric touch, to ridicule his own republic, and throw it into everlasting contempt."

In the summer that followed the founder's death, no American leader stood to deliver his eulogy. In France, however, the paeans poured forth. French republicans beatified the man who "ripped lightning from the sky, and the scepter from tyrants." Paris vendors sold Franklin's likeness, carved (they swore) from Bastille stones. In portraits, his face shone alongside those of Voltaire and Rousseau: "Liberté, Égalité, Fraternité" personified. Louis XVI supposedly had Franklin's image painted, too—at the bottom of his Sèvres chamber pot.

Franklin died before French revolutionaries would prove Poor Richard's maxim "A Mob's a Monster: Heads enough, but no Brains." He would never read how a young Madame Tussaud watched red-capped Jacobins seize wax heads from her tutor's display cases to parade through the streets on pikes, soon to be replaced by real ones, including the king's.

Franklin, incidentally, had known the guillotine's namesake, having once served with Joseph-Ignace Guillotin on a royal committee that debunked the efficacy of Franz Mesmer's hypnotic treatments. Mesmer had ended his sessions for patients by playing the hauntingly pitched notes of the glass armonica, invented by Franklin, the hub around which the Western Hemisphere then seemed to spin.

In June 1790, two months after Franklin's Philadelphia funeral, a drafter of the Declaration of the Rights of Man and of the Citizen solemnly announced to the silent French National Assembly, *"Franklin est mort."* The Comte de Mirabeau, his porcine face sagging with gravitas, continued: "Long enough, court etiquette has proclaimed hypocritical mourning periods. Nations should wear mourning only for their benefactors."

Mirabeau proposed that for three days members of the National Assembly don black. The Revolutionary War hero Lafayette—who had received a lock of Franklin's hair, cut postmortem—seconded, and the motion passed unanimously. The edict proved embarrassing for one representative, who was forced to borrow a much taller man's dark coat. Three years before unleashing the Reign of Terror, Maximilien Robespierre skulked around Paris in an oversize jacket, resembling a child playing dress-up.

Two days later, at the Palais Royal, mourners heard the first official eulogy anywhere for Franklin. A speaker related that on the day Franklin signed the Treaty of Paris, he had marveled aloud, "Could I have hoped at my age to have experienced such happiness?"

Three thousand Parisians packed into the Halle aux Blés, or Grain Exchange, whose tall wooden dome inspired the design of the U.S. Capitol. At the center of the black-draped hall stood a bust of Franklin. In his encomium, a bishop who had stormed the Bastille proposed placing a pyramid to honor Franklin in the middle of the Atlantic Ocean. He did not say how.

At the Académie des Sciences, a eulogizer credited Franklin's Pennsylvania Constitution as the French ideal. At the Académie Royale de Médicine, Marie Antoinette's physician proclaimed, "One man is dead, and two worlds are in mourning."

In their own ceremony, Parisian printers arranged the tools of their trade around Franklin's bust, making a shrine to "Saint Benjamin," the patron saint of printers.

"Franklin was born as poor as the poorest among us," one printer pronounced, "but he had the courage not to be ashamed by poverty." The line recalled Poor Richard's maxim "Having been poor is no shame, but being ashamed of it is." Take pride in your trade, the Frenchman continued, for a free press topples tyrants. As he spoke, colleagues set his words in type, inked them onto paper, and delivered the pages across Paris only moments after the event. When viewed from Franklin's own perspective, could any tribute have topped that?

Today Franklin's likeness sits on a pedestal in the city's square de Yorktown, near the site of the château where he lived with Benny and Temple during the war. His bronze gaze studies the traffic on rue Benjamin Franklin. The memorial was a gift from Philadelphia, in gratitude for the Statue of Liberty, and has oxidized to the same shade of green. If Franklin could turn his head slightly to the right, he could see the Eiffel Tower's Crown. At night it gleams like a lighthouse, shining from the far shore of the Seine. But for Franklin, always, it is just a short swim away.

4

The Morals of Chess

In the month following Franklin's death, Boston's selectmen made national news by reading his will aloud at a town meeting. "The extracts are lengthy," reported the *Gazette of the United States* in May 1790, "and contain many of those judicious and elegant maxims and observations for which the Doctor is justly celebrated."

Boston accepted his £1,000 first. Its town clerk grandiloquently—if naïvely—promised that "every step to carry into full effect his benevolent plan will be cheerfully pursued by those, who he was pleased to constitute his Trustees, and rising generations will for ages Bless the Name of their illustrious Friend & Benefactor."

Philadelphia's belated acknowledgment read like it had finally escaped from bureaucratic molasses—and also gave a taste of what was to come. The city council resolved "that the Mayor be desired to notify the Executors of the Will of Doctor Benjamin Franklin that the Corporation do accept the Legacy left to them by Doctor Franklin; and that they will receive the same at any time when the Executors will pay it."

Franklin had requested that his loans to tradesmen begin within a year. In the twelve months that would pass before the first borrowers were approved, his other beneficiaries received their gifts. As with the bequests to his main inheritors, these smaller gifts give a deeper understanding of who Franklin was at his death and how he wanted to be remembered.

"One of the greatest Comforts of Life, to old People," Franklin once observed to his sister Jane, was one "their Friends should endeavour to accommodate them in. When they have long liv'd in a House, it becomes natural to them, they are almost as closely connected with it as the Tortoise with his Shell, they die if you tear them out of it. Old Folks and old Trees, if you remove them, tis ten to one that you kill them."

To Jane he kept his word: in addition to a £50 annuity to cover her living expenses, "I give and devise to my dear sister," Franklin wrote in his will, "a house and lot I have on Unity Street, Boston, to her and her heirs and for ever." Jane lived there, in the shadow of the Old North Church, until her death. The house was razed in 1933 to enlarge the Paul Revere Mall, celebrating his lantern flashes from the church's steeple. Today tourists following the inlaid red bricks marking the Freedom Trail unknowingly step through her former front door.

"My dear brother supplied all," Jane wrote to Sally in the fall of 1790. "Whatever other pleasures were, as they mostly took their rise from him, they passed like little streams from a beautiful fountain."

After leaving £300 to be divided among the children, grandchildren, and great-grandchildren of his six surviving siblings, Franklin apportioned his four-thousand-volume library among a favorite cousin, his grandsons, and the Philadelphia institutions he had founded. Most were scientific texts. One of the only novels was *Robinson Crusoe,* which Franklin had loved as a teen. It told the tale of a boy his age, also "satisfied with nothing but going to sea," who runs away from home, receives nothing from his father's estate, and yet manages, after years as a castaway, to strike it rich.

In Franklin's previous will—written in 1757 as the forty-one-year-old embarked on a voyage to England—he had concluded by giving "sincere Thanks to God" for "a loving and prudent Wife and dutiful

Children." These lines do not appear in his final will, whose only hint of piety is seen in his gift of his only (and new) Bible to his godson, the grandchild of his former London landlady. As if to balance a depiction of Eden with a scientific eye, he additionally left the boy a "botanic description of plants, in folio, with colored cuts."

While the gift of these books may have further endeared Franklin to his friends, his will's apparent lack of devotion may have cast him further from his former peers. "Had the Doctor left a deathbed Testimony in favour of religion," observed one congressman after the Senate refused to join the House in mourning, "it might have brought many of our pretended Deists to some serious Consideration: for I do believe that a man who has the reputation of great wisdom and uncommon insight into the work of nation, dying calmly & with satisfaction, has a tendency to lure thereof a careless turn of mind."

Also among the books that Franklin left in his bequests was his volume of Samuel Johnson's *A Dictionary of the English Language*. The masterwork, published in 1755, might never have been finished had Franklin succeeded in luring its author from London. In 1750, he had entreated Johnson to "undertake the Management of the ENGLISH EDUCATION" at the Philadelphia Academy, the secondary school he was helping to start.

Franklin admitted feeling unqualified to write a curriculum. "The Trustees have put it on me," he wrote Johnson, "for which I am indeed very unfit, having neither been educated myself (except as a Tradesman) nor ever concern'd in educating others." Even in his accomplished middle age, Franklin sought reassurance of his abilities. "You have never mention'd any thing to me of my Electrical Papers," he nudged his older brother John, after sending him an account of the kite experiment. "So I conjecture you have either not had time to read them, or do not like them."

Samuel Johnson politely refused Franklin's repeated invitations to lead his academy, demurring that he was too old (he was then forty) and too rustic (he actually lived in the capital of the English Enlightenment). But after reviewing Franklin's plans to promote "good reading and speaking," Johnson reassured him that "nobody would imagine that the draught you have made for an English education was done by a Tradesman. I cannot pretend to be qualified to criticize much on things of this kind having never had anything that could be called an Education myself, the most of what I *did* learn being of such a cobweb kind that the best thing I could do with it was to forget it as fast as I could."

Four decades later, Franklin similarly distanced himself from Philadelphia's school, pointedly choosing not to include it as a beneficiary in his will. At first glance, this might not have seemed such a slight. In the months after Franklin's death, the board of the Pennsylvania Hospital gathered to consider its benefactor's bequest: a "great folio ledger" whose columns showed the fees for printing and postage that Philadelphians still owed him. Franklin hoped the people listed would "be induced to pay or give as charity" their outstanding balances to the hospital. Its board members grew nonplussed as they turned the ledger's crinkling pages. "Many of the debts are small," the meeting's minutes reported, "numbers of them are due from persons unknown, and all of them from thirty to sixty years old."

Despite Franklin's benevolent intentions, the hospital would be the only entity to turn down his parting gift. The Philadelphia Academy would not be given that option. In the event that the public or press wondered why Franklin had severed ties with the school, since grown into a college, his executor held a copy of the caustic letter Franklin had sent to its leaders in the months before his death. The six-thousand-word polemic provides a window into his thinking at the time that he decided to add the loan scheme for tradesmen to his will.

In the letter, Franklin accused the college's trustees of subverting his intention of providing a "Public Education for our Youth." His founding idea, he wrote, had aimed "no farther than to procure the Means of a good English Education." After raising £2,000 from donors (the same amount that—perhaps not incidentally—he would later commit to stake his loan scheme), these "Persons of Wealth," Franklin lamented, had compelled him to add instruction in "the learned Languages" of Latin and Greek.

Slowly but insidiously, as Franklin was away in London, the school's leadership—blue bloods who counted themselves among "the principal Gentlemen of the Province"—set about to enroll the offspring of upper-crust Philadelphians. The academy would not, as Franklin had intended, serve as a great leveler, but rather erect a wall of snobbery, behind which the gatekeeping classicists promised to "promote and establish" privileged students in "Business, Offices, Marriage, or any other thing for their Advantage preferable to all other Persons whatever even of equal Merit."

The English curriculum withered as enrollment plummeted, and the faculty thinned. As the founding trustees died, adherents of the college's new mission replaced them. Book learning usurped utilitarian instruction in skills such as public speaking and accounting.

Franklin regretted raising his voice so late. "I am the only one of the original Trustees now living," his letter concluded, "and I am just stepping into the Grave myself . . . To make what Amends are yet in my power, I seize this Opportunity, the last I may possibly have. I seem here to be surrounded by the Ghosts of my dear departed Friends, beckoning and urging me to use the only Tongue now left us, in demanding that Justice to our Grand children that our Children have been denied."

And so, in his last will and testament, Benjamin Franklin, unlike countless donors to come, did not leave money to a college, let alone to one that he had founded. When viewed alongside his letter to the Philadelphia Academy, Franklin's concurrent creation of his loan scheme reads like a protest. If £2,000 could establish a small city school that, within only four decades, had grown into the University of Pennsylvania, what opportunities could the same amount of money create for skilled tradesmen across the next two hundred years?

Franklin put his faith in America's future into the hands of its working class. While living in Paris, he had promised would-be immigrants that unlike Europeans, Americans "do not enquire concerning a stranger, *What IS he?* but *What can he DO?* If he has any useful art, he is welcome; and if he exercises it and behaves well, he will be respected by all that know him." Such skilled newcomers would "have no need of the Patronage of great Men; and every one will enjoy securely the Profits of his Industry."

This may seem a bit rich coming from the man who would complain about having to pay for his own postage, and who donned a black velvet suit and white silk stockings to sup at Versailles. But the trappings of high society were never a natural fit for Franklin. Marie Antoinette had seen right through his disguise. Glimpsing Franklin for the first time, as he stood, wigless, "among the decorated ministers of the great powers of Europe," the queen doubted that genius pulsed "under such a modest and simple exterior." What had Franklin been, she asked a courtier, before becoming the American ambassador? "An apprentice printer" came the reply. In France, sniffed Marie Antoinette, Benjamin Franklin would have risen to become, at most, a bookseller.

French revolutionaries mourned him throughout the fervid summer of 1790. In the United States, as the mulberry tree at the heart of Franklin Court dropped its leaves, the death of comparably minor personalities, including the former Massachusetts governor James Bowdoin (Harvard class of 1745), had produced dozens of memorials. As winter approached, no American had yet to deliver Benjamin Franklin's eulogy.

A packet from Paris sat unopened on George Washington's Mount Vernon desk. (The federal government was trundling south, to the new national capital of Philadelphia.) The envelope, stuffed with French letters of condolence and transcripts of Parisian memorials, gave Washington pause. The sender had addressed it to "The President and Members of the American Congress." The Constitution clearly separated the executive and legislative branches. Who, then, should break the envelope's seal?

Washington decided to forward the package without comment to the president of the Senate. John Adams (Harvard class of 1755), also noticing its dual address, returned the envelope, unopened, to Washington. The president then passed this diplomatic hot potato to his secretary of state, who finally broke the seal. Seeing that its French senders had addressed their letter to Congress, Thomas Jefferson sent the parcel back to Adams. Now it was December; eight months had passed since Franklin died.

Would he have been surprised or stung by these events? Franklin had fallen from public favor before, only to see his esteem rebound. He possessed a patient and calculating mind. Listed among the pages of his library's inventory, one title stands out. Some thirty years earlier, Franklin had written to Deborah from London, requesting that she send him some things. "Among my Books on the Shelves," he wrote, "there are two or three on the Game of Chess; One in French bound in Leather . . . You may know the French one, by the Word *échecs* in the Titlepage." She mailed it to him. Franklin, an avid player throughout his life, would go on to write the first essay on the game in America, "The Morals of Chess," published four years before his passing.

"Chess is not merely an idle amusement," Franklin contended. "For life is a kind of chess, in which we have often points to gain, and competitors or adversaries to contend with, and in which there is a vast variety of good and ill events, that are, in some degree, the effects of prudence or the want of it. By playing at chess, then, we may learn: *Foresight,* which looks a little into futurity, and considers the consequences that may attend an action: for it is continually occurring to the player, 'If I move this piece, what will be the advantages of my new situation? What use can my adversary make of it to annoy me? What other moves can I make to support it, and to defend myself from his attacks?'"

Chess also taught its players circumspection, by requiring them to keep an eye on the entire board. *"Lastly,"* Franklin concluded, "we learn by chess the habit of *not being discouraged* by *present* bad appearances in the state of our affairs, the habit of *hoping for a favourable change,* and that of *persevering in the search of resources.* The game is so full of events, there is such a variety of turns in it, the fortune of it is so subject to sudden vicissitudes . . . that one is encouraged to continue the contest to the last."

Through his last will and testament, Franklin played on. After his moves had toppled a real-life king, he cautioned a friend in France in 1788, "We must not expect that a new government may be formed as a game of chess may be played, by a skillful hand, without a fault. The players of our game are so many, their ideas so different, their prejudices so strong and so various, and their particular interests independent of the general seeming so opposite, that not a move can be made that is not contested."

"You know we have two parties with us," Alexander Hamilton told a British diplomat in the winter of 1790. "There are gentlemen, who think we ought to be connected with France in the most intimate terms; there are others who are at least as numerous, and influential, who decidedly prefer an English connexion."

John Adams made his allegiance clear when Congress returned to session that December. He finally deigned to read France's condolences for Franklin's death, mailed six months earlier. The vice president "looked over the letter some time," wrote Senator William Maclay in his diary, "and then began reading . . . and then said some sarcastic things against the National Assembly for abolishing Titles."

Maclay, a reedy, high-browed man whose portrait could stand for Ichabod Crane's, loathed Adams. He detested the vice president's "self-conceit," "vacant laugh," and tendency to sit like "a monkey just put into breeches." What irritated Maclay most was Adams's very face, which often bore "the most silly kind of half smile which I can not well express in English. The Scotch-Irish have a word that hits it exactly —smudging."

Facing the classroom-size Senate from his canopied dais in Philadelphia's new Congress Hall, Adams dismissed France's respects with indifference. Alone among his twenty-six peers, Maclay rose to a boil. "I could not help remarking," he recorded, "that this whole Matter was received and transacted with a coldness and apathy that astonished me . . . There might be others who indulged the same sentiments. But 'twas silence all!"

The matter dragged through the winter, until Thomas Jefferson finally convinced Congress to grant George Washington the authority to respond to France as president. The motion passed on February 22, 1791, the president's fifty-ninth birthday.

Maclay, still smarting over the Senate's display of a "coldness that was truly amazing," foresaw a botched job. "I cannot help painting to myself the disappointment that awaits the French Patriots," he wrote in his diary, "while their warm fancies are figuring the raptures that we will be thrown into, on the Receipt of their letter, and the information of the honors which they have bestowed on our Countryman, and anticipating the complimentary echos of our Answers, when they find that we, cold as Clay, care not a fig about them, Franklin or Freedom."

In the end, Washington assigned Alexander Hamilton the task of writing the letter, which the president then signed.

At Washington's birthday party, which counted John Adams and most of Congress among its guests, Philadelphia's merchants stood to raise a pointed toast, honoring France, Lafayette, and "the memory of Doctor Franklin."

The battle over his legacy was fought in close quarters. The President's House, Congress Hall, and the Pennsylvania State House (today's Independence Hall) all stood within blocks of Franklin's tombstone. In the state house, William Maclay's younger brother Samuel convinced his fellow Pennsylvania state senators to circumvent Congress and send their own letter of gratitude to France. From the grave, Franklin occasioned one of the earliest tests of the government that he had helped to create.

"It is the first step of the kind that has been taken by a sovereign state," the French ambassador reported to Paris. "They tell me that other states of the union will at once follow the example of Pennsylvania."

When Virginia's governor asked Thomas Jefferson whether such independent actions undermined the country's foundational, and nascent, separation of powers, the secretary of state replied, "I am of [the] opinion that all communications between nations should pass through the channels of their Executives." But here, for his friend Franklin, he made an exception.

In Paris, the National Assembly heard Pennsylvania's letter read alongside Jefferson's own thank-you, to which he added a brief civics lesson, explaining that it was not Congress, but rather the executive branch, through its State Department, that transacted American diplomacy. Once their applause died down, the French politicians pledged everlasting amity with the United States and called for a new trade treaty with its fellow revolutionaries.

This resolution only confirmed John Adams's fears. Fretting that a rival would emerge to challenge his ascension to the presidency, Adams wrote to the painter John Trumbull, "There is a French interest at work to this purpose as deep as it is wicked. Panegyricks upon panegyricks come from Europe upon some characters in order to lessen others." He suspected that universities poisoned the youth against him. "Politicks are carried on instead of Philosophy in learned and scientific Academies." The news was fake, too. "Newspapers from Georgia to New Hampshire Magazines are Cooked and dress'd. The populace are made the dupes of their own feelings."

Trumbull, known as the painter of the Revolution, did not reply. Adams had misjudged the young man's allegiances.

"I wish you to be his patron," Trumbull's father had written to Benjamin Franklin in Paris eleven years earlier. "Nothing can give me more pleasure than to hear from you, that his manner of improving his Time, and his Companions, meet your Approbation."

Franklin brought Trumbull to the attention of Benjamin West, "the American Raphael," in London, who remained—even after the war—as Surveyor of the King's Pictures and president of the Royal Acad-

emy. "As to you I owe my introduction to him," Trumbull wrote to
Franklin, five months before the founder died, ". . . I must beg leave
still to consider you as my patron." In order to "render some distant
service to Posterity," Trumbull told Franklin that he had "begun a series of pictures of the great Events of the Revolution."

These four large oil canvases still hang in the Capitol's Rotunda. In
the painting titled *Declaration of Independence,* Franklin stands at a table draped with the document's drafts. Standing beside him, Thomas
Jefferson feigns innocence as his right foot appears to step on the toes
of the short, sullen man shown on his right: John Adams.

In February 1791, Philadelphia's civic leaders finally moved to end
the embarrassing inertia over Franklin's official eulogy. The American
Philosophical Society voted on which of its members would stand to
honor Franklin.

He had founded the institution — today housed in a two-story redbrick building opposite Independence Hall — in 1743, for the promotion of "useful knowledge"; the term *philosophy* then meant science and
technology. The ballot to select his eulogizer ended in a tie between the
society's two vice presidents, David Rittenhouse and William Smith.
The former, remembered today as the namesake of Philadelphia's elegant and most popular public square, was the logical choice: Franklin's
close friend had inventoried his estate. But John Adams's opinion of
Rittenhouse may have cost him some votes. The vice president judged
the astronomer to be "totally ignorant of the World, an honest Dupe
of the French Revolution."

Evincing his nonconfrontational nature, Rittenhouse ceded the
honor to the Reverend William Smith. As a result, Benjamin Franklin's eulogy would be delivered by someone he had loathed. Ironically,
Franklin himself had invited his antagonist to America.

In 1752, Samuel Johnson had finally ended Franklin's hopes that
the writer might lead his new school. "I must beg my Good Friends to

excuse me," Johnson apologized, "and I pray God they may be directed to a better Choice." Instead, providence provided Franklin with William Smith. After reading the Anglican minister's writings, Franklin hired him as provost of the Philadelphia Academy in 1753.

Their schism started two years later, during the French and Indian War. After the pacifist Pennsylvania Assembly refused to supply British forces under General Edward Braddock marching west to drive the French out of present-day Pittsburgh, Franklin rounded up horses and wagons himself, guaranteeing their owners compensation from his own savings.

After a disastrous defeat, whose fatalities included Braddock himself ("I luckily escapd witht a wound," a young George Washington told his mother, "tho' I had four Bullets through my Coat, and two Horses shot under me"), Franklin and his fellow assemblymen demanded that the Penn family — exempt, as the colony's proprietors, from taxation — help to fund the rematch. It was then, two decades before the Revolution, that Franklin memorably declared, "Those who would give up essential Liberty, to purchase a little temporary Safety, deserve neither Liberty nor Safety."

The Penns kept a closed purse. The expedition succeeded anyway, opening the headwaters of the Ohio River to colonial settlers. Seeking favor, William Smith offered to spy on Franklin for the Penns, assuring them that their opponent "always did and still does treat me as his Bosom-friend."

Poor Richard may have advised his readers to "love your Enemies, for they tell you your Faults," but a clear-eyed Franklin wrote that Smith had "scribbled himself into universal Dislike here." Although he stopped speaking to the duplicitous minister, in 1756 Franklin related that "Smith still endeavours to keep up a Flame, but is become universally odious, and almost infamous."

In 1758, Smith accused Franklin of stealing another scientist's electrical discovery — the alleged victim refuted the charge — and claimed that Franklin had begged or bought his honorary degrees from St. Andrews and Oxford.

"I made that Man my Enemy by doing him too much Kindness," Franklin reflected. "'Tis the honestest Way of acquiring an Enemy. And since 'tis convenient to have at least one Enemy, who by his Readiness to revile one on all Occasions may make one careful of one's Conduct, I shall keep him an Enemy for that purpose."

William Smith escalated his attacks. In 1764, he led the whisper campaign against Franklin's reelection to the Pennsylvania Assembly, tarring him as a lecher. One ditty that he circulated went:

> Franklin, though plagued with fumbling age,
> Needs nothing to excite him,
> But is too ready to engage,
> When younger arms invite him.

Smith also alleged that Franklin's illegitimate son, William, had been born to a servant named Barbara, a "Kitchen Wench" and "Gold Finder," or privy cleaner. Presenting no evidence but the lie that he demanded become true, Smith charged that Franklin had allowed the woman to starve before he "stole her to the Grave, in Silence" without "a *Groan,* a *Sigh* or a Tear."

Franklin lost that election for the assembly seat that he had easily held for the previous thirteen years. Still William Smith was not sated. Franklin, he fulminated in public, was "foul," "crafty," "a very bad man" with a "wicked and virulent spirit," who bore "the most unpopular and odious name in the province."

This was the man who would deliver Benjamin Franklin's American eulogy.

It is certain," Franklin wrote as Silence Dogood in 1722, "that those Elegies which are of our own Growth, (and our Soil seldom produces any other sort of Poetry) are by far the greatest part, wretchedly Dull and Ridiculous." Seven decades later, his own memorial proved it.

In the Dogood essay, the sixteen-year-old Franklin humorously suggested a template for a tribute that would hold an audience's attention. "Having chose the Person," Franklin wrote, "take all his Virtues, Excellencies, &c. and if he have not enough, you may borrow some to make up a sufficient Quantity: To these add his last Words, dying Expressions, &c. if they are to be had; mix all these together, and be sure you *strain* them well. Then season all with a Handful or two of Melancholly Expressions, such as, *Dreadful, Deadly, cruel cold Death, unhappy Fate, weeping Eyes,* &c. . . . Let them Ferment for the Space of a Fortnight, and by that Time they will be incorporated into a Body, which take out, and having prepared a sufficient Quantity of double Rhimes, such as, *Power, Flower; Quiver, Shiver; Grieve us, Leave us; tell you, excel you; Expeditions, Physicians; Fatigue him, Intrigue him;* &c. you must spread all upon Paper, and if you can procure a Scrap of Latin to put at the End, it will garnish it mightily."

William Smith ignored this simple recipe, producing a loaf of words that would not rise. Standing in the pulpit of Philadelphia's German Lutheran Church on the morning of March 1, 1791 — over ten months since Franklin's death — the reverend faced the largest collection of dignitaries seated together to that point in American history. President Washington and his entire cabinet were in attendance, along with the Senate and House of Representatives, the justices of the U.S. Supreme Court, and the Pennsylvania legislature.

Smith had once hoped to be named the first Anglican bishop in America. He looked the part, with a chiseled face, alabaster forehead, and swept-back raven hair whose color matched his cassock. Yet he had been passed over for the episcopate, rumor had it, in part for being "too fond of the grape." The president of Yale, a Congregationalist minister and friend of Franklin's, branded Smith "a contemptible drunken Character!" He was also "immoral, haughty, irreligious, and profane, *avaricious* and covetous, a consummate Hypocrite in Religion and Politics!"

Now in his sixties, with thin white hair, sagging cheeks, and a bulbous nose, Smith bellowed from his pulpit: "Citizens of Philadelphia!

Luminaries of Science! Assembled Fathers of America! Heard you not that solemn interrogatory? Who is *He* that now recedes from his labours among you? . . . Is it HE—your FRANKLIN?—It cannot be!"

It be—for nearly an hour, it be. Smith began by quoting from Pericles's commemoration of battle-slain Athenians. Many *thee*s and *thou*s followed, along with the fact that Franklin had invented the fireplace flue. None of his other discoveries, apparently, warranted mention.

How could so many words say so little?

Thomas Jefferson avoided public speaking (sometimes feigning illness to escape it) and so wrote out his remembrance, which William Smith read aloud. Jefferson reminded the many Federalists filling the pews that France's period of mourning for Franklin had been "the first instance of that homage having been paid by a public body of one nation to a private citizen of another." When Parisians had asked if he was the man who had come to replace Franklin as ambassador, Jefferson had replied, "No one can replace him. I am only his successor."

After the highest echelon of American political life exited the church, the reverend resumed his downward spiral. Smith became "a habitual drunkard," a physician remembered, who, as he lay upon his deathbed, "never spoke upon any subject connected to religion or his future state. He descended to his grave without being lamented by a human creature. Not a drop of kindred blood attended his funeral."

A rare marker of William Smith's legacy can be found two hundred miles west of Philadelphia, in Huntingdon, the town he had founded on a tract of land granted by the Penn family. There, starting at the bank of the Juniata River, a visitor can walk the length of the main road he named for himself. William Smith Street's three stubby blocks end near Penn Street. At their junction sits an office named—appropriately, given the town's location on former Oneida land—Colonial Real Estate.

Legend holds that after listening to his eulogy of Benjamin Franklin, William Smith's daughter approached him outside the church and said, "I don't think you believed one-tenth part of what you said of old

Ben Lightning-rod. Did you?" The good reverend answered only with a sly smile.

Franklin's will was a masterstroke that ensured he would have the last laugh. He planned for his loan scheme to self-perpetuate for two hundred years. It required no external investments, only the continuous lending of money to an increasing number of borrowers at 5 percent interest, who promised to settle their debt within a decade. The accumulated interest would be added to the fund's capital, allowing more loans to be made, resulting in the repayment of more interest and an exponential increase in the balance overall.

Franklin died thinking that his idea would be a surefire success. In the seven years preceding his passing, a similar "sinking fund"—created by Richard Price, his London friend who had published the English translation of Fortunate Richard's will—had paid down £10 million of Britain's national debt.

But Franklin did not live to see the kingdom's series of treasury-bleeding wars that ended only with Napoleon's defeat at Waterloo. By then, British ministers had drained Price's fund to plug budgetary shortfalls. No matter how sound an investment appeared on paper, national changes of fortune and human mismanagement could sink even the cleverest designs.

Franklin expected unpaid "virtuous and benevolent citizens" to administer his loan scheme at a time when American financial institutions were just being born. In 1782, he had participated in the country's first initial public offering. In a show of support, Franklin paid $400 for one share—and a 0.1 percent ownership—of the Bank of North America. (He eventually increased his holdings twelvefold, leaving the annual dividends to his sister Jane.) The Bank of Massachusetts—since subsumed into the Bank of America—started two years later, followed by Alexander Hamilton's Bank of New York, the predecessor of today's BNY Mellon.

Shares of these three banks were the first to be traded on the New York Stock Exchange, which opened in 1792, two years after Franklin's death. He did not anticipate the seismic impact of equities on American finance any more than he expected the U.S. dollar to one day become the world's most dominant currency.

In 1787, Franklin had designed the first general-circulation national coin, a unit of the Continental dollar. The copper penny was called the Fugio cent, for its caption, Latin for "I fly." Franklin placed the word next to the engraving of a sundial, implying "Time flies." Beneath the image, he added the maxim MIND YOUR BUSINESS.

But Franklin, like most Americans in the aftermath of independence, largely conducted his transactions in foreign currency, calculating prices, wages, and savings in British pounds sterling, and paying in an admixture of European specie and South American coins, made from that continent's abundant reserves of silver and gold. Even after Congress made the dollar the official currency in 1792, many Americans continued to use denominations of Mexican silver money. Until the federal government banned foreign currency in 1857, Mexican reales—called "bits"—were the most commonly used coin, with "two bits" equal to 25 cents. Not until the California gold rush of 1849 would the United States hold its own reserves of bullion. This explains Franklin's stipulation, in his will, that the required guarantors of each loan pledge to repay the sum not in American dollars, but in "Spanish milled dollars, or the value thereof in current gold coin."

Shortly before he died, and after his return to Philadelphia, Franklin found in his house a letter, mailed to him ten years earlier, that had been mislaid and never forwarded to him in Paris. Unfolding the dormant pages and then reading its loving descriptions of children—including his godson—who had since aged into adulthood, Franklin felt a magical spark from reanimating "*Words* that had been, as somebody says, *congeal'd in Northern Air.*"

He hoped that his bequests would produce the same stirring effect in generations of Americans. As spring blossomed in 1791 and his public remembrances at last concluded, Franklin's executor transferred

£100 to Boston's "free grammar schools," as dictated by his will, to be "put out to interest, so continued at interest forever," to fund annual prizes for their top students. Next, he resolved Temple's petulant refusal to surrender a stack of books that his grandfather had earmarked for others, and then remitted £1,000 to both Boston and Philadelphia. Franklin had staked the bet. He trusted his hometowns to prudently play the long game, and his fledgling nation to carry on without him.

"I begin to be almost sorry I was born so soon," Franklin once told a friend, "since I cannot have the Happiness of knowing what will be known 100 years hence."

Act II
AFTERLIFE

———

1791–1904

5

Dr. Franklin's Legacy

In 1889, ninety-nine years after Benjamin Franklin's death, the treasurer of his gift to Boston opened a letter from his Philadelphia counterpart and read:

> *Dear Sir:*
>
> *Will you please send me a copy of the last report of the Franklin Fund, also any information concerning the use you propose to make of it at the expiration of the first one hundred years. We have not yet decided what disposition we will make of our fund at that time. A copy of our last annual report is mailed you this day.*

As the centennial of Franklin's death approached, so, too, did the first disbursement of his legacy to his two hometowns. If his instructions had been followed, Franklin presumed that his gift to each city would have grown to £131,000, or $581,640. He directed that Boston could spend £100,000 (or, if his projections were wrong, 100/131 of the money's total) on public works. The remaining £31,000 (or 31/131 of the total) was to be lent to young artificers for another century, at which point he expected the final payout to total £4,061,000, or $18 million. "I hope it will have been found," Franklin wrote of his loan scheme in his will, "that the institution has had a good effect on the conduct of youth, and been of service to many worthy characters and useful citizens."

Philadelphia was to undertake the same division and reinvestment of its monies. Initially, Franklin had suggested that the city spend the £100,000 on purifying its drinking water, "bringing, by pipes, the water of Wissahickon Creek into the town, so as to supply the inhabitants, which I apprehend may be done without great difficulty, the level of the creek being much above that of the city, and may be made higher by a dam. I also recommend making the Schuylkill completely navigable."

As an advocate for public investment in infrastructure, Franklin would have been pleased to see that the city had independently completed these improvements. On his visit in 1842, Charles Dickens noted that "Philadelphia is most bountifully provided by fresh water, which is showered and jerked about, and turned on, and poured off, everywhere. The Waterworks, which are on a height near the city, are no less ornamental than useful, being tastefully laid out as a public garden, and kept in the best and neatest order."

In addition to being dammed to create a reservoir, the Schuylkill River had also been improved for shipping. These changes mooted Franklin's proposed use of his centenary disbursement, leading the manager of "Dr. Franklin's Legacy"—as Philadelphia called his bequest—to write to his counterpart, asking how Boston planned to put its gift to use.

Samuel McCleary Jr., the treasurer of the "Franklin Fund"—as Boston's account became known—received the letter at his office in the elegant, mansard-roofed Equitable Building, rising eight stories in the heart of the financial district. On his walk to work, McCleary regularly passed under the gaze of the man whose money he had been entrusted to protect. Although Benjamin Franklin's Milk Street home had burned down in 1811, his likeness perched in an architrave of the office building that still stands on its site. Over the entrance, pigeon-stained stone letters flanking his bust celebrated the BIRTHPLACE OF FRANKLIN.

McCleary, like Franklin, was a child of the North End, born in the cradle of the American Revolution. His childhood Lafayette Avenue home, near the Old North Church, faced Bunker Hill across the harbor. An ancestor had died there while evacuating rebels from the rail-fence line. In 1775, in the aftermath of that costly redcoat victory (with casualties felling one-third of Britain's three thousand troops), Franklin had warned a British friend, "Enough has happened, one would think, to convince your ministers that the Americans will fight, and that this is a harder nut to crack than they imagined." In addition to his post as treasurer of the Franklin Fund, McCleary also served as president of the Bunker Hill Monument Association, the custodian of the granite obelisk crowning the battlefield.

After Boston's incorporation in 1822, McCleary's father, Samuel Sr., had served as the first city clerk, a nominally nonpartisan post, second-in-command to the mayor. Born that same year, the younger McCleary later reflected that he had come of age alongside his hometown. "Every mayor of the City of Boston from 1822 to 1883," he wrote, "has taken me by the hand."

Samuel Sr. had sharp, aquiline features, a face that seemed designed to appear on currency. His son inherited only his high brow, which turned to baldness in middle age, juxtaposed with his mother's doe eyes and Cupid's bow lips. He looked like a gentle bookworm, and behaved like one, too, excelling at the free Boston Latin School that Franklin had loved in his single year of attendance, before his father had pulled him out to work. Upon graduation, Samuel Jr. had been awarded one of the silver medals that Franklin's £100 bequest continued to award to the city's top students.

McCleary next crossed the Charles River to attend Harvard College. To give a sense of what $1 bought at that time, his 1839 enrollment cost $106.63. McCleary's tuition included charges of $37.50 for instruction and $8.19 for "Wood or other fuel delivered from the College Wharf." (At the time of this writing, he would have been invoiced $72,356, a sum that did not include firewood.)

McCleary's papers—on reserve at the Massachusetts Historical Society, where he served as its "cabinet-keeper"—reveal a likeable, perspicacious man. In one assignment at Harvard, he reflected on the societal shifts resulting from a sped-up era of railroads, tabloid newspapers, and quack medicine. "Is it true that as the world grows wiser it grows less poetical?" (In sum: *no.*) "Is anonymous criticism on the whole favorable to Morality and Truth?" (*No.*) "Does phrenology hold promise as a science?" (*Certainly,* McCleary responded sarcastically, provided one can alter their skull shape as easily as they can improve their mind.)

McCleary graduated in 1841 as part of a class that bridged the Revolutionary and Civil Wars. His fellow alumni included Paul Revere's grandson and five future Union army officers. Two other classmates rose to the U.S. Supreme Court; another founded Wellesley College. McCleary remained on campus for a law degree, studying alongside the future U.S. president Rutherford B. Hayes. His own prospects, however, were constrained by his father's declining health. McCleary spent more time assisting his dad at the city clerk's office than at his own law practice. When the elder McCleary finally retired in 1853, the city's aldermen unanimously voted for his son to succeed him.

Samuel McCleary Jr. held the post for another thirty years, during which time he assumed the management of Franklin's gift. Despite last visiting Boston in 1763, its benefactor would have recognized many of the landmarks McCleary passed on his morning commute from his Beacon Hill town house to his Milk Street office, including the King's Chapel, Boston Latin School, and Old South Meeting House.

Franklin would have been lost, however, had he wandered beyond the Common's Boston Massacre/Crispus Attucks Monument (which Samuel McCleary had raised funds to build). Since Franklin's eighteenth-century death, nineteenth-century Boston had turned its back on the waterfront to face new railroad tracks and depots. The city

Samuel McCleary Jr. as he appeared at the start of his management of the Franklin Fund.

filled in the millpond where Franklin had learned to swim, and lopped off 40 percent of Beacon Hill. Atlantic Avenue sliced across the Long Wharf. Steam shovels widened the isthmus known as the Neck to create neighborhoods such as the West End and Back Bay.

Boston's new center congealed around a plaza named for the painter John Singleton Copley, who had immigrated to London in 1774. While overseas, Copley suspected that he had been swindled on the sale of his Beacon Hill estate. Its purchasers quickly flipped the land, now crowned by the Massachusetts State House's golden dome. Copley died in 1815, having never set foot in America again. But how many of the Bostonians crossing Copley Square in the autumn of 1889—the women in high-shouldered, bustle-plumped dresses; the bowler-hatted men erect from stiffened collars and frock coats—knew that?

Even fewer, if any, likely were aware that their city would soon unwrap a hundred-year-old present from its most famous son.

In his office, the sixty-seven-year-old Samuel McCleary held the letter from his Philadelphia counterpart, who asked how Boston planned to spend Franklin's money. McCleary was Brahminhood personified, and a public servant of such probity that, at a time when Philadelphia's Republican Party corruption rivaled New York Democrats' Tammany Hall venality, he kept a separate drawer in his work desk to hold supplies for his personal use. Pulling it open revealed dozens of Benjamin Franklins, whose profile adorned the ultramarine one-cent postage stamp.

The man colleagues called "Stalwart McCleary" had once independently compiled a report sketching the management of the Franklin Fund from 1791 to 1866. Over the decades of his own oversight of the money, he had kept a neat ledger, updating its balance as the one-hundredth anniversary of the benefactor's death approached.

We can only imagine Samuel McCleary's thoughts as he paged through the pamphlet that Philadelphia's treasurer had included with his inquiring letter. That city's annual report listed Franklin's legacy among dozens of other charitable funds established by later Philadelphians supplying food and coal to widows, relief to yellow fever victims, and scholarships for orphans. In contrast to Boston, no single, dedicated manager had been assigned to shepherd Franklin's gift.

What did McCleary's face look like when he at last learned the balance of Philadelphia's account? Did he rapidly flip the page, looking for the actual total, and then flip back to the printed number and wonder—feeling a dip of disappointment or a surge of civic pride—how in the world that figure could be correct?

Franklin had calculated that after one hundred years, the £1,000 each he left to Boston and Philadelphia would mature to the equivalent of $582,164. McCleary knew that, after some initial setbacks, by 1889 Boston's fund had appreciated to $368,741.12.

He stared at Philadelphia's balance: $89,058.07.

Over four times less than Boston's total.

To use the parlance of the time: *What the blazes had happened?* Samuel McCleary would not be the only person asking that question. Later that year, in a lawsuit filed against the City of Philadelphia, Benjamin Franklin's descendants would demand an answer—and all of their ancestor's money.

One of Franklin's clearest contributions to our understanding of electricity was to describe it as a fluid, moving in streams. Though composed of opposing particles, the weightless, elastic substance ceaselessly circulates—like heat, like money—ever returning to a state of balance. An electrical current also can be reversed, as easily as time can be rewound on the page.

Ninety-eight years earlier, in March 1791, Franklin's executor sent drafts for £1,000 (equal, he wrote in his ledger, to $4,444.44) to both Boston and Philadelphia. How large was Franklin's bet on the "rising generation" of young skilled workers? Given the variable cost of labor and materials, comparing money across eras is not as simple as calculating an exchange rate. Adjusting only for inflation, Franklin's bequest would equate—at the time of this writing—to two gifts totaling $266,000. At first glance, the amount doesn't scream largesse. In our time, it would at best stake but a few blue-collar businesses. Using only inflation as a metric, however, undersells the true size of his wager.

In 1751, Franklin raised £4,000 for the construction of America's first hospital, since subsumed into the University of Pennsylvania. In 2017, the school broke ground on a five-hundred-bed addition that cost $1.5 billion. The result of Franklin's fundraising had built an entire medical center. Today that amount would pay only for a single bed.

In the early 1780s, Franklin collected £374 ($1,661) to build a new home for the American Philosophical Society, which still resides there. He gave lavishly to the project; his £100 donation was more than four times the £23 provided by Robert Morris, Philadelphia's richest man.

At decade's end, the dying Franklin's bill from his druggist, tallying palliatives purchased across a year, came to a little over £15. After his death, his executor received an itemized invoice for "erecting a tomb stone in Christ Church burial ground over the late Doctor Franklin." It included charges for "setting up the marble," 875 common bricks, 200 blocks, 3 bushels of lime, "half a load of sand," 24 water table bricks, "foundation planks and boards," and hauling. The laborious job's total cost came to a little over £4.

Calculating the "economic power" of Franklin's bequest reveals a much more generous outlay for his loan scheme. Based on its share of the gross domestic product at the time, the £2,000 ($8,888.88) he left to Boston and Philadelphia would equate today to approximately $1 billion.

That estimate, however, could grossly overstate Franklin's munificence. The size of his gift mattered less than its intent. In our own era of crumbling public infrastructure and a shortage of skilled workers, imagine what a philanthropic grant of that size, for that purpose, could do.

In his will, Franklin calculated that the maximum amount of money needed "to assist young married artificers in setting up their business" totaled £60 (or $266 at the time). He forbade his money's managers to loan more than that amount. (Four decades earlier, Poor Richard had observed, "Most People return small Favors, acknowledge middling ones, and repay great ones with Ingratitude.") He further directed the lenders to "keep a bound book or books, wherein shall be entered the names of those who shall apply for and receive the benefits of this institution."

Boston's ledgers reside in its city archives, housed in a nondescript warehouse tucked behind the West Roxbury Home Depot at the end of a dead-end road. The oversize volumes' leather bindings dust a read-

The title page of Boston's Franklin Fund ledger.

er's hands with red rot, the leprosy of old books. Their covers crack and creak like long-forgotten doors, opening a portal into the past.

A bricklayer named Daniel Tuttle received the first Franklin loan. A coppersmith and another mason, perhaps the tradesman under whom Tuttle had apprenticed, guaranteed repayment in gold.

Other borrowers in 1791 used family members as guarantors. The £60 loan to Thomas Eayres listed the silversmith's father-in-law: "Paul Revere, Gentleman."

Boston's first class of loan recipients could have built and operated an entire village. The ledger's elegant cursive entries belie the din each entrant made with their tools. In addition to Tuttle's trowel and Eayres's anvil, the mute pages summon the sounds produced by a housewright, a glazier, and a cabinetmaker; a blacksmith, a founder, and a candlemaker; a saddler and a shoemaker; a jeweler and a hairdresser; a distiller, a cooper, and a baker.

Only one printer applied in 1791, but he soon withdrew his application. No note explains why, but Samuel Etheridge reappears in the ledger two years (and five crinkling pages) later, when his loan of $200 was approved — dollars having replaced pounds after the Coinage Act of 1792. Etheridge would repay his loan over ten annual installments, as his new business prospered by printing folios of George Washington's writings. One of Etheridge's own apprentices would become mayor of Boston and then governor of Massachusetts.

That chain of events illustrated Franklin's faith in the potential of skilled workers, and the importance of assisting them from the first. He had lived in a time of no safety nets. Franklin's abhorrence of debt was not a smug affectation, but was earned through experience: he knew the precariousness of unskilled labor, and how it curtailed mobility. His mother, Abiah Folger Franklin, had been born to an immigrant indentured servant who had married the teacher who, for 20 shillings, had purchased her freedom. Skilled tradesmen often could depend only on themselves. Franklin's father, Josiah, had trained as a fabric dyer in the heart of cosmopolitan London. After refusing to disavow his Congregationalist faith and adhere to the Church of England, he had crossed the Atlantic, to land in a port of ten thousand that grazed its cows on the Common. Tinting fine cloth would not feed his family here. Josiah became a soap maker and tallow chandler, less of a laborer and more of a public utility. His candles were estimated to light one-third of Boston's homes.

The town was then a near island — smaller in area than today's Central Park and connected to the mainland only by the Neck. Walking out under the blue ball that hung, in lieu of a shop sign, over his family's Union Street front door, a young Franklin passed shops owned by workers who made things with their hands, including bricklayers, turners, joiners, and braziers. "It has ever since been a Pleasure to me," he recalled in his autobiography, "to see good Workmen handle their

Tools." It also, he wrote, motivated him from a young age to learn how to make and fix things himself, fueling his later inventions.

After leaving school at age ten (the required books cost money, and Benjamin was one of thirteen surviving children), Franklin joined his father "cutting Wick for the Candles, filling the Dipping Mold and the Molds for cast Candles, attending the Shop, going of Errands, etc."

This offhand description, which he recorded in his memoir, makes the job sound like a lark. In fact, it was smelly, squishy tedium. The tallow used in candles came rendered from leaf suet, the hard fat surrounding cattle and sheep kidneys. The ten-year-old Franklin—besmeared with filth and fat and blood and foam—pushed carts filled with animal carcasses to his fuggy home, perfumed by the suet as it boiled down for hours. Next, the boy ladled the viscous fat into molds, setting the wicks before it hardened. A twelve-hour day produced 250 candles.

"I dislik'd the Trade," Franklin laconically wrote in his memoir, "and had a strong Inclination for the Sea." He wanted to be a sailor, but after his older brother Josiah was lost on a voyage, his father "declared against it"—unswayed, apparently, by Franklin's self-designed swim training to survive a wreck. Instead, the boy was apprenticed, at age twelve, to the printshop owned by his brother James, who published one of America's first newspapers, the *New-England Courant,* whose name included the French word for running, to evoke a messenger on horseback. Franklin foundered under his brother's harsh tutelage. Five years into his nine-year contract, the seventeen-year-old broke colonial law by betraying his indenture and bolting to Philadelphia. Benjamin Franklin's first bet was on himself.

By the summer of 1791, Boston, following its benefactor's wishes, had lent the entirety of his cash gift to young tradesmen. The ink had dried on its ledger's oversize pages before Philadelphia had even published its first call for applications.

Because it had been the capital of a proprietary colony, Philadelphia had long been run more like a medieval English city than an American one, with officers plucked from the elite for life. Governance took a back seat to spoils. The mayor and aldermen, for example, regularly leased the Delaware River's public wharves to themselves, pocketing the profits. Franklin had filled the vacuum of social services with those "charitable, public foundations" that John Adams had admired on his first visit.

Franklin had lived long enough to see Philadelphia at last transfer its levers of municipal government to elected officials. The charter of 1789 did not, however, delineate executive, legislative, and judicial authority. As a result, the city's government became a patchwork fiefdom of select councils; the public wharves, for example, came under the self-serving rule of "port wardens." Each council, not the mayor, could appoint its members. Opaque offices often did not know (or want to know) what their counterparts were up to. For the next hundred years, Franklin's generous foresight would be diminished by this lack of transparency.

Things began promisingly enough when, in the spring of 1791, a three-man committee convened to vet the first bunch of loan applicants. Unlike Boston's board of selectmen and clergy, each of these Philadelphians had known Franklin personally.

Isaac Wharton belonged to the family of Quaker scions whose elders had frequently corresponded with Franklin in London and Paris. George Roberts was the son of a merchant who belonged to the Junto, or Leather Apron Club, the civic improvement group that Franklin had founded in 1727. Matthew Clarkson was a former director of the subscriber-funded Library Company, America's first lending library, created by Franklin in 1731.

On May 26, 1791, the men approved the fund's first loan, £97 to the shoemaker John Grant. A tobacconist and currier acted as guarantors. Their signatures score the first yellowed page of Philadelphia's "Bond Book," which, redolent of their trades, smells of smoky leather.

The ledger does not explain why Grant's loan, along with ten others for the same amount, exceeded—by over 50 percent—the £60 limit Franklin had set in his will. Perhaps this was because the four other Philadelphia borrowers approved in that first year received sums well below this figure. Lending a higher amount raised the risk of a greater default, however, which could hobble the fund's accumulation right out of the gate. The race had just begun, and already Philadelphia was veering off the course that its benefactor had so carefully plotted. Franklin's own main heirs, meanwhile, weren't faring much better.

The following summer, in 1792, seven Philadelphia tradesmen received loans. The preprinted agreements had been produced by Franklin's grandson Benny, working at the Market Street printshop that fronted Franklin Court. He had also set the type for the notice calling for more applicants that appeared on the front page of his *General Advertiser* newspaper.

Benny had made quick use of his inheritance, taking over the publication—soon to be renamed the *Aurora*—only five months after Franklin's death. "I am sending you some of my papers that may please you," he wrote, in French, to their former neighbor in Paris, "and some copies of praise for the Great Man . . . I miss him."

Benny also shared some "good news, however. I'm no longer little Benjamin, I'm big bearded Benjamin, and married—yes, at 22. *What, married?* Yes, well married. If you knew her you would like her."

Margaret Markoe, called Peggy, worked beside him as co-owner of the paper, just as Deborah had once labored beside Franklin. Although men would crowd latter-day depictions of early urban America, Peggy's position was actually not that unusual. Two of Philadelphia's other leading printers at the time were women. One had inherited the business upon the death of her father, the other after her husband had passed away. Women owned and managed approximately one-fifth of Philadelphia's inns and taverns, while others worked as midwives, nurses, teachers, tinkers, tailors, bakers, and seamstresses.

During the Revolutionary War, Franklin's daughter, Sally, then a mother to three young children, had co-founded the first interstate women's organization, the Ladies Association of Philadelphia, which collected money to give to the underpaid Continental Army. After George Washington feared that his soldiers would squander the donations on alcohol, the organization instead purchased linen and sewed 2,200 uniforms. "I am very busily imploy'd in cutting out and making shirts," the thirty-six-year-old Sally wrote to her father in Paris. "I hope you will approve of what we have done."

Benjamin Franklin's enlightened thinking did not brighten every corner of his mind. Even as he daily encountered evidence of women's capacity for learning and work, it was his Quaker neighbor, the abolitionist Anthony Benezet, who in 1755 founded North America's first

Dr. *Franklin's* Legacy.

THE Committee appointed by the Corporation to manage the Legacy of One Thousand Pounds Sterling, from the late Dr. BENJAMIN FRANKLIN, to the inhabitants of this City, and for Loaning the same to such married Artificers as are under 25 years of age, who have faithfully served an Apprenticeship in the City, and can give two respectable Citizens as their Sureties, to repay One's tenth Part of the Principal annually, with an Interest of Five per Cent—Do hereby give Public Notice, that a small Part of that Sum is still on hand, ready to be loaned to such as are entitled, and desirous to participate in the advantage which may result therefrom, so as not to exceed Sixty Pounds Sterling, nor less than Fifteen Pounds, to one Person.

Such as incline to apply, will produce to George Roberts, Joseph Ball, Michael Hillegas, James C. Fisher, or Joseph P. Norris, who are the present Committee, such Credentials as will establish their Applications, before the 15th Day of September next.

The Application should be accompanied with those Credentials and Documents, proving the Age, Apprenticeship in this City, good Moral Character, Marriage, Occupation or Trade, and Place of Residence of the Applicant (as none but Persons living in this City, appear to be entitled to any Part of the Loan) with the Names of the two Persons who are willing to become their Sureties.   t&f11A.

Philadelphia, July 21, 1792.

A call for loan applicants published in Benny's newspaper.

public school for girls. Franklin's Philadelphia Academy, while unique for being America's first secular college, limited enrollment to men.

His loan scheme was restricted, too. In his will, Franklin explained that he aimed to pay forward the support that he had received from two men when he was twenty-three. These Junto members had surprised Franklin by offering him a low-interest loan to buy out his printshop partner, "often seen drunk in the Streets, and playing at low Games in Alehouses, much to our Discredit." For the price of £30 and a new saddle (which the partner mounted to ride out of town), Franklin, thanks to the men who looked out for him, had found his foothold.

The first woman does not appear in the Franklin ledgers until 1796, when Priscilla Patten, "widow," would guarantee the loan of the Boston rope maker Nathaniel Patten, who was perhaps her son.

Yet in 1792, as excerpts from Mary Wollstonecraft's *A Vindication of the Rights of Women* began appearing in the American press, a curious advertisement appeared in Benny's newspaper. "TO BE LET," the notice announced; "The Mansion HOUSE / Of the late Dr. FRANKLIN." Beside it ran another item, headlined NOTICE OF SALE OF FRANKLIN'S FURNITURE AND HOUSEHOLD GOODS. This post listed furniture, stoves, kitchenware, a sedan chair, a harpsichord, and dozens of other items that Sally had inherited but was now selling at auction.

TO BE LET;

The Mansion HOUSE

Of the late Dr. FRANKLIN.
Its central and retired situation is well known.
Enquire of the Editor of the General Advertiser

Concurrently, Louis XVI's lavish gift began to lose its luster. Sally followed the letter of her father's decree, if not its spirit. She removed the portrait's outer circle of diamonds not to make jewelry, but to finance her first trip overseas. But would Franklin really have begrudged her?

For her entire life, Sally had watched as he took her brother William, nephew Temple, and son Benny to Europe. Sally had remained behind in Philadelphia, obeying her music, writing, and French tutors, as well as her absent father. "You know I have many Enemies," he wrote when she, as a mature twenty-one-year-old, had admitted to skipping church. ". . . You must expect their Enmity will extend in some degree to you, so that your slightest Indiscretions will be magnified into crimes . . . It is therefore the more necessary for you to be

Miniature Portrait of Louis XVI, 1784, showing only the inner ring that once held diamonds.

extreamly circumspect in all your Behaviour that no Advantage may be given to their Malevolence. Go constantly to Church whoever preaches."

Sally had dutifully cared for Deborah after her strokes, tended to the upkeep of Franklin Court, and gave birth eight times. Now, as she neared fifty, it was her turn to leave home. The French Revolution's Reign of Terror ruled out visiting her first choice of Paris, so instead Sally took her fifteen-year-old daughter, along with her husband, Richard, to the other city she had longed to see: London.

Sarah (Sally) Franklin Bache.

They lodged near, but not with, her estranged brother William, who had married his landlady. He was embarrassed that their Maryle-bone town house, unlike his former New Jersey governor's mansion, was not big enough to accommodate guests. William's surviving letters do not reveal if he still smarted over their outsize inheritance, but Sally and her family stayed for two years.

After a lifetime of seeing likenesses of her father, Sally sat for her first portrait as an adult. She looks healthy and youthful on the canvas, with rosy cheeks and loosely worn hair. Her clothes would have been fashionable in 1793 Paris: an over-the-shoulders fichu, and a headscarf that resembled the Phrygian cap worn by revolutionaries.

Franklin might have noticed that in the painting she wears no jew-elry. He might also have spotted the lace. From Paris, he had once scolded Sally for wasting money by ordering some of the fabric from France. "Your sending" for it, he wrote, "disgusted me as much as if you had put salt into my strawberries." He suggested a more frugal means of acquiring the material: "If you wear your cambric ruffles as I do, and take care not to mend the holes, they will come in time to be lace." But now Sally was beyond her father's reproach.

As Sally traveled and Benny worked to make the *Aurora* America's most read newspaper, the third of Franklin's main inheritors neglected his gift.

In the autumn of 1790, Temple had made a start, sailing to Europe to gather his grandfather's uncollected manuscripts. Franklin had kept a messy desk, and visitors to his Paris study had been amazed to "be-hold papers of the greatest importance scattered in the most careless way over the table and floor." Beyond the task of navigating this forest of foolscap, Temple would have to prune its fifteen thousand pages for publication.

The translator he had hired to help produce a French edition of Franklin's letters quickly begged off the job. "It is necessary to sort these materials," he wrote to Temple at the start of 1792, "to add those which are lacking, to order them among themselves, to fill the intervals with a Short and instructive account of what happened, and thus to provide, instead of a Collection which would be good to consult only for the makers of history, a complete monument to the works of Franklin which excites and satisfies the curiosity of all those who have heard of him. This work is, I will confess, much beyond my strength; and I believe it is only suitable for you."

Temple ducked the challenge. Instead, he cashed in on his grandfather's connections, ignoring Poor Richard's 1738 warning that "there is much difference between imitating a good man, and counterfeiting him." In London, Temple acted as the agent for Robert Morris —known as the financier of the Revolution—in his 1792 sale of over one million acres of New York State forestland. Today the town of Franklinville (population three thousand) survives as a testament to his role in brokering the deal. For his quick work, Temple netted a windfall of £7,000, which, in his porous hands, would dissipate as easily as it had come.

Temple could not be roused to work, even as letters and portions of Franklin's autobiography appeared in the American press, and an incomplete edition was published in London, compiled from the copy Franklin had left with friends in France. Temple, too, had left part of himself behind in Paris, which—along with his temporary riches —may explain his reluctance to return there. Seven years earlier, Temple, just like his father and grandfather before him, had fathered an illegitimate son. The boy, named Théodore, died (like little Franky) of smallpox before turning five.

In London, Temple tried reconnecting with his exiled father, but he soon found William to be a nag, constantly urging him to begin editing Franklin's papers. Temple said he preferred to find and marry a "woman possessed of such a fortune" that would allow him to retire. He settled for seducing his stepmother's married sister, who gave birth to an illegitimate daughter called Ellen. This made William both her uncle and grandfather, and—after Temple absconded—her guardian.

For the second successive generation, a Franklin father and son would not speak for the next thirteen years.

William thought the infant Ellen bore a striking resemblance to Franklin, which calls to mind a baby sporting bifocals. After William's wife — recalling Deborah's demise — became incapacitated by a stroke and declined into death, an elderly William became a single parent. "I must resign myself," he wrote, "for the remaining Days of my Existence to that Solitary State which is most repugnant to my Nature."

Of all Franklin's beneficiaries, Benny stayed truest to his grandfather's dying designs. In Philadelphia, he put his inheritance to productive use, benefiting from publishing in a boomtown. In the decade after it became the national capital, Philadelphia's population tripled to nearly 100,000. The ensuing competition for wood — as a building material and fuel source for homes, government buildings, and large institutions such as the Pennsylvania Hospital — impacted cabinet and furniture makers, including one of the city's first Franklin loan recipients. By the turn of the nineteenth century, Adam Hains had given up his trade, advertising his workshop's stock at reduced prices or in "exchange for Groceries," before the mayor appointed him as Philadelphia's firewood inspector.

The *Aurora* profited from Thomas Jefferson's suggestion to move local ads like Hains's to the publication's last page. These could be "torn off or omitted for distant customers," Jefferson advised Benny, thus creating "a paper of general distribution, thro' the states." At a time when most dailies counted five hundred subscribers, the *Aurora* enjoyed nearly four times that number.

Throughout the 1790s, the newspaper published congressional transcripts, foreign news that Benny translated from French, and contributions from his grandfather's circle, including Thomas Paine and Edmond-Charles Genet.

Benny shared his grandfather's taste for satire, mocking what he saw as the Federalists' aloofness from farmers and tradesmen. John Adams carped that the "paper begins to maul the President for his Drawing Rooms." Adams had known Benny as a little boy in Paris. In Philadelphia, the vice president kept a wary eye on him as an independent man.

After George Washington's reelection in 1792, Benny attacked the president's unrepentant ownership of slaves. Washington rotated nine enslaved Black men and women from Philadelphia back to Mount Vernon before they attained the freedom granted by Pennsylvania law after six months of continuous residence in the state. "I wish to have it accomplished," Washington instructed his private secretary, "under pretext that may deceive both them and the Public."

The *Aurora* was appalled that "Liberty's Apostle should be seen with chains in his hands, holding men in bondage." Washington remained characteristically mute, but newspapers such as the aptly named *Porcupine's Gazette* bristled at Benny's incessant attacks on the president and his allies. Its editor charged that Benny was in the pay of France. His distaste for Federalist patronage belied the fact that for decades the Franklins had profited from government posts.

The *Porcupine* attacked Franklin's inheritors, too. If Americans "have read the old hypocrite Franklin's will," one editorial fulminated, "they must have observed that part of his library is left to a certain grandson. [Temple] spent several years in hunting offices under the Federal government, and being constantly rejected, he at last became its most bitter foe." The charge alluded to the rumor that Temple had sold the copyright for his grandfather's papers to the British Crown, which was suppressing their publication.

The same column tarred Benny as an "atrocious wretch (worthy descendant of *old Ben*)," who knew "that all men of any understanding set him down as an abandoned liar, as a tool and a hireling." Other articles branded him "the Market Street Scoundrel" and—confusing his provenance with Temple's—"the son of one of Dr. Franklin's bastards." His critics didn't like the looks of him either. "He is an ill-looking devil," the *Porcupine* continued. "His eyes never get above your knees. He is of a sallow complexion, hollow-cheeked, dead-eyed . . . like that of a fellow who has been about a week or ten days on a gibbet."

Lightning Rod Junior stood firm. In 1795, Benny learned that President Washington had quietly dispatched Chief Justice John Jay to London to negotiate an end to ongoing hostilities with Britain. On his return home that June, the Senate read the agreed-upon terms under secrecy. "We are all hanging by the eye lids about this confounded treaty," Benny wrote. "I fear it will go down."

After a senator leaked a copy to Benny, the *Aurora* (presaging the publication of the Pentagon Papers nearly two centuries later) rushed the secret government document into print. Peggy wrote that crowds waited two hours outside their Market Street office to receive the broadsheets hot off the press. Yet after lobbying from President Washington, the Senate ratified the treaty twenty votes to ten, just meeting the required two-thirds margin.

The United States, Benjamin Franklin's grandson warned readers, again found itself under the thumb of a king. "Mr. Washington has at length become treacherous even to his own fame, what was lent to him as a harmless general must be withdrawn from him as a dangerous politician."

Yet Benny would have done well to heed Poor Richard's warning: "He that lies down with Dogs, shall rise up with fleas." His antipathy for Washington and the Federalist press blinded him to the mendacity of Thomas Paine's scurrilous pamphlet *Letters to George Washington*, in which Paine accused the president of, among other things, leaving him to rot in a French prison during the Reign of Terror. (Paine's zealotry next turned to attacking Christianity. When he died in 1809, only six people attended the funeral of the man who wrote *Common Sense*.)

Benny published Paine's pamphlet, as well as forged wartime letters —ostensibly penned by Washington—which purportedly revealed the great general to have been secretly allegiant to the king. "This man," Washington wrote of Benny, "has celebrity in a certain way, for His calumnies are to be exceeded only by his Impudence, and both stand unrivalled."

Surprisingly, the *Aurora* celebrated John Adams's election in 1796. Benny predicted that Adams would "not deign to become the *President of a Party,* but the PRESIDENT OF THE UNITED STATES." But soon he recanted, dubbing Adams "the Duke of Braintree" (Massachusetts), and "president by three votes," for his margin of victory in the Electoral College. He also attacked the president for sending his son John Quincy on diplomatic missions, which Benny read as a sign that the presidency was becoming a hereditary institution, like the monarchy from which his grandfather had helped to wrest the country free.

The First Lady rose to her husband's defense by landing a low blow. Writing in the rival *Porcupine's Gazette,* Abigail Adams contrasted Benny's lineage with the "conjugal character of the President, who has never given his children or grandchildren cause to blush for any illegitimate offspring."

Benny showed uncharacteristic restraint by not replying in print. But by then, the *Aurora*'s readership had dwindled in proportion to its vitriol. Twice in 1797, Benny was physically assaulted for his writing. In another instance, a mob smashed the *Aurora*'s front door. Peggy stood firm inside, just as Deborah had defended Franklin Court three decades before.

In the spring of 1798, as Federalists in Congress drafted a new law against seditious speech, Thomas Jefferson cautioned that its true intent was to suppress dissenting newspapers by muzzling their owners. Benny, he told James Madison, "has been particularly named."

The Federalists did not see themselves as a political party, but rather as the government itself. Invective against them was considered an incitement to revolt. Charged with "false, scandalous and malicious writing against the government of the United States," Benjamin Franklin's grandson was the first person arrested under the Alien and Sedition Acts.

Released on bail in July, with his trial scheduled for October, the twenty-nine-year-old refused to back down. The first test of the First Amendment was at hand. "Printers," Benny warned his readers, "are subjected to prosecution for every sentence in their papers which the

The editorial cartoon *See Porcupine in Colours Just Portray'd* shows the editor of the Benny-bashing *Porcupine's Gazette* transcribing the invective of Satan and the British Lion. Lady Liberty weeps over a portrait of Benjamin Franklin.

eye of a jealous government can torture into an offence." The *Aurora's* circulation soared. Benny wrote that the increase exceeded his "most sanguine expectations."

Also rising was the death toll from the latest yellow fever epidemic. That same week, the *Aurora* reported "one hundred and eleven new cases for the last 48 hours." Five days later, the paper published a Health Office notice that admitted, "The best skills of our physicians have proven unequal in the contest with this devouring poison. We believe you will think, with us, that the preservation of health is only to be attained by flight."

President Adams and most of Congress bolted Philadelphia. Benny stayed put. "If Federalist attacks and sedition prosecutions can't intimidate him," the *Aurora* proclaimed, "neither will the yellow fever!" Above this boast the paper printed a quote from Poor Richard: "He's the best physician that knows the worthlessness of most medicines." Yet Benjamin Franklin had penned this sardonic quip before disease had claimed the life of four-year-old Franky.

On September 3, Peggy gave birth to their fourth child, a boy named Hartman, after her mother's maiden name. The paper's next issue announced that "the malignant yellow fever is conquering the *Aurora*. Eight who work at the paper will die." That Friday, it reported that "Benny continues feverish and sick. We are all worried. Today, if only as a precaution, Benny makes out his will."

Scrawled on the front and back of a single sheet of paper, Benny passed Franklin's printing press to Peggy, "to be by her used according to her own good sense, firmly confiding from the tenderness and love which I have in every shape experienced from her uniformly." He also hoped she would educate their children to be "attached to the immutable principles of civil Liberty." (Six decades later, Hartman would cap a career building lighthouses by commanding the U.S. Army Corps of Engineers during the Civil War.)

On September 10, one month before Benny was to stand trial for libeling the president, the *Aurora* wrote that "Philadelphia at this time is nearly desolated, & though but few inhabitants [are] left, we behold hearses continually carrying corpses to their graves." Later that day, Benjamin Franklin's cherished grandson joined them.

"The printer is dead," exulted the Alien and Sedition Acts' enforcer, Secretary of State Timothy Pickering, "as, I am informed, is his mischievous newspaper contained."

The *Aurora* endured. Peggy, nursing an infant, took over as editor, refusing several offers to sell the press, fearing that any buyer wanted only to shut it down. Thomas Jefferson would credit the *Aurora* for helping him win the presidential election of 1800, and, as he put it, "maintaining the republican ascendancy" by defeating the Federalists.

From his retirement on a Massachusetts farm, in 1807 John Adams reflected, "I have often heard Dr. Franklin Say, 'that one of the Pleasures of old Age was to outlive ones Ennemies.' This Sentiment also never failed to disgust and Shock me . . . If this could have been a Source of pleasure to me, I Should have had a Surfeit of it."

Then, in one long, extraordinary paragraph, Adams dished out how his adversaries met their demise. One diplomat "became a Vagabond." A journalist "drank himself into his Grave." Another reporter "drowned in a river." Yet another perished when his house burned down, with "his Wife and Children in it." Alexander Hamilton was sent "to his long home by a Pistol Bullet through his Spine."

Adams remembered Benny as "one of the most malicious Libellers of me. But the yellow Fever arrested him in his detestable Career, and Sent him to his Grandfather from whom he inherited a dirty, envious, jealous and revengfull Spight against me, for no other cause under heaven than because I was too honest a Man."

While it is tempting to allow Poor Richard to make an arch reply, Benny should have the last word before he exits the stage.

He was buried near his grandfather and parents in the Christ Church Burial Ground, but who remembers him today? The cemetery's official map omits any mention of him. No stone marks his grave.

A short walk away on Market Street, the *Aurora*'s office still fronts Franklin Court. No plaque beside its dust-shrouded windows explains how, in his finest moments, young Benny had carried on his grandfather's ideals through his trade. "*The Freedom of the Press* is the *Bulwark of Liberty*," a twenty-one-year-old Benny wrote in his newspaper's first edition. "An impartial Newspaper is the useful offspring of that Freedom. Its object is to inform . . . If the PEOPLE are enlightened the Nation stands and flourishes; thro' ignorance it falls or degenerates."

The *Aurora*'s painted wooden sign, hanging discreetly from rusted hooks over the brick sidewalk, can stand as Benny's memorial. The words BENJ. FRANKLIN BACHE, PUBLISHER are crowned by the newspaper's motto, which also elegantly evokes the spirit that animated his grandfather's last will and testament: SURGO UT PROSIM. "I rise that I might serve."

6

"A name that will disappear with him"

In 1800, ten years after Benjamin Franklin's death, only one American in twenty lived in a town of more than 2,500 people. Four out of five Americans farmed land. Of these 4 million farmers, nearly 900,000 were enslaved. Farmers used tools that Franklin would have recognized, clearing trees from the land and setting their houses at a distance from others, unlike the clustered dwellings of European villages. Their rooms, plagued by insects and vermin, smelled of the barnyard and privy. They wore mud-caked clothes cleaned with chamber lye, or concentrated urine. These Americans set their day by the sun, furrowing the land with moldboards, and at night burning candles made the same way as a ten-year-old Franklin had produced them in his father's shop.

In American cities then, young craftsmen such as coopers and blacksmiths largely used the same tools as their grandparents. Those trades, manufacturing a blend of necessities for the body and belly, comprised the majority of the first generation of Boston's Franklin loan recipients. Carpenters were the most represented profession in Philadelphia's ledger, followed by shoemakers, tailors, and housepainters. In

1799, the year after yellow fever killed Benny, Joseph Fox became the first Philadelphia printer to receive a loan.

In these first ten years, Philadelphia borrowers repaid nearly all of Franklin's money. The ledger's opening pages reveal only one large delinquency, an amount recovered by the sheriff. The borrowers included bakers and glaziers, potters and harness makers, coppersmiths and wheelwrights. Also: a bricklayer named Oliver Cromwell. Turning the musty pages of each loan agreement can feel like reading an old swashbuckling story, bringing the same sense of relief when the last line reveals that a character has made it through. Three cheers for the cabinetmaker Christopher Pigeon, who repaid his debt on time. And a compassionate wag of the head for Paul Revere's son-in-law, one of only two Boston defaulters. Records show that "Thomas S. Eayres a Madman" suffered a breakdown, perhaps occasioned by the unexpected death of his wife. The silversmith then vanished from the page.

As the nineteenth century began, the trades listed in the ledgers start to change. Boston's loans in the year 1800 went to as many hatters (two) as housewrights and blacksmiths. Franklin thought that producing "superfluities" wasted labor to feed vanities and fuel conspicuous consumption. "Our Eyes," he wrote in 1784, "tho' exceedingly useful, ask when reasonable, only the cheap Assistance of *Spectacles,* which could not much impair our Finances. But *the Eyes of other People* are the Eyes that ruin us. If all but myself were blind, I should want neither fine Clothes, fine Houses nor Fine Furniture."

In addition to the hatters, for the first time Boston's class included a tailor, a furrier, a bookbinder, and an upholsterer: fine clothes, fine houses, fine furniture.

Philadelphia's borrowers in the year 1800 included a silversmith born on July 4, 1776. Liberty Browne would fulfill his name's promise, repaying Franklin's faith in the working class. At his workshop, located near Franklin Court on Chestnut Street, Browne produced finely etched silver plates and tankers that command high prices at auctions today. In 1801, Browne entered politics as a Jeffersonian Democratic-Republican, winning a vote to be an election inspector.

Seven years later, he was elected to Philadelphia's thirty-two-seat city council. Shortly after settling his $250 loan, which with interest totaled $318.75, he rose to become the powerful body's president in 1813. (That same year, another Franklin loan recipient, John Clawges Jr., ran for the Pennsylvania House of Representatives. Along with his fellow Federalist candidates, he lost to a Democratic-Republican slate led by William J. Duane, a former *Aurora* cub reporter who had married Sally's daughter Deborah.)

In 1808, Boston applicant number 175, the bricklayer Charles Wells, used his $100 loan to launch a career as a successful builder. After repaying his loan and serving as a city alderman, he became Boston's fourth mayor, in 1831, "elected," one historian recorded, "as a protest of the middle classes against what they thought was the high-handed and extravagant way" that Wells's predecessors had managed the city's affairs. Wells served two terms, then followed a Franklinian trajectory, first becoming president of the Massachusetts Mutual Fire Insurance Company and then volunteering to lead the Massachusetts Charitable Mechanic Association, whose founding chairman had been Paul Revere. The philanthropic organization trained apprentices and established America's first free public secondary school.

As mayor, Wells extended Boston's central streets, including Tremont, which was lengthened to reach Roxbury, then a separate town. America was expanding, too. The ripples of two unrelated events far from Boston and Philadelphia would soon wash against their waterfronts, altering both cities in ways that Franklin had not foreseen.

In 1785, the inventor John Fitch wrote to Franklin seeking backing for a new technology "of the first Magnitude, not only to the United States but to every Maratime power in the World." Two years later, Franklin and other delegates took a break from the Constitutional Convention to watch a demonstration of Fitch's steamboat on the Delaware River. The eighty-one-year-old was unimpressed by the slow-moving craft and refused to invest. In his will, Franklin also failed to consider how mechanization might upend the apprentice system, skilled tradesmen, and his loan scheme.

In 1793, three years after Franklin's death, Secretary of State Thomas Jefferson—whose office evaluated patent applications—received, from a man named Eli Whitney, "a description of my machine for ginning Cotton." Jefferson eagerly replied, requesting a model so he could see how this so-called cotton gin ("gin" being short for "engine") removed the plant's seeds. He granted the patent the following spring. Whitney next informed Jefferson of his method for manufacturing rifles using interchangeable parts. After fulfilling an order for ten thousand muskets, Whitney became the federal government's chief arms manufacturer.

Other developments spun forward the world that Franklin knew. In 1802, a French weaver invented the automated loom. The following year, Napoleon—seeking funds to fight his war against Britain—offered to sell the Louisiana Territory to the United States for $15 million. With a stroke of President Jefferson's pen, the country doubled its landmass. The 1804–1806 expedition led by Meriwether Lewis and William Clark revealed its bounty. Soon Robert Fulton's improved design of the steamboat paddled settlers west. In the nineteenth century's first decade, the nation's population increased a whopping 35 percent, to 7.2 million. Kentucky and Tennessee joined the Union, followed by Ohio. Migrants pushed their farms and towns to the Mississippi River and beyond.

While schoolchildren often learn his name in association with his cotton gin, Eli Whitney was also the forefather of American mass production. His guns armed settlers and soldiers encroaching on Native American territory, while his machine made growing cotton—and slavery—more profitable than ever. Many of the newly appropriated southwestern lands were planted with cotton. The ginned bales would soon be fed into textile mills whirring thirty miles north of Boston in the Merrimack River town named for Francis Cabot Lowell, the man who helped launch the American industrial revolution after a plucky feat of espionage.

Unlike Benjamin Franklin, James Watt jealously shielded his patents, which included engines that used water and steam to generate what Watt called "horsepower." On a trip to England and Scotland in 1810, Lowell toured mills using this advanced technology to drive automatic looms. Forbidden to take notes, and knowing that his papers would be searched upon his leaving Britain, Lowell memorized the machines' components so he could build them from scratch upon his return to Massachusetts. In 1814, his Boston Manufacturing Company, converting raw cotton to cloth, opened on the banks of the Charles River, ten miles upstream from the millpond where a young Franklin had struck upon the idea of strapping wooden paddles to his hands to gain speed. "I remember I swam faster by means of these palettes," Franklin wrote of his invention of swim fins, "but they fatigued my wrists."

Little did Franklin expect that rapid advances in technology would threaten to exhaust his loan scheme within a generation after his death. In his will, Franklin had acknowledged that his two-hundred-year wager supporting skilled artificers was susceptible to the "accidents to which all human affairs and projects are subject in such a length of time." He seemed to imply that the funds could be mismanaged, never suspecting that his intended recipients would so soon be replaced by gears, steam, and steel.

The Philadelphia that Franklin had known was quickly fading, too. In December 1799, the Continental Army veteran Henry Lee (father of the future Confederate general Robert E. Lee) lodged at Franklin Court. There, he wrote George Washington's famous funerary address, proclaiming him to be "first in war, first in peace, first in the hearts of his countrymen."

The following year, the national capital moved to Washington, D.C., stunting Philadelphia's economy. The 1807 Embargo Act and the War of 1812 further curtailed the maritime trade upon which the city's merchants and financiers depended.

After Franklin's daughter, Sally, died of cancer at Franklin Court in

1808, her husband, Richard Bache—who, under the terms of Franklin's will, had freed the enslaved man named Bob—shared the space with the African Free School, founded to instruct Black children. After Bache's death in 1811, his inheritors tore down the storied compound to build rows of small rental homes.

Of Franklin's main heirs, only Temple remained. After abandoning his infant daughter in London, he crossed the Channel and dropped off the map. His own collected letters show a gap of fourteen years, stretching from 1797 to 1811. We do know that he did not heed John Adams's warning that he should publish Franklin's works before others beat him to the profitable punch. In 1799, while stationed in Italy during the Napoleonic Wars, the French author of the novel *Dangerous Liaisons* carried with him an unauthorized edition of Franklin's autobiography, printed in Paris. "Be sure you buy Franklin's *Memoirs*," Pierre Choderlos de Laclos wrote to his wife, "and give them to our son to read. Franklin had a formula for happiness within the common man's reach, and there is nobody I would rather have our son emulate than him."

American newspapers revived the rumor that Temple had sold out to the British. In 1805, Benny's widow, Peggy, taking matters into her own hands, announced that the *Aurora* would publish a tranche of Franklin's papers that Temple had failed to secure. In London the following year, one of Franklin's closest friends followed suit, bringing out three volumes of correspondence. Its preface exonerated Temple of duplicity, but not his dereliction of the duty Franklin had entrusted to him. Another collector of Franklin's papers complained that Temple was "a slow coach, honest, earnest, proud of his charge, opinionated, laborious and fussy; but at the same time he was an unmethodical muddler, an incompetent editor, and uncommonly dilatory in his habits." As Poor Richard once quipped, "'Tis hard for an empty Bag to stand upright."

In 1812, Temple finally wrote to his exiled father in London, asking for help collating Franklin's papers. William readily agreed, confiding to a friend that he could not "bear the thoughts of dying at enmity with one so nearly connected."

Temple never showed up. His personal battles, or Napoleon's war against Britain, kept him rooted in Paris. His surviving letters do not, unfortunately, include any observations of what it was like to live in the French capital during the monarchy, republic, and then empire. What would his grandfather have made of that progression, let alone the news that many of their friends and associates, including their favorite neighbor, had perished at the guillotine?

William died the next year, 1813, at age eighty-three. He had lived nearly as long as his famous father, albeit in ignominy. In his own will, he passed what remained of his estate to Temple's illegitimate daughter, whom he had raised as his own child. William's final wish was to be buried "with as much frugality as is consistent with decency in the same grave in St. Pancras Church Yard in which my late beloved wife was deposited."

The St. Pancras Old Church graveyard's Hardy Tree. William Franklin's tombstone purportedly stands among the jumbled markers.

No trace of his plot remains. The cemetery was a notorious haunt of grave robbers who sold their spoils to anatomy schools for practicing dissection. (In *A Tale of Two Cities,* Jerry Cruncher brings his son to St. Pancras for some nocturnal "fishing.") During the railway age, this patch of Mornington Crescent became latticed with tracks ending at nearby King's Cross station. Its architect ordered his assistant, a young man named Thomas Hardy, to disinter dozens of bodies and move their bones to a communal pit. The future author of *Far from the Madding Crowd* next arranged the tombstones in rings around an ash tree. The last trace of Benjamin Franklin's firstborn son is said to stand among these moss-furred markers, entwined by roots that continue to grow.

For most of this era, from 1802 to 1815, Philadelphia's loan scheme was overseen by a man who also left a scant trail, appearing less as a solid character than a misty apparition. Even the one known portrait of George Baker looks ghostly.

His presence is seen clearest through the section of Philadelphia's ledger filled in by his hand. For the first time, the treasurer recorded the home address of each guarantor, attended borrowers' bankruptcy hearings, and listed each man's trade. Thanks to Baker, we know that the Henry Miller who received a loan in 1802 dealt in alcohol, and that Samuel Tatern (did it rhyme with *pattern?*) worked as a tailor.

Under Baker's tenure, no fewer than four tradesmen received loans each year. As the first generation of borrowers repaid their notes, the number increased to as many as ten. In 1809, Baker also recorded receiving $180.13 in counterfeit currency, another setback—like defaults—that Franklin had failed to account for when calculating his principal's growth. It was an incongruous lapse for the man who, as Poor Richard, had observed, "Tis against some Men's Principle to pay Interest, and seems against others Interest to pay the Principal."

In 1816, Franklin's Philadelphia fund received a surprise boost from faraway Scotland. In his will, the chemist John Scott left "to the Corporation of Philadelphia who are entrusted with the management of Dr. Franklin's Legacy the sum of Three thousand Dollars . . . to be applied to the same purposes as Dr. Franklin's Legacy." Scott also gave an additional $4,000 to be placed in an account whose earned interest was to fund the awarding of copper medals to "ingenious men and women who make useful inventions." The American Philosophical Society still annually awards the John Scott Medal, which comes with a prize of $10,000, funded by his bequest.

Who was John Scott? "A biographer's nightmare," concluded one historian. "He published neither books nor papers and references to him are few and brief." Edinburgh directories showed him working as a druggist there for thirty years, before dying in London in 1815. How he had heard of Franklin's loans, and why he chose to support them, remains unknown.

The money that Scott directed to Franklin's scheme doubled the amount available to Philadelphia tradesmen to $520. The additional funds could not bail out existing borrowers, whose missed repayments spiked during the War of 1812, which ended in 1815. The unpaid amounts included the $64.57 owed by the cabinetmaker Nixon Albertson, the bricklayer Lewis Foote's default of $86.36, the tailor George Cox's evasion of $218.96, and the bookbinder John M. Boddy's reneging on $294. Mr. Boddy turned out to be a stiff, repaying only $36.

Other names in Philadelphia's ledger could have doubled as Franklin's pen names: John Death, Francis Hammer, Philip Reap, Frazier K. Work, and the alliterative all-stars Daniel Deal, Gilbert Gaw, Marmaduke Martin, William Wile, and Samuel Stackhouse (who was, fittingly, a home builder). Stackhouse defaulted for a loss of $256.98. His fellow carpenter Isaac Kite Jr. also fell behind—and was named in a suit to collect payment—but did not drift away, finally settling his account in full over ten installments.

On paper, Philadelphia's Franklin Legacy looked to be on solid footing. An 1817 city audit certified that Franklin's $4,444.44 gift, plus the outstanding loans and interest of $10,812.11, added up to

$15,256.55. The amount approached the $15,803 that Franklin had estimated the balance to reach at this point.

Yet many of the outstanding balances on loans taken during the War of 1812 would end up being written off during a housecleaning that would not take place for another thirty years. Defaults gained steam during the Panic of 1819, the nation's first peacetime financial crisis. The ledger's entries for 1820 showed Franklin's money moving backward, ending the year with $12,105.57. In the next two years, the fund lost 20 percent of its value. Philadelphia's bequest would never regain its momentum.

In 1814, the year that Napoleon was exiled to Elba, the fifty-four-year-old Temple, in Paris, finally began seriously working on his grandfather's gift to him. It would be convenient if a letter existed that showed Temple had been moved at last to act by a sense of honor — or even Poor Richard's exhortation "But dost thou love Life, then do not squander Time; for that's the Stuff Life is made of." The truth appears more mundane: Temple's London publisher persuaded him to receive the clerk that its office was sending across the reopened Channel to help him.

John Adams once remarked that producing Franklin's biography could not be done without also offering the reader "a complete history of the philosophy and politics of the eighteenth century. Such a work would be one of the most important that ever was written; much more interesting to this and future ages than the 'Decline and Fall of the Roman Empire.'"

Temple made an admirable attempt. In three years, beginning in 1816, he produced six volumes of his grandfather's papers and correspondence, including an authorized edition of his autobiography. In the preface, the roué winked at his critics. "Nations," Temple wrote, "as well as individuals have their periods of infancy and decrepitude, of moral vigor and wild derangement."

These were Bible-size tomes. The first volume of the American printing ended on page 519 with Franklin's famous mock epitaph, wherein he wrote that he would return in a new, more elegant edition. In a way, through his work, Temple had made it true.

In another volume's afterword, Temple excerpted accounts of Franklin's funeral—"All the bells in the city were muffled"—and the mellifluous French tributes, but omitted William Smith's insipid eulogy. Temple also included most of Franklin's last will and testament, though he excised his grandfather's bequest to the turncoat William —a belated act, perhaps, of filial respect.

The illegitimate son of the illegitimate son of one of the Western world's most famous men at last seemed to stand on his own. John Adams sent his approval. "I am pleased," he wrote Temple, "to see you at length appearing on the stage of human Affairs."

In 1823, Temple wed his longtime companion in Paris. Under the terms of Franklin's will enacted thirty-three years before, their union finally canceled the £3,500 Temple owed to his grandfather.

He died a few months later, of unknown causes, at age sixty-three. In his handwritten will, Temple left most of his paltry estate to his daughter, Ellen, who had been raised by his father in London. To his wife, Hannah Collier, he gave "all the property of whatever nature it may be that I die possessed of—or have a right to—in France." That meant the mother lode of Franklin's manuscripts.

Collier packed them in crates, which moved with her back to her native England. In 1827, the Boston editor Jared Sparks, embarking on a project to tell the history of the United States using its protagonists' own words, sailed to London to view Franklin's in the original. Collier said she no longer had the papers. Whether they had been lost or sold remains unclear. In 1831, a large cache of Franklin's writings was at last discovered in the building where she had lodged on St. James's Street. For years, a tailor had been cutting the pages into sleeve patterns.

Sparks next searched for the trove of Franklin papers that Temple had left in Philadelphia with a friend. The man had died and passed them to his own son, who, Sparks learned, stored the manuscripts in a stable. The family often reached into the tall stack to give a handful of pages to guests as souvenirs.

Temple was buried in Paris's Père-Lachaise Cemetery. His simple tombstone, in French, identifies him as the grandson of Benjamin Franklin. The epitaph, written by his wife, insists:

> He has always been worthy of a name
> That will disappear with him.

Franklin's loan scheme faced its own demise, although, as industrialization gathered steam, the threat was not immediately apparent. At first, young women transplanted from rural areas — not urban tradesmen —filled the Charles River mills. Boston's Franklin Fund continued to lend money to skilled workers. The ledger's entries for 1814 show disbursements of $200 to a "coach & chaise painter," a wheelwright, a tailor, a mason, a saddler, a painter, a glazier, and a shoemaker.

But the die had been cast. Jennies and looms and rollers and lathes would rapidly transform Franklin's hometowns and cause his money's managers to question the viability of his supposed far-seeing bequest.

Philadelphia, which had ended the eighteenth century as the Athens of America, would finish the nineteenth as its Manchester.

Boston would become the nation's wealthiest city, driven by the textile factories owned by a group of investors known as the Boston Associates, part of the group that would come to be called Brahmins, after India's highest caste. Their mills, a visiting Charles Dickens noted, were "owned by a Company of Proprietors, but what they call in America a Corporation." Most Boston mill stock was closely held by a handful of linked families who reaped the profits of shares that paid handsome annual dividends upwards of 20 percent.

While Franklin's last bet would remain in play, the rules of the game had changed in his absence. In the twenty years since Boston had received Franklin's gift, 156 young tradesmen had received loans. Starting in 1811, when a Harvard-educated lawyer took over the books, only 135 further loans would be made—across the next eighty years.

The falloff was due, in part, to the mechanization of work such as shoemaking and printing. It is true that Franklin had failed to foresee labor's shift from workshop to factory. But a variety of trades still operated, and thrived, across the nineteenth century. Far less visible were the innovations in finance occurring at this time. Anyone could notice a large, fuming factory. Harder to glimpse was the new professional class that began managing the wealth these companies produced.

New England's textile mill proprietors hired third parties to handle their estates, ensuring that their favored descendants and charities would receive their fortunes. These accounts, or "trusts," were shaped by a landmark ruling that still governs their management today. It also granted the overseer of Boston's Franklin Fund the power to steer the benefactor's money as he saw fit.

In 1823, the Long Wharf merchant John McLean—who, coincidentally, lived at Franklin Place, the crescent of elegant town houses built near the founder's birthplace—left in his will a trust holding $50,000 in mill stock. He designated as its custodians Jonathan and Francis Amory, directing the brothers to pay all dividends to his widow. Upon her death, the entire account was to be disbursed equally to the Massachusetts General Hospital and to Harvard, for the endowment of a teaching post. (Still funded today, the inaugural McLean Professor of Ancient and Modern History was the Franklin manuscript-hunter Jared Sparks.)

After Jonathan Amory died in 1828, his brother Francis resigned from overseeing McLean's trust. Harvard and the hospital sued him, alleging that he was financially liable for the portfolio's decline from its starting value. A probate court cleared Amory of wrongdoing, but in 1830 the case was appealed to the Massachusetts Supreme Judicial Court.

Evincing Boston's tight circle, one of Francis Amory's attorneys was Lemuel Shaw, a man who had witnessed McLean's will and actually may have drafted it, just as he had written Boston's city charter. Shaw would be appointed chief justice later that year. (Herman Melville cagily dedicated his first novel to him, a year before marrying Shaw's daughter Elizabeth.)

In *Harvard College v. Amory*, the court again absolved Amory of wrongdoing. "All that can be required of a trustee to invest," its opinion ruled, "is that he shall conduct himself faithfully and exercise a sound discretion. He is to observe how men of prudence, discretion, and intelligence manage their own affairs, not in regard to speculation, but in regard to the permanent disposition of their funds, considering the probable income, as well as the probable safety of the capital to be invested."

This still-recognized "Prudent Person Rule" fostered the growth of the trustee as a profession. As a center of textile manufacturing and a port thriving from new trade routes to Asia, Boston presented its trustees with both a stockpile of assets and the latitude to invest them as they wished.

Lemuel Shaw's close friend William Minot (Harvard class of 1802) took over the law firm started by his father (Harvard class of 1778) and became Boston's most prominent trustee. Minot's central Boston office, at 39 Court Street, stood adjacent to the former site of the printshop where Franklin had once slipped pseudonymous articles under its front door, hoodwinking his older brother James, who published them in the *Courant*.

In Silence Dogood's fourth essay for the newspaper, the sixteen-year-old Franklin, perhaps exorcising his resentment at being pulled from formal schooling, mocked "Parents, who, blind to their Childrens Dulness," sent their offspring to Harvard, "where, for want of a suitable Genius, they learn little more than how to carry themselves handsomely, and enter a Room genteelly, (which might as well be acquir'd at a Dancing-School,) and from whence they return, after Abundance of Trouble and Charge, as great Blockheads as ever, only more proud and self-conceited."

Now one of these graduates controlled his dying gift to Boston. Turning the ledger's brittle pages scored by his handwriting reveals a precipitous increase in Franklin's money—and a simultaneous corruption of the founder's grand design for the endurance of the working class.

"Until within the last twenty years," the loan scheme's treasurer William Minot wrote dispassionately in 1836, "no great care was taken in accumulating the fund. It is now carefully attended to."

7

Boston: Grubby Boys and Angel Fish

The word *project* is one of the nouns Franklin used most in his memoir, appearing thirty times. *Ingenious* and *ingenuity* crop up seventeen times, usually to describe his father, uncles, and other craftsmen Franklin admired. While his contributions to electrical and political science are well-documented, Franklin's role as a catalyst of modern American philanthropy is often overlooked. As we will see, he inspired at least one Gilded Age tycoon to create the template of contemporary giving.

But who inspired Benjamin Franklin's charity? Despite—or be-cause of—his lack of schooling, Franklin found his first role models on the shelf. "All the little Money that came into my Hands," he wrote of his Boston childhood, "was ever laid out in Books." His favorite title then was *The Pilgrim's Progress,* followed by Shakespeare's plays and Milton's *Paradise Lost.*

"There was also a Book of Defoe's," Franklin remembered in his memoir, "called *An Essay on Projects,* and another of Dr. Mather's, call'd *Essays to do Good* which perhaps gave me a Turn of Thinking that had an Influence on some of the principal future Events of my Life."

That modest "perhaps" understated the fact that Franklin lifted from their pages the kernels of his earliest philanthropic ideas.

A bankrupt Daniel Defoe wrote *An Essay upon Projects* while hiding in Bristol from a London creditor empowered to imprison him. Published in 1697, two decades before *Robinson Crusoe* brought him fame, *Projects* laid out Defoe's ideas for social improvement. These included the education of women, the creation of unemployment benefits, a lottery to benefit charity, fire insurance, proportional taxation based on income, mortgage interest capped at 4 percent, and a public assistance scheme called the Friendly Society for Widows. As Silence Dogood, a sixteen-year-old Franklin transcribed thirteen hundred words of Defoe's text—without crediting him—in an essay proposing an "Office of Ensurance for Widows" for Boston.

Defoe had also suggested the formation of "friendly societies," or "people entering into a mutual compact to help one another in case any disaster or distress fall upon them." The Reverend Cotton Mather had made a similar suggestion in his *Essays to Do Good* and formed twenty neighborhood mutual benefit societies (one for every church) across Boston. Franklin's father, Josiah, had joined one. Meetings began with a set of questions put to the group, asking which community problems needed solving and whether anyone had been observed behaving scandalously. The twenty-two-year-old Franklin would borrow this idea to create, in Philadelphia, his Junto, which discussed less ecumenical matters. Its bylaws also required pauses between questions long enough to drink a glass of wine.

"When I was a Boy," a seventy-eight-year-old Franklin wrote to Cotton Mather's son, "*Essays to do Good* gave me such a Turn of Thinking as to have [an] Influence on my Conduct thro' Life; for I have always set a greater Value on the Character of a *Doer of Good*, than on any other kind of Reputation; and if I have been, as you seem to think, a useful Citizen, the Publick owes the Advantage of it to that Book."

In Philadelphia, a young Franklin had quickly learned a lesson that remains applicable to philanthropy today. At the time, giving was

more commonly called charity (the word Franklin used), and donations were usually collected by a church. In 1730, as the twenty-six-
year-old attempted to raise money to build the colonies' first library,
Franklin realized that people were reluctant to donate to a cause that
would elevate his reputation above their own.

"I therefore put my self as much as I could out of sight," he related in his autobiography, "and stated it as a Scheme of a *Number of
Friends,* who had requested me to go about and propose it to such as
they thought Lovers of Reading. In this way my Affair went on more
smoothly, and I ever after practis'd it on such Occasions; and from my
frequent Successes, can heartily recommend it. The present little Sacrifice of your Vanity will afterwards be amply repaid."

In our current era of virtue signaling and philanthropic grandstand-
ing, Franklin's advice to silently do good seems quaint. It is true that,
as he later admitted, the library did benefit himself, perhaps more than
any other Philadelphian. Like many autodidacts, Franklin's lack of formal schooling remained a phantom limb that he constantly scratched.
"This Library," he wrote, "afforded me the means of Improvement by
constant Study, for which I set apart an Hour or two each Day; and
thus repair'd in some Degree the Loss of the Learned Education my
Father once intended for me."

When raising funds to build the Philadelphia Academy, Franklin
told potential donors that the school's funding was "not as an Act
of mine, but some *publick-spirited Gentlemen;* avoiding as much as
I could, according to my usual Rule, the presenting of myself as the
Author of any Scheme for Benefit."

From the itinerant preacher George Whitefield, who compelled his
audience of commoners to contribute the coins in their pockets to
fund the construction of an orphanage, Franklin learned the cumula-
tive power of small donations. The Penns and colonial gentry were not
given to large contributions; the term *noblesse oblige* would not enter
the lexicon until 1837. Yet, Franklin realized, much could be accomplished when the public pitched in pence upon shillings, and pistoles
upon pounds.

As much as he downplayed his own philanthropy, Franklin came to realize that sometimes the best way to get people to donate to your cause was to publish the names of those who had already contributed. Friends would not want to appear miserly, and foes would not want to look outspent. He noted, too, a trend that remains unchanged in America today: those with the least money usually give the most readily, just as a young Franklin had done. "Perhaps," he reflected, "thro' fear of being thought to have but little."

When raising money to build the Pennsylvania Hospital, the project's progenitor, Dr. Thomas Bond, had urged Franklin to make public his own donation. "The subscriptions afterwards were more free and generous," Franklin recalled. By convincing the state assembly to match any amount raised up to £2,000, Franklin secured "an additional motive to give, since every man's donation would be doubled . . . The subscriptions accordingly soon exceeded the requisite sum."

The colony's assembly, Franklin gleefully recorded, "conceiv'd they might have the credit of being charitable without the expense." But he had outfoxed them. "I do not remember any of my political maneuvers, the success of which gave me at the time more pleasure." He had invented the matching grant.

This burst of philanthropic ingenuity arrived in the aftermath of his retirement from printing, at the age of forty-two. Just as he had not named his projects after himself, Franklin did not boast about his giving. He was not above some self-effacing moralizing, however. In a letter to his sister Jane, he reprinted a poem that portrayed Faith, Hope, and Charity (the rungs of Jacob's ladder, which led to heaven) as the floors of a house. "Don't delight so much to dwell in these lower Rooms," Franklin told her, "but get as fast as you can into the Garret; for in truth the best Room in the House is *Charity*. For my part, I wish the House was turn'd upside down; 'tis so difficult (when one is fat) to get up Stairs; and not only so, but I imagine *Hope* and *Faith* may be more firmly built on *Charity*, than *Charity* upon *Faith* and *Hope*."

The plumper middle-aged Franklin told his mother that in his retirement, "I read a great deal, ride a little, do a little Business for my

self, more for others." This 1750 letter includes prescient updates on
William, then nineteen, who had "acquir'd a Habit of Idleness, but
begins of late to apply himself, and I hope will become an industrious
Man." The seven-year-old Sally was his opposite, an avid reader and
dancer who "grows a fine girl. Perhaps I flatter my self too much; but
I have hopes that she will prove an ingenious sensible notable and
worthy woman."

The forty-four-year-old Franklin concluded, "So the Years roll
round, and the last will come; when I would rather have it said, *He
lived usefully,* than, *He died rich.*"

After becoming treasurer of Boston's Franklin Fund in 1811, William Minot chose accumulation over usefulness. Perhaps this is not
surprising. Unlike his Philadelphia counterparts, the twenty-eight-
year-old Minot did not himself see the results of Benjamin Franklin's
industrious philanthropy. In Boston, the only reminders of Franklin
that a citizen gamboling about town might notice were his parents'
gravestone at the Granary Burying Ground near the Common, or
the sign marking Franklin Street, dedicated when William Minot was
twelve.

Minot's papers, held at the Massachusetts Historical Society, reveal
no affinity for the man. Minot had not won a Franklin medal at school
and did not write an introspective book manuscript, like his successor
as Franklin's Boston treasurer, about "trifles," the "slight circumstances
that make or mar the happiness of life." In it, Samuel McCleary would
marvel that "the flying of a common paper kite by a printer gave us the
magnetic telegraph . . . We cannot tell what will be the result of any
one act, or what effect it will have in the future. It may make us rich
and it may make us poor. But one thing we do know. We know that
a right action will bring no misery. These are things worth reflection."

William Minot betrayed no such uncertainty. In his lone surviving
portrait, an elderly Minot resembles John Adams: ruddy cheeks, bushy

eyebrows, and a seemingly electrified bald pate, wild with uncombed strands of white hair. His mouth is even shaped into a self-satisfied smudge.

Given the events that would unfold in Philadelphia—and annoyingly to those who wanted to see Franklin's scheme play out in his birthplace—Minot may have chosen the correct course. But in curtailing loans to young tradesmen, he also undermined Franklin's conviction that America's future depended on public-facing citizens forged from skilled labor. William Minot did not belong to that class.

You may give a Man an Office," said Poor Richard, "but you cannot give him discretion." But Franklin had never met a Boston trustee. Just as today's airline pilots speak to passengers in the clipped voice modeled on the maverick Chuck Yeager's unflappable drawl, contemporary trustees trace their silence back to their early-nineteenth-century forefathers. William Minot stands foremost among them.

"Boston trustees are a secret lot," a lawyer once explained to a meeting of the American Bar Association. "They not only don't advertise, but they are reluctant to tell you anything about their business. One of them describes his beneficiaries to me as 'members of my financial family.' The old Boston trustees took a rather serious and aloof position. They managed the trust on the idea it was their own business. They were acting as a father substitute (in the Freudian sense), acting for members of their financial family, and they felt more responsible to the court than to their beneficiaries."

As a group, they were very good at their jobs. Trustees in Boston, birthplace of the mutual fund, tended billions of dollars for families —such as the Ames, Forbes, and Peabody fortunes—and the endowments of universities, including Harvard and MIT. The sociologist who popularized the acronym *WASP* to describe America's white Anglo-Saxon Protestant aristocracy found that although at the start of the nineteenth century twice-as-populous Philadelphia was the richer city,

Boston was far more enterprising, and better at making its inherited wealth last longer.

Elite Bostonians tended to follow their fathers in work. A descendant of the textile merchant defendant in *Harvard College v. Amory* went on to become president of the National Association of Cotton Manufacturers. One of his sons developed Harvard Law School's first course on accounting. Another son, Cleveland Amory, displeased the family by devoting his post-Harvard life to advocating for animal rights, inspiring his successful trilogy of memoirs beginning with *The Cat Who Came to Christmas*.

Amory's first book, *The Proper Bostonians,* is a series of astringent anecdotes about his caste. "Boston's First Family fortunes," he wrote, "have long been tied up beyond the reach of any power save possibly, as one financial writer put it, the Communist International . . . The power of the trustee, as long as he is by court definition a 'prudent' man, is close to absolute . . . Almost all these trustees are themselves First Family men . . . The total power and resources of Boston's Family trusts have never been figured, but some years ago one of the city's trustee officers alone paid three percent of Boston's total tax levy."

That man was William Minot's son, who had followed his father into the family business. In 1895, William Minot Jr. controlled more assets "than any financial institution in Boston." Sunlight still illuminates Copley Square because in 1893 he lobbied for a building height restriction around its perimeter—which also drove up rents in the offices he owned there. "It was the city," he said, "that made the square so beautified." But it was the trusts that empowered a Minot to sculpt it.

In 1811, the year William Minot became treasurer of the Franklin Fund, thirty-six artificers received sums averaging $200. Minot's ledger from that year records the repayments, and also a cash balance of $1,386.86. After twenty years, Franklin had predicted the fund's value would have risen to nearly $12,000. In actuality, due to delinquent repayments, Boston's account held 25 percent less, or about $9,000. Still, its starting value had more than doubled, validating (if only partially) Franklin's faith in his class.

On paper, per Franklin's instructions, Boston's selectmen—and, after incorporation, its aldermen and mayor—managed his gift, alongside designated ministers. In practice, however, William Minot worked alone. In his audit of the fund in 1866, the year Minot at last stepped down, Samuel McCleary discovered that the appointed clergy had not attended a meeting for forty-four years. They had finally convened only to vote on Minot's successor.

Minot began his stewardship of Franklin's money by chasing defaulters draining its principal. In his will, Franklin had hoped that a "virtuous and benevolent" citizen would manage his scheme "gratis." Ledger entries show that Minot charged the fund $10 a year in postage and classified advertisements spent on "notifying bondsmen," as well as a 2.5 percent commission on any recovered sums. In 1813, he recouped $426, earning a fee of $10.65. At year's end, Minot recorded that Franklin's pool of money was growing at last. "The amount of the fund," he wrote, "exclusive of bad debts, was $9,666.54, as nearly as could be ascertained."

And then, a change. In 1818, Minot approved loans to a carpenter and a baker, a bookbinder and a boot maker, a builder of cabinets and a man who made pianos. But for the first time, Franklin's money was handed to a banker, too. As fewer tradesmen applied for loans (and Minot did not seek them), the account's cash on hand grew to the point that he, as a prudent man, reinterpreted Franklin's desire "that no part of the money will at any time be dead, or be diverted to other purposes, but be continually augmenting by the interest."

"I yesterday received an order of the Trustees of the Franklin Fund," Minot recorded in the ledger, "to deposit $2000 in the checker of the Manufacturers Bank."

How and when Minot received such an order is unknown; the committee's minutes do not record it. But if William Minot—the respected son of the august jurist chosen to deliver George Washington's eulogy at Boston's public memorial—had suggested the idea himself, who were they, a committee of increasingly absent selectmen and disinterested clergy, to say no? Like Franklin's borrowers, the account would pay 5 percent interest. The bank, however, carried no risk of default and freed Minot from chasing down late payments from men who proved Poor Richard's observation that "Creditors have better memories than debtors."

An auditor soon after praised Minot's action, noting that it "had a salutary effect . . . The loss the fund will eventually sustain will be very small."

In 1819, Minot topped up the bank deposit to $3,000. As Bostonians endured the worst financial panic to that point in their country's history, Franklin's money went into a vault, not out to entrepreneurs. That Christmas, Minot decided to pause filing lawsuits against "delinquents of the Fund," he wrote in the ledger, since "compulsive measures at this season would be attended with distressing consequences to their families."

So William Minot was not a total Scrooge (still unborn; in 1819, Charles Dickens turned seven). But that holiday season was also one of mourning in Minot's town house, which faced the Common at 61 Beacon Street. After he had married Louisa Davis, the daughter of the Massachusetts solicitor general, in 1810, she had given birth to two boys and one girl. In the winter of 1819, their third son, Francis, died before reaching his third month. Did Minot even know that the Franklins had also lost a son with that name?

Minot did not record this event, or these years, in a diary. He was his father's son. In a failed attempt to keep one, the elder Minot had written on an opening page: "I have frequently resolved to keep a journal; but never could be brought to put it into practice. Of what should it consist? Of resolutions and relapses; of many faults and few virtues; of fears without danger, and misfortunes without forecast. Of what avail would such a picture be?"

William Minot would do better, but only in fits and starts, and seldom confiding his emotions to posterity. A typical laconic entry among his papers reads like the one in his datebook for April 14, 1865: "President Lincoln assassinated."

Minot's wife, Louisa, an oil painter belatedly recognized as among the earliest artists of the Hudson River school, appeared more ebullient, composing a book of verse she dedicated to their daughter, Mary. It included the poem an eighteen-year-old Louisa wrote after meeting her future husband, revealing the charms of a young William Minot. "I love the enchantment you spread," she wrote, "the quick throb that you shot through the heart."

Minot's own papers sketch a decorous man, with fleeting glimpses of a doting father (one most grateful for "the uniform and invariable love of my children"), a Unitarian (paying $33.75 for six months' use of a pew at King's Chapel), a bourbon drinker ($25.50 for an order of seven gallons), and a self-aware Brahmin. A receipt for the purchase of a "beaver hat" ($9.10) is followed by one, dated a month later, acknowledging Minot's payment of his annual dues to the Massachusetts Society for the Prevention of Cruelty to Animals ($5).

To dig through the boxes of William Minot's papers is to sink your hands into numbers. The figures filter through your fingers, replacing the tools upon which Benjamin Franklin had placed his bet.

In 1820, even as defaults had slowed, Boston's Franklin Fund trustees met "to devise some mode to secure the fund against lapses." Minot, acting as secretary, recorded that the board instructed him to invest any unloaned money "so as to gain interest."

Poor Richard observed that "Men and Melons are hard to know," and they are even more so across the gulf of time. A charitable interpretation of Minot's actions might argue that he acted to ensure that Franklin's seed money would safely grow, realizing the benefactor's wish that Bostonians would have a large amount to spend on the centenary of his death. On the other hand, given Franklin's desire to see skilled laborers rise to join the "general happy Mediocrity," as he called the middle class, Minot's stewardship honored the letter of the founder's unique bequest, but not its intent.

Unlike his Philadelphia counterparts, Minot did, at least, put the money in a savings account, instead of using it for "other purposes," such as sinking it into the stock market. Franklin's aversion to speculation was born of experience, resulting in one of his biggest public missteps. While working as Pennsylvania's representative in London in 1761, he had taken receipt of £26,618 earmarked for the colony during the French and Indian War. Rather than transferring the money straightaway, a wary Franklin followed the Pennsylvania Assembly's order to temporarily invest the enormous sum "in the publick funds." He placed the entire amount in government annuities after London colleagues assured him that, with the European theater of the conflict (where it was called the Seven Years' War) sure to end soon, he could easily realize a 20 percent return. Ministers, Franklin was told, had already picked out the horses that would pull their coaches to the peace conference.

The horses remained in the stable, the war bled on, and the market crashed. Franklin watched his bet lose, lose, and lose again. We can feel his heart sink upon opening the letter from the assembly that had just completed its weeks-long voyage from Philadelphia, instructing Franklin to immediately settle the colony's outstanding debts. Franklin was reduced to begging door-to-door for credit. Every banker turned him away until one finally granted a loan, requiring no "other Security from you, than that which we have in your Character."

Even though Franklin had acted on explicit orders, and despite the fact that he managed to reverse the loss within a year when the market improved — netting a £6,400 profit — his political opponents, including his future eulogizer, the Reverend William Smith, tarred him as a profligate gambler of the public's money.

The mark against his character stung more than losing reelection to the assembly. "Experience keeps a dear school," Poor Richard observed, "but Fools will learn in no other." In his will, Franklin clearly stated that if either Boston or Philadelphia refused his loan scheme's terms, "the money of course remains in the mass of my Estate."

William Minot walked a fine line, and one that would lead to lawsuits. In 1820, Boston's Franklin Fund showed a balance of $11,767 (equivalent to $273,000 at the time of this writing), about one-third less than the $18,294 ($425,000) that Franklin had expected after thirty years. The $3,000 that Minot had deposited in the Manufacturers Bank was earning 5 percent annually, but now he shopped for a better return. Later that summer, Minot diverted that money, plus an additional $1,500, to a Suffolk County bond that paid 6 percent.

In 1822, Boston incorporated. Selectmen became aldermen, and —after the abolition of property-owning requirements for voting and office holding—a mayor was elected. The newly created city council demanded transparency from other committees run by Boston elites, such as the almshouse-managing Overseers of the Poor. Perhaps because it was not officially a public charity, or because its steward was above reproach, William Minot's oversight of the Franklin Fund escaped such scrutiny.

Boston philanthropy began its turn away from the public-facing mutual aid societies that Franklin knew and toward faceless boards of private institutions managing large endowments. Writing as Silence Dogood, Franklin had thumbed his nose at his birthplace's social hierarchy, then dominated by Puritans. Brahmins replaced them. "The great family trusts," Cleveland Amory scornfully observed a century later, "stand between the Bostonians and the activities of contemporary life like the transparent but all too solid glass which separates the angel fish of an aquarium from the grubby little boys outside."

In 1827, William Minot began sinking Benjamin Franklin's money behind that partition. The textile magnate John Lowell called its new home "the best institution on earth . . . the *first* of the *sort* in the whole world. It is in truth so. There is no institution either in Europe or America, of this character. It is *eminently* the *Savings bank of the wealthy.*"

Ironically, the mastermind behind this new breed of bank was cut from Franklinian cloth. All but forgotten today, the story of "Nat the

Navigator" once appeared beside Franklin's in best-selling juvenile biographies with subtitles such as *Sketches of Some Men of Mark Who Rose from Obscurity to Renown.*

Born in Salem in 1773, Nathaniel Bowditch was at age ten, like Franklin, pulled from school to work alongside his father. At twelve, Bowditch left the family's cooperage to be indentured as bookkeeper for a chandler who outfitted trade ships. During his apprenticeship, Franklin admitted that as a sixteen-year-old publishing as Silence Dogood, he had been "perhaps too saucy and provoking." Bowditch swore he would be no "idle 'prentice," and during his indentures taught himself algebra and calculus. At age sixteen he tackled Latin, so he could read classic mathematical treatises, including Isaac Newton's *Principia Mathematica,* in the original.

Both men smacked of the sea. Unlike most of his fellow founders, Franklin was not rooted to the land, either as a plantation owner or a gentleman farmer. Bowditch made his mark not on city streets, but upon salt water. After shipping out on a voyage to Asia, the highbrowed twenty-three-year-old trained the entire crew, including the cook, how to navigate by lunar observation. Each man, the captain told a surprised inquirer on shore, had mastered the art. Bowditch, ever humble, "sat as modest as a maid, saying not a word, but holding his slate pencil in his mouth."

While Benjamin Franklin was the first to chart the Gulf Stream, he sailed exclusively as a passenger. Some of his most relaxed prose was written on the quarterdeck of the ship that took the twenty-year-old home from London in 1726. Franklin recorded leaping overboard to swim with dolphins, seeing a rainbow made by moonlight, and slowing to parley with a passing Dutch fluyt. That occasioned an observation that he could still make today. "We are apt to fancy the person that cannot speak intelligibly to us proportionally stupid in understanding," Franklin wrote in his diary, "and when we speak two or three words of English to a foreigner, it is louder than ordinary, as if we thought him deaf, and that he had lost the use of his ears as well as his tongue." At the journey's end, Franklin disembarked back in Philadelphia, where Deborah and glory awaited.

For Nathaniel Bowditch, the ocean meant work, but also an escape from his proscribed station in life. Both men had calculating minds. A young Franklin used to pass the time — "which I still think I might have employed more usefully" — by amusing himself in creating "magic squares" of numbers whose rows, when added together, equaled the same sum. Next he moved on to magic circles, eddying whirlpools of digits whose rings totaled 360. Franklin sent his designs to an English friend with whom he shared his nascent thoughts on electricity, allowing that number play perhaps was not "altogether useless, if it produces by practice an habitual readiness and exactness in mathematical disquisitions, which readiness may, on many occasions, be of real use."

During his own downtime on a voyage to Spain, Nathaniel Bowditch spotted and corrected five hundred errors in the longitudinal tables appended to the London-published *New Practical Navigator*. As Bowditch set off for Batavia (present-day Indonesia) in 1799, an American publisher urged him to ferret out all of the book's mistakes. Bowditch soon realized that its tables — calculated by the Cambridge-educated British astronomer royal and commissioner of longitude — were "nothing but a tissue of errors from beginning to end."

A self-taught son of an American tradesman once again transformed an Englishman's idea into his own. After Bowditch's eight thousand hand-calculated corrections, the book was published, in his name, as *The American Practical Navigator*. ("Diligence," as Poor Richard put it, "is the Mother of Good-Luck.")

Because most vessels could not afford a chronometer, Bowditch's *Navigator* quickly gained renown as the "Seaman's Bible," or simply "the Bowditch." The book aided the burgeoning American sea trade, as well as its whalers. In Herman Melville's *Moby Dick*, Ishmael warns "ye ship-owners of Nantucket" not to hire a daydreaming crewman who ships with Plato "instead of Bowditch in his head." (American

NATHANIEL BOWDITCH

whalers, the narrator added, were distinguished by a "long line of har-pooners" who had "something better than royal blood." Descended from Franklin's maternal Nantucket forebears, they were "all kith and kin to noble Benjamin.")

Just as Franklin had felt intellectually unqualified to contribute to the Philadelphia Academy, a thirty-three-year-old Bowditch declined Harvard's offer to join its faculty as a math professor. Having "not received a Collegiate education," a friend wrote, "he did not think himself adequate." John Adams was delighted that Massachusetts pro-duced a scientific mind that rivaled the "Franklinian Democrat" Da-vid Rittenhouse. "We have a Bowditch, his Superior," Adams wrote to Thomas Jefferson. The latter tried hiring Bowditch to teach at the University of Virginia. Instead, this young, best-selling, world-sailing savant anchored himself behind the desk of a Salem fire and marine insurance company.

While asking Nathaniel Bowditch to file paperwork and calculate dividends seems akin to hiring his contemporary Jane Austen to compose greeting cards, Bowditch appreciated the time the job afforded him to pursue his own interests. He also excelled at the drudgery of recalculating rows upon rows of numbers, work usually performed by assistants dubbed "computers." Among Bowditch's admirers was the mathematician Charles Babbage, who sent him the designs for his steam-powered calculating machine, the forerunner of the computer.

Bowditch's reputation also brought an invitation from Boston to help raise money to expand its Massachusetts General Hospital. To build Pennsylvania's medical center, Benjamin Franklin had personally donated £25 and enlisted dozens of subscribers. Nathaniel Bowditch funded his project from a remove, through the sale of life insurance policies. The annuities were untried in the United States. Bowditch first had to recalculate the only existing actuarial tables, which were based on English life spans.

At this point, the men's philosophical paths diverge. Franklin inveigled the Pennsylvania Assembly to match his fundraising and then applied his expansive talents to break new ground in science, diplomacy, and literature. Bowditch lobbied the Massachusetts legislature to allow the hospital's life insurance company to accept money in trust and then sank further into his sums, becoming America's prototypical investment banker. In a State Street office near William Minot's, his business quickly transformed into a repository for Boston's railroad and textile wealth.

In the first seven years, Bowditch's balance sheet showed approximately $250,000 in policies and annuities—but twenty times that amount in deposits. His clients formed a register of upper-crust Boston, including twenty-one trusts in the name of Perkins, nine for the Cabots, and eight apiece for the Eliot and Sears families, along with Harvard University.

In January 1827, William Minot recorded a deposit in the Franklin ledger: "Cash invested in the Life Hospital Insurance Co. $10,000." Money that Benjamin Franklin had left to benefit the working class would now help underwrite the ascendant aristocracy. Bowditch used his company as a sort of venture capital fund. Earlier that week, he had announced a 7 percent dividend on its stock, the start of a run of positive returns that would not pause until 1939, the last year of the Great Depression.

The Massachusetts Hospital Life Insurance Company initially derived revenue from a combination of bank stocks and mortgages on farms in the Berkshires, loaned at the federally set rate of 6 percent. Bowditch, whose bent toward mathematical order and precision led to his creation of time sheets, standardized printed forms and a filing system that would become standard in American offices, grew frustrated at farmers' irregular payments. What did unwavering adherence to a "firm due date" set by a stranger mean to villagers accustomed to settling accounts as the season's harvest allowed, face-to-face with people they knew?

After Bowditch threatened foreclosures, the Massachusetts press and its politicians turned against "the *grappling-irons* of this giant monopoly," run by "rich capitalists" with "special privileges." In 1827, foreshadowing the populist sentiment that would propel Andrew Jackson to the presidency the following year, the Commonwealth's centrist governor, Levi Lincoln, warned that the "high minded and independent yeomanry" would soon be working their land as "Lessees of Corporations." One critic charged that although the rich extolled the Massachusetts Hospital Life office, "among the poor farmers, it is called the *Death Office;* because its immense capital, which is more than five millions, being loaned upon real estate, devours their lands like a beast of prey."

In 1831, when Alexis de Tocqueville visited Boston researching his hallmark book *Democracy in America,* he found a city characterized not by Tea Party patriotism, but by Beacon Hill gentility. Boston society, Tocqueville wrote, "quite closely resembles the upper classes of Europe. Luxury and studied elegance are the norm. Nearly all the women speak French well, and all the men we have seen thus far have been to Europe. Their manners are distinguished, and intellectual subjects are the heart of their conversation. In Boston there are a fair number of people who have nothing to do and therefore pursue the pleasures of the mind."

The Harvard (and Franklin-papers-hunting) historian Jared Sparks told Tocqueville, "Real property is almost never divided anymore in Massachusetts. The eldest child almost always inherits all the real estate." When the Frenchman asked what became of the other children, Sparks replied, "They migrate to the West."

Nathaniel Bowditch's office would not be providing mortgages to these homesteaders any more than Benjamin Franklin's will. Bowditch instead turned the Massachusetts Hospital Life Insurance Company's gaze inward, away from rural lending and toward securing metropolitan millions. He created what we would recognize as an investment bank, or, as he put it, "a species of Savings Bank for the rich and middle class of Society."

Unlike Franklin's intended beneficiaries, these magnates seldom defaulted on their loans, even during the Panic of 1837, second only to the stock market crash of 1929 in American financial disasters. Nine out of ten mills closed then, and nearly half of the banks failed. The following decade became known as the Hungry Forties. Bowditch, meanwhile, reported to the company's board that he anticipated only a small loss on a single note.

Bowditch would later burn most of his correspondence. Frustratingly, we can largely only deduce his own thoughts from between a ledger's lines. William Minot's sporadic diary holds no mention of his peer, nor any intrusion of contemporaneous news, such as the formation of the Republic of Texas following the Battle of the Alamo (1836) or Queen Victoria's coronation (1837). Instead, in two of the longest entries, Minot vented his anger at the outgoing seventh president, Andrew Jackson, who had refused to renew the charter of the Second Bank of the United States and then vetoed an attempt to revive it.

"Gen. Jackson has exercised unlimited sway by the force of his popularity," Minot wrote. "He is the idol of the lower classes but generally and particularly detested by people of education . . . Posterity must

settle his character. His enemies consider him passionate yet crafty &
an hypocrite & unforgiving in his resentment. His attempts to introduce a specie currency prove him to be wholly ignorant of political
economy."

On this point, at least, William Minot agreed with Benjamin Franklin, who in 1729 had argued for the "Nature and Necessity of a Paper
Currency." Relying on limited-circulation specie—coins minted from
precious metals—for transactions, Franklin wrote, created high interest rates, suppressed demand for goods, and discouraged "Labouring
and Handicrafts Men (which are the chief Strength and Support of a
People) from coming to settle in it, and induces many that were settled
to leave the Country . . . It is the highest Interest of a Trading Country
in general to make Money plentiful."

One hundred eight years later, William Minot wrote in his 1837
diary that to limit a run on specie, Boston's banks were refusing to
disburse coins. "It is an unexpected shock to most of our Citizens but
is rendered necessary by the call for silver & gold to remit to England
in payment of our debts. Never since the Revolutionary War has the
distress of the country equaled the present."

That year, Minot approved only a single borrower. For the first time,
Franklin's money went to a "gold beater," a craftsman who, instead of
minting new coins, hammered the precious metal into decorative leaf.

Nathaniel Bowditch's steady hand and dazzling returns prefigured
Warren Buffett's leadership of Berkshire Hathaway. Who could fault
William Minot for choosing to invest with his firm? Benjamin Franklin, for starters. By 1836, only 6 percent of his money was being lent
to Boston tradesmen. Three decades later, in Minot's final year as treasurer, the amount fell to less than 1 percent.

Glimpses of life behind the transparent, if impenetrable, aquarium
glass: In 1840, Minot would accept the invitation to become an officer
of Bowditch's Massachusetts Hospital Life Insurance Company, a seat

he would hold for twenty-four years. His son later would become its president.

After purchasing a piece of land from the Boston scions the Welds, Minot built a sylvan estate on Jamaica Plain's rolling hills. His daughter named the house Woodbourne, after the estate in Sir Walter Scott's *Guy Mannering*. In a letter, William Minot Jr. described their spread's bucolic bliss: "Our roses are just out," he wrote. "Our honeysuckles too. The new mown hay, almost half a ton, lies spread on the garden lot. The pears are shaping themselves. Strawberries ripening. Raspberries well formed. The laurels are opening new leaves. All is green, growing, gracious." Having earlier crossed the Atlantic to make the Grand Tour, he added, "England and Switzerland are full of beautiful scenery, but the avenue through our pine trees had a charm surpassing anything I saw in Europe."

His father, the captain steering Benjamin Franklin's class-conscious gift, did not publicize the availability of his loans, or the course he had set for the money. Readers looking for mention of William Minot in the press would only have found him listed in *"Our First Men": A Calendar of Wealth, Fashion and Gentility*, the directory of Boston's aristocracy.

At the end of 1836, William Minot replied to a letter sent by the chair of Philadelphia's Committee of Legacies and Trusts. Skipping cordialities, Minot said that the inquiry should not have been addressed to the Boston mayor, but to "me, as Treasurer." Next he reported that since the fund's inception in 1791, 255 loans had been granted to tradesmen. Since assuming his post in 1811, he had approved 91 borrowers, "of which fifty, at least, have been repaid (in whole or in part) by sureties, and on four of these are balances which cannot be collected."

Four failures out of 346 loans equaled a default rate of 1.2 percent. Compared with the losses on their own books, the managers of Franklin's Philadelphia gift might well have done a double take upon reading that minuscule figure.

Minot admitted to Philadelphia that his granting of new loans av-

eraged "for the last five years, not more than one a year." He blamed
a shortfall in applicants but failed to recognize that, beyond Woodbourne's sprawling grounds, Boston's population in the 1830s would
increase by a third, to 84,000. The number of census-recorded heads
of household who identified as "skilled artisans" would rise by the
same proportion, to 2,560. Furthermore, a $200 Franklin loan could
still stake a small business in an era when tradesmen earned between
$1.50 and $2 a day.

Referring to Franklin's stipulation that applicants must be wed,
Minot wrote, "The improvidence of early marriages may be fairly
inferred." His presumption ignored the fact that the median age at
which Bostonians married had remained constant, too.

In an intimation of widening class divisions, Minot also told his
Philadelphia counterpart that perhaps would-be borrowers simply
could not find guarantors who trusted them to repay. The ledgers cannot be used to confirm or refute this claim. Minot, in keeping with
his predecessors, failed to record who had actually remitted each in-
stallment. Did Paul Revere repay his silversmith son-in-law's loan, or
was the madman's debt covered by his other guarantor, "Christopher
Minot, Gentleman"? If William Minot ever paged back to the ledger's
start, he might have noticed that his own uncle had backed one of
Boston's first recipients of Franklin's money.

In his reply to Philadelphia, Minot also failed to mention the 6 percent penalty that he charged on late payments (contravening Franklin's
instructions), or the fact that Boston's business owners increasingly
wanted their young employees clocking in to factories, not apprenticing to a trade. By mid-century—a time when Henry David Thoreau
sought out the "tonic of wilderness" at Walden Pond—this new form
of impersonal labor saw workers seated in the type of Bowditchian
offices that Herman Melville would satirize in his story "Bartleby, the
Scrivener." The title character rebels against deskbound drudgery, refusing every order by uttering only, "I would prefer not to."

When it came to disbursing Franklin's gift, William Minot expressed much the same sentiment. He focused only on the bottom line. Franklin had calculated that after forty-five years, Boston's fund would hold $39,933 (equivalent to $1.2 million at the time of this writing). Minot told his Philadelphia counterpart that the thirteen outstanding loans, plus the $22,739 he had deposited in the Massachusetts Hospital Life Insurance Company, equaled $24,325, or 40 percent less than what Franklin had predicted.

"It is apparent from these facts," Minot concluded, "that the benevolent intentions of the donor have not been realized."

When seen through William Minot's gimlet gaze, Franklin's ambitious scheme had failed. But as Poor Richard once observed, "Half the Truth is often a great Lie."

It is true that Franklin's confident forecast had not accounted for even a single default. Nor had he foreseen that the American banking system would mature to the point of readily offering loans charging less than 5 percent interest—and free of his age and marital restrictions. But Boston did not suffer a lack of financial wizards. The most famous, Nathaniel Bowditch, worked in a neighboring office. Instead of proposing revisions to Franklin's benevolent scheme, Minot laid Franklin's wishes to rest.

"Money not required for actual use," Minot reported, "is placed in the Life Insurance Company, where it increases at the rate of about five and one-third percent a year."

In 1837, Nathaniel Bowditch refused to see a doctor about his abdominal pains, arguing with his son that he had to balance the company's books and did not have "leisure to be ill." Stomach cancer took him shortly before his sixty-fifth birthday, but not before he corrected the proofs of the final book of his translation, from the French, of Pierre-Simon Laplace's five-volume *Treatise of Celestial Mechanics*. Did he know that Laplace and Franklin had been friends in Paris, where they had proved to Louis XVI that lightning rods could safely defend stores of gunpowder? We cannot say. Bowditch tossed a lifetime's worth of notes into the flames. A mathematician to the end, he asked his children in his final moments to stand around his bed in the order of their births.

Bowditch had confided to a friend that his work would become obsolete and he would become a footnote, if he was remembered at all. A poem that appeared in a Boston newspaper after his death in 1838 acclaimed him, with unintentional irony, as a "Child of this, our great Republic, brother of the toiling poor." Bowditch left the bulk of his estate to the Salem libraries and societies that had supported him. The Bowditch house, at 9 North Street, is now the offices of Historic Salem, Inc., one of America's oldest heritage conservation organizations. A short street bordering People's Park in Berkeley, California, is named for him. In 1867, the U.S. Navy bought the copyright to his *American Practical Navigator*. To this day, every one of its vessels keeps an updated copy of the Bowditch on board.

In 1844, a group of Brahmins convened to remember Bowditch with what would be America's first life-size bronze statue. "It seems to me," the committee's treasurer, William Minot, wrote upon inspection, "to be a perfect likeness of a man who all the world respected and delighted to know." The marker still tops Bowditch's lonely grave, located in Mount Auburn Cemetery, across the Charles in Cambridge. Nothing here suggests his unsung role in modern finance, let alone his connection to the second man that Boston would cast in bronze. The seated Bowditch cradles a globe, a sextant, and a volume of his *Treatise of Celestial Mechanics,* looking ready to ship out. But his landed friends turned this self-taught navigator's memorial so that he forever faces away from the sea.

By 1852, the balance of Boston's Franklin Fund had tripled in value over the preceding fourteen years, to $67,115 (equivalent to $2.4 million at the time of this writing). The mayor and aldermen routinely endorsed Minot's annual report. In 1853, the ledger notes their suggestion that Franklin's money deposited in Bowditch's company "remain there as a permanent investment." That year, William Minot approved two loans, to a ship carver—who repaid in full—and a sailmaker, gone with the wind before repaying a penny.

Only two tradesmen received loans in the next three years, even as remembrances of Franklin peaked during the sesquicentennial of his birth. In the spirit of its subject, a public collection in 1856 saw two thousand people donate their spare change to fund a statue of Boston's famous son. Minot's Franklin Fund successor, Samuel McCleary, kept the receipt for his $10 contribution. If Minot chipped in, the proof is not among the thirty-four volumes of papers he left behind.

Boston declared September 17, the day of the statue's unveiling, a one-off public holiday. Booming cannons and clanging church bells kicked off the crisp and bright late-summer day. Evergreen wreaths garlanded the graves of Franklin's parents, kites flew over the Common, and printed Poor Richard quotes fluttered on flags. Among the most popular was "He that hath a Trade hath an Estate."

A procession five miles long began at the Granary Burying Ground, where, in 1827, Boston had replaced the worn tombstones of Franklin's parents with a tall granite obelisk. (Confusing tourists, the marker's bronze letters say only FRANKLIN. Franklin himself would likely be more confounded by a nearby plaque that says the cemetery includes "Josiah Franklin and Wife," instead of her name, Abiah, which Franklin—"their youngest son, in filial regard to their memory"—had directed to be inscribed on their tombstone.)

The parade snaked along the waterfront where Franklin had played as a child, and then past the places where he had been born, lived, and worked. It took two and a half hours for the militia, firefighters, clergymen, college presidents, and civic leaders to complete the route in carriages, followed by horse-drawn flatbeds constructed and adorned by Boston tradesmen.

These floats represented seventy trades, beginning, alphabetically, with AGRICULTURAL IMPLEMENT MAKERS and ending with WOODEN WARE MANUFACTURERS. Bakers tossed biscuits hot from the oven, and sweet snowflakes flurried around the sugar refiners. The piano makers played instruments built in 1706 and 1856. The barbers welcomed people aboard for free haircuts, and the electricians dared the crowd to grasp apparatuses that emitted a slight shock. Printers tossed out reproductions of the first edition of the *New-England Courant* that listed Franklin's name on its masthead.

"Carlyle speaks of the opera as an 'explosion of all the upholstery,'" wrote one observer. "This was an explosion of all the industries. No trade carried on in Boston was unrepresented." Members of the city's charitable societies, followed by boys and girls from the public schools bearing bouquets of flowers, formed the rear. "Probably, at no time was there a greater number of persons in the city. Never were the sides of the streets more crowded with spectators." With special omnibuses and trains bringing in revelers from outside town, Boston's population that day increased threefold, to an estimated 300,000 people, "arrayed in holiday attire."

See the badges and ribbons. Hear the brassy peal. From London, Thomas Carlyle himself wrote, "Long life to Franklin's memory! We add our little shout to that of the Bostoners in inaugurating their monument for him." Philadelphia's mayor sent a rather possessive message that read, in full: "Philadelphia claims a share in the renown of him whose name is identified with American liberty, learning, and lightning." But that city had no memorial to Franklin to call its own.

At the unveiling of Boston's Franklin statue—now standing in front of the Old City Hall—Robert Charles Winthrop, a descendant of the Pilgrim who wrote of founding the Puritan "city upon a hill," lamented that Franklin had not been a more "earnest student of the Gospel of Christ." He lauded Franklin's philanthropy, however, especially his late-in-life embrace of abolitionism. The crowd cheered. Boston had recently declared martial law after the extradition of the escaped slave Anthony Burns back to Virginia under the country's controversial new Fugitive Slave Act.

"Never forgetting," Winthrop continued about Franklin, "the difficulties under which he had struggled as a Boston apprentice, he has left ample testimony of his desire to relieve Boston apprentices from similar trials in all time to come." He did not mention that by that time, Franklin's desire had all but been extinguished. Or that the man responsible for this worked from an office only a short walk away. But did Winthrop even know?

He pulled a string, the thirty-one-starred American flag shrouding the statue fell away, and the audience applauded. "Behold him!" bellowed Winthrop. "Coming back to give austere lessons and generous examples to the moderns . . . with a perpetual desire to be a doer of good!"

"Boston kept open houses that day," one witness gushed. Tradesmen, academics, politicians, and priests shared tables, "and the noise of banqueting was everywhere heard." The day ended in fireworks. The city's printed record of the celebration ran to 412 pages. William Minot's name does not appear once.

Two years later, at the 1858 dedication of the central Boston Public Library building, former Harvard president Edward Everett—who enjoyed a lucrative side career as a touring orator celebrating "Franklin the Boston Boy"—announced to the mayor and the crowd gathered in Copley Square that he had "the satisfaction of presenting the first volume given to the library. I offer this copy of Franklin's *Autobiography.* If there is one thing on earth which would have gladdened his heart could he have anticipated it, it would be the knowledge that his native city, in two generations after his death, would fund a library like this, to give to the rising generation."

After loquacious conjecture about the Boston sites a resurrected Franklin might visit (five years later, at Gettysburg, Everett would speak for two forgettable hours before President Lincoln delivered his immortal two-minute address), he added, presumably pausing at every comma, that "inasmuch as the accumulating fund which he bequeathed to the city has proved almost wholly unavailing for the primary object of the bequest, it deserves consideration whether, when it has reached a significant magnitude, as it will before the end of this century, the interest of the fund, if it can be legally done, might not advantageously be appropriated, as a permanent endowment for the support of the library."

Everett also called on Bostonians to each donate at least one book to fill its shelves. William Minot is not listed among the attendees. His wife, Louisa, was on her deathbed that month, an event that marked Minot's withdrawal from public life.

"It's very difficult," Minot wrote in his diary, "and most distressing to believe that she is to be taken from me. The companion of my life more than 47 years." Six days later, his shaky handwriting recorded, "My poor dear Louisa died at 20 minutes before 6 today, aged 70."

In a letter to friends, Minot described his late wife much as Franklin had sketched Deborah, praising "her candor, good sense and gentleness . . . She found her happiness in making others happy." Yet William Minot could also write with an intimacy that Benjamin Franklin did not permit himself on paper. "It is very hard," Minot confessed, "to part with my best friend."

Minot's Franklin Fund ledger ends abruptly that year. Beneath his final entry for 1858, his successor, Samuel McCleary, penciled, "There seem to be no further accounts at hand."

Even if the Bostonians and national press assembled at the Boston library's opening had heard Edward Everett pronounce Franklin's fund to be "almost wholly unavailing," his scheme still limped on. Minot retired in 1866. Samuel McCleary's subsequent ledger lists the names of fifteen Bostonians (but not their trades) approved for Franklin loans before the 1890 centennial of his death.

Not until then, as the fund's first payout to his hometowns neared, would anyone demand to know what Franklin's custodians had been doing with his money for the past hundred years.

8

Philadelphia: Anybody Could Have Done It

I f America's intellectual traditions came through the port of Boston, and an equally strong anti-elitist bent emanated from the port of Philadelphia, then it should not be surprising that the Bostonians who handled Franklin's money left an easier trail to follow. All were Harvard graduates (honorary, in Bowditch's outlier case), whose portraits and papers await visitors in the efficient modern city archive and at the Massachusetts Historical Society, where the wainscoted reading room's sun-dappled windows face the leafy fens.

Searching Philadelphia's austere city stacks feels more like visiting an inmate whom the weary wardens can't quite produce. A visitor perches beneath sickly sodium lights on a cold metal chair that clangs like a jailbreak alarm when pulled out from the table, and rifles through legal boxes of uncollated records that the lone, overworked clerk has managed to find. Unlike in Boston, the system has not been digitized, and is barely even analog. Requests are written on a call slip the size of a tax form. Because the archive shares a wall with a new Target superstore, I half expected to be brought, instead of documents, a box brimming with canned goods and kitty litter.

A mile-long walk along North Sixth Street—past the encampment beneath the approach to the Ben Franklin Bridge (how might he have solved homelessness?), past Isamu Noguchi's shiny *Bolt of Lightning* sculpture that towers over Franklin Square, and across the cobblestone street from Independence Hall—brings you to the redbrick quietude of the American Philosophical Society, the main repository of most things Franklin.

In 1954, after discovering the Franklin loan books in a "dark, dusty basement corner of the City Treasurer's office," the mayor had them transferred to the APS. Its library's carpet absorbs every footfall, and wished-for materials fan out upon oak reading tables large enough for a game of Ping-Pong. Here, however, the other silent researchers don't poke through your papers and say, as the leathery tattooed man at the city archive had scoffed, "Benjamin Franklin, huh? I know that guy."

Everyone in Philly knows a guy. But this man, an unemployed housepainter killing time (he could have used a Franklin loan), surprised me. "You gotta write about Deborah," he said. "She ran their businesses when he was gone all those years, but she always gets the shaft. You know that line from *Hamilton*? 'Let's follow the money and see where it goes'? You can really learn a lot about the founders that way."

Philadelphia's Franklin loans were recorded by a series of bureaucrats appointed as treasurer by the city council. There was no single custodian, no Society Hill version of William Minot here. Unlike Boston's neatly organized books, Philadelphia's ledger is harder to read. Turning its pages feels like witnessing a demonstration of the new Halloween tradition brought by Irish immigrants to the city's streets: see Franklin's money transform from a ripe pumpkin to a hollow, gap-toothed jack-o'-lantern.

In 1820, the shoemaker Peter Fox borrowed $331.50, then disappeared. Tilbert Taw, a tailor, repaid only 10 percent of the $292.50 that he was advanced. The skin dresser David Pearson made but three repayments of his $218.40 loan. An umbrella maker totally folded, and a chair painter paid but once. In 1829, the $331.50 loaned to the tailor Lewis J. Miller turned out to be a total loss.

Although, not every loan was squandered: in 1827, a wheelwright named Benjamin Franklin—how could his application have been refused?—borrowed $260, then repaid, in ten installments, the interest-added amount of $331.50. Most of the other borrowers also fulfilled their obligations. Perhaps the goldbrickers did, too; the record does not show whether the defaulters had attempted to start their own businesses and simply failed. Franklin believed that being one's own boss was a one-way ticket to mobility. "Strange," observed Poor Richard, "that he who lives by Shifts, can seldom shift himself." Franklin's projections for his money presumed that his borrowers would find success, as he had, or that their backers would cancel their debts, as in his will he had struck out the money that his heirs owed his estate.

But the guarantors of Philadelphia's Franklin loans also started reneging. So much so that in 1829 the city council passed three resolutions to protect Franklin's gift. Rather than promising to repay a loan in gold, at least one of the co-signers had to own Philadelphia real estate, whose value could cover a loss. Second, when a payment was missed, "a warrant of attorney shall accompany each bond, containing an authority to enter judgment immediately." The third edict forbade women to stand as sureties. This last amendment seems odd—and ironic, given Franklin's reliance on, and trust in Deborah, and their daughter, Sally. The new rule was perhaps a conservative reaction to the movement growing then advocating for a woman's right to own property in her own name.

These bandages did not stanch the bleeding. In 1831, seven Philadelphians received loans. Three repaid not a penny.

Following the path of Franklin's Philadelphia money is a walk through soupy fog. His fund's treasurers left behind no diaries, no boxes of personal papers. Their names also seldom appeared in newspapers. When nineteenth-century Philadelphia bureaucrats did see their names in the press, the headlines were often ones they wanted buried, not preserved. In his series of exposés on nineteenth-century civic mismanagement, the muckraking journalist Lincoln Steffens crowned "corrupt and contented" Philadelphia as "the worst-governed city in the country." It beat even New York, then under the thumb of Tammany Hall.

When Alexis de Tocqueville visited Philadelphia in 1831, he struggled to translate a new term he learned from the American Philosophical Society's elderly librarian, who had known Franklin personally.

"Our Walnut Street Prison is in terrible condition," John Vaughan told Tocqueville. "This was not the case when the Quakers ran it, but when the political party opposed to the Quakers won the elections some time ago, the Quakers were forced out of all the posts they held."

"But what does politics have to do with the prisons?" Tocqueville asked.

"Nothing, to be sure," Vaughan replied. "But people are eager for all kinds of jobs, and when a party wins, it seizes the opportunity to reward its supporters."

Vaughan said that this was one of the effects of the "spoils system," which Tocqueville, finding no French equivalent, called the *"système Populaire."* "Men of talent are seldom selected," he wrote in his notebook. "Politics governs all appointments. Connections and intrigue play as big a role here as in monarchies. Only the master is different."

Vaughan had conveniently forgotten that during Franklin's lifetime, the champion of meritocracy had been pilloried by his peers and in the press for the posts granted to his son William (governor); grandson Temple (secretary); and son-in-law, Richard (postmaster). In Philadelphia, it had long been useful to know a guy.

Commissioned in 1826 by its subject, the painting *Pat Lyon at the Forge* shows a brawny man standing proudly defiant with his tools. The Philadelphian looks every bit the Franklin ideal. "I do not desire to be represented in this picture as a gentleman," Lyon told the artist, "to which character I have no pretensions. I want you to paint me at work at my anvil, with my sleeves rolled up and a leather apron on."

Pat Lyon at the Forge, 1826–27.

Today the painting hangs—ironically enough—in Boston, in its Museum of Fine Arts. Smudging from a nearby frame is John Adams, whose 1823 portrait is dominated by the dark, empty space above his head, as if blackened by thoughts of Franklin. Among the "paughtraits" (as John Singer Sargent came to mock his work depicting the "Upper Classes"), Pat Lyon looks like he has crashed a genteel party.

Lyon insisted that his portrait's background include the Walnut Street Jail, where he had been wrongly imprisoned for three months on suspicion of bank robbery during the yellow fever epidemic that killed his wife and child (along with Benny). After his release, Lyon used his awarded settlement to stake what became a lucrative business manufacturing hand-pump fire wagons.

In 1824, his partner, Samuel Vaughan Merrick, co-founded Philadelphia's Franklin Institute for the Promotion of the Mechanic Arts. Its library, laboratory, and lecture hall aimed to spread "useful knowledge" from its building, located one block west of Independence Hall. Franklin's great-grandson, Alexander Dallas Bache, who would become the first president of the National Academy of Sciences, edited the institute's journal. One early paper saw him attempting to fix the date of Franklin's experiment to ascertain whether northeast storms originated in the southwest. On horseback, Franklin had galloped behind a whirlwind for a mile, adding storm chaser to his list of achievements.

Ralph Waldo Emerson said that the 1820s were a time when you could hardly meet anyone who did not have a plan for the world in their vest pocket. Philadelphia's tradesmen proved unprepared for the designs destabilizing their own community, including the Erie Canal, whose opening sapped work from the city's wharves. While Philadelphia remained the nation's financial capital — the colonnaded Second Bank of the United States, designed to resemble the Parthenon, was completed in 1824 — a series of economic panics convulsed local businesses.

As the defaults piled up across the decade, the custodians of Philadelphia's Franklin fund faced a decision. In 1824, its ledger showed a balance of $23,059, nearly twice as much as the $13,222 total that spurred William Minot to quietly steer Franklin's money away from the men who fed Boston's forges. Should Philadelphia continue making loans — still sufficient to start a small business — to the point of bankrupting Franklin's legacy?

Pat Lyon's strapping portrait can stand for Philadelphia's spirit in this era. In 1823, Boston chose as its mayor a former U.S. congressman (and future Harvard president), Josiah Quincy III. The Philadelphia mayor, Robert Wharton, was a former hatter's apprentice who admitted to having a "decided distaste for learning." He was elected a record sixteen times.

Boston made twenty-seven loans in this decade. Philadelphia approved sixty-five. Yet turning the crinkling pages of Philadelphia's ledger reveals an added overleaf that lists seventy-nine borrowers who had fallen behind in their payments. Given these defaults, in 1828 Philadelphia's auditor—making a soft approximation—penciled in a balance of $9,919.50, a calamitous 43 percent slide in only four years. Boston's fund pulled ahead, ending 1828 with $15,782. It would never trail Philadelphia again.

Franklin, however, would likely not have cheered this development. "I wish, indeed," he had written in his will, that the cities "both undertake to endeavour the execution of the project, because I think that, though unforeseen difficulties may arise, expedients will be found to remove them, and the scheme be found practicable." In a decade that saw the last of the founding fathers exit the public stage, Franklin's faith in the "rising generation" appeared to have been misplaced.

But what did this generation of Americans know about Franklin? Three decades after Franklin's death, Temple's edited volumes of his grandfather's papers appeared to large sales and mixed notices. "Franklin had but little imagination as a writer," sniffed Boston's *North American Review.* "Though he occasionally discovers some play of fancy in particular expressions, . . . we will not vouch however that [they are] not stolen, for he was not very conscientious about committing such petty larcenies."

Temple's editions of Franklin's works at least allowed its subject to speak for himself. In 1818, the itinerant preacher Mason Locke Weems published *The Life of Benjamin Franklin: With Many Choice Anecdotes and Admirable Sayings of This Great Man, Never Before Published by Any of His Biographers.* These morsels had never previously appeared because Weems had made most of them up. This was the man who, eager to inflate sales of his *Life of George Washington,* painted the apocryphal cherry tree onto the stained glass of American history.

Poor Richard observed that "Historians relate, not so much what is done, as what they would have believed." Parson Weems's "Ben" spoke in melodramatic utterances that often ended in exclamation points. The book ends not with his last will and testament, but upon his deathbed, where readers find Franklin gazing piously at a painting of Christ on the cross. "Happy Franklin!" his story concludes.

No such portrait hung at Franklin Court. In fact, in the month before he died, Franklin wrote to a Yale minister who asked if he had accepted Jesus: "I have some Doubts as to his Divinity," Franklin replied, "tho' it is a Question I do not dogmatise upon, having never studied it, and think it needless to busy myself with it now, when I expect soon an Opportunity of knowing the Truth with less Trouble."

Every generation discovers Franklin for themselves. In addition to Weems's Christian Franklin, adherents of his autobiography—reprinted an estimated 120 times by mid-century—elevated Franklin as the Buddha of Betterment and shepherd of "self-made men," as Frederick Douglass dubbed his class in a popular speech with that title. (The cult of Franklin was almost exclusively male. Perhaps as a consequence of downplaying Deborah's contributions to his success, along with the fact that his loans were restricted to young men, we do not find Franklin in the writings of Louisa May Alcott, Sojourner Truth, or his distant cousin Lucretia Mott.)

"It was [1827], about my fourteenth year," remembered an Irishman who had immigrated to Pennsylvania, "that I happened upon a dilapidated copy of the autobiography of Dr. Franklin. It delighted me with a wider view of life and inspired me with new ambition—turned my thoughts into new channels. For so poor and friendless a boy to be able to become a merchant or a professional man had before seemed an impossibility; but here was Franklin, poorer than myself, who by industry, thrift and frugality had become learned and wise, and elevated to wealth and fame."

After he rose to become owner of the powerful bank that bore his name, Thomas Mellon positioned a life-size statue of Franklin at the entrance to his office. "I regard the reading of Franklin's autobiography," Mellon wrote, "as the turning point of my life."

Another young man decided to "try America" after reading Franklin's memoir in Scotland. After founding the *New York Herald,* James Gordon Bennett revolutionized newspapers, introducing a daily weather report, stock listings, and illustrations. In 1844, New York's newly elected mayor, James Harper, hung a portrait of Franklin in City Hall. Reading Franklin's autobiography as a farm boy had inspired him to apprentice as a printer. Although Harper founded the publishing company that still bears his name, the street-sweeping Franklin might have been as impressed by the mayor's edict banning pigs from Manhattan's streets.

Born in a small Ohio town in 1847, Thomas Edison later told Henry Ford that the first book he read, at age nine, explained Franklin's electrical experiments. Another admirer, the *New-York Tribune* editor Horace Greeley, so resembled Franklin in appearance that his peers called him "the Late Franklin." The son of a Vermont farmer, Greeley had left home at fifteen to apprentice as a printer. One of the nineteenth century's most memorable quotes is attributed to this poor man's Poor Richard, who urged readers: "Go West, young man."

In 1847, the Missouri printer Orion Clemens bought the *Hannibal Journal,* writing to his mother that by living austerely on bread and water, he was "closely imitating" Franklin. He attempted to goad his teenage brother to work harder by constantly quoting Poor Richard. Just as Franklin had fled his hard-driving older sibling James, so did Samuel Clemens escape Orion. He did go west—and became Mark Twain. Orion moved to Iowa to open the Benjamin Franklin Book & Job Printing Office, where he worked on a manuscript about the failure of the American Dream.

In a facetious early essay, published three years before the title of his first novel would give the Gilded Age its name, Mark Twain wrote that Franklin "early prostituted his talents to the invention of maxims and aphorisms calculated to inflict suffering upon the rising generation of all subsequent ages . . . With a malevolence which is without parallel in history, he would work all day and then sit up nights and let on to be studying algebra by the light of a smouldering fire, so that all other boys might have to do that also or else have Benjamin Franklin thrown up to them. Not satisfied with these proceedings, he had a fashion of living wholly on bread and water, and studying astronomy at meal time—a thing which has brought affliction to millions of boys since, whose fathers had read Franklin's pernicious biography."

Twain concluded by noting how Franklin "was always proud of telling how he entered Philadelphia for the first time, with nothing in the world but two shillings in his pocket and four rolls of bread under his arm. But really, when you come to examine it critically, it was nothing. Anybody could have done it."

Franklin hoped that his last will and testament would persuade Americans to follow his example. The dying wishes of his fellow founders Washington, Hamilton, Adams, Jefferson, and Madison only amplify the uniqueness of his bequests, as well as their shared moral failings. It can be hard to appreciate what a radical step this was. While in life these six men grappled with the question "What does America mean?" only Franklin felt compelled to continue his answer from the grave. He was also among the few founders to die solvent.

George Washington's will transmitted the eight thousand acres of Mount Vernon—down to the "liquors and groceries on hand"—to his wife, Martha Dandridge Washington, into whose landed family he had married. He hoped, but did not order, that she would free the farm's three hundred slaves during her lifetime. A little over a year later, she finally acquiesced. "In the state in which they were left by the General," wrote Abigail Adams, "she did not feel as tho her Life was safe in their Hands." She did not record how these enslaved men, women, and children must have felt.

Washington's $25,000 presidential salary (the equivalent of millions when compared with what the average laborer earned) equaled 2 percent of the entire federal budget. He left bank shares worth $4,000 to an Alexandria school for orphans. Others were earmarked for the expansion of the James ($10,000) and Potomac ($22,200) Rivers. One hundred shares were transmitted to the Virginia academy that became Washington and Lee University. Fifty shares funded the endowment of "a University to be established within the limits of the District of Columbia." He hoped that George Washington University's location would eradicate students' "local attachments and State prejudices," which he—perhaps remembering his treatment by Benny—blamed for "disquietude of the Public mind."

Alexander Hamilton hastily wrote his two-paragraph will two days before his 1804 duel with Aaron Burr. He left everything in a letter (prepared in case "an accident should happen to me") to his wife, Elizabeth. The man who designed the repayment of America's war debt himself died broke. Attached to his will was a four-page list of amounts he owed. His widow presented the document to Congress, which, only after twelve years of her entreaties, finally awarded her a pension for Hamilton's service in the Continental Army.

John Adams owned a forty-acre farm named Peacefield and a prosperous law practice. Like Washington, he had married into wealth; Abigail hailed from the Massachusetts Quincys. Adams died in 1826, on July 4—a date he had refused to call Independence Day because in 1776 the Second Continental Congress had actually voted to sever ties with Britain on July 2. For all of the acerbity that filled his lengthy letters, Adams left a pithy will of less than two dozen paragraphs, directing his executor (son John Quincy, then the sixth American president) to open a bank account for his youngest son, Thomas.

Thomas Adams, like his brother Charles—who died at age thirty of cirrhosis—would today likely be diagnosed as an alcoholic. Adams's will ensured that Thomas's children would be provided for by depositing $21,000 in an account earning 6 percent interest. The children received quarterly payments that did not reduce its principal. At the age of twenty-one, they could withdraw $3,000 for use as a sort of start-up fund. If Adams's benevolent scheme drew inspiration from Benjamin Franklin's, he (unsurprisingly) never acknowledged it.

As he expired, John Adams, age ninety, supposedly rasped: "Thomas Jefferson survives." If true, then Adams died not knowing that he would be remembered for being wrong. The eighty-three-year-old Jefferson actually had passed away only hours before.

Thomas Jefferson had inherited three thousand acres from his father, to which he added two thousand more—also tilled by slaves at the lash—and built for his home the architectural wonder Monticello. (The design of its Great Clock, which still bongs the hour, was inspired by Franklin's Chinese gong.) Jefferson died mired in debt. In 1815, he had sold the bulk of his books to Congress to replace those that the British had torched during the War of 1812. Much of what Jefferson had netted in that sale had gone to his creditors.

He rebuilt his library with the help of Lewis Descoins Belair, an immigrant bookseller in Philadelphia then paying off a $260 Franklin loan. Belair sent Jefferson curated lists of available titles of interest, mostly scientific works written in French. The young entrepreneur also flattered his famous customer by naming the mutual aid society he formed to maintain the salaries of ill or injured tradesmen the Jefferson Benevolent Institution of Pennsylvania. (Upon his death in 1875, Belair gave $24,000 in cash, plus the residue of his large estate, to eight Philadelphia charities, including the Apprentices' Library, established in 1820 to aid the education of young tradesmen.)

The one public gift in Thomas Jefferson's last will and testament presented what remained of his library to the University of Virginia. He left most of his estate to a grandson and daughter, and freed three of his slaves and two of their apprentices, named Madison and Eston. Jefferson did not note that they were his sons. Their mother, the enslaved Sally Hemings, had negotiated the freedom of her unborn children as a condition of returning with Jefferson from Paris, where she had served as his maid.

The only clue of Jefferson's special concern for the boys is seen in his will's codicil, where he "humbly and earnestly" entreated the state legislature to permit them to live freely in Virginia "where their families and connections are." Sally Hemings was never legally emancipated. She lived in Charlottesville with Madison and Eston until her death in 1835.

James Madison died the following year. As the nation's fourth president, he had kept as his valet an enslaved man named Paul Jennings, who would write the first White House memoir. Madison's will did not free the families who worked his five thousand acres. He left small donations to three college libraries and funds for the publication of a "careful and extended report of the proceedings and discussions" of the Constitutional Convention.

No such report existed. In his eighties, Madison obsessively rewrote his correspondence to shape his legacy and attempted to collate his fifty-year-old notes taken as the convention's chair. Under immense, self-harming mental stress, Madison worked to the point of physical collapse, spending over a year in bed. He died of heart failure, with the work unfinished.

His insolvent wife, Dolley, sold his papers to Congress. Before the sale went through, the Madisons' erstwhile White House servant often brought the former First Lady food. "I occasionally gave her small sums from my own pocket," Paul Jennings recounted, "though I had years before bought my freedom of her."

In Philadelphia in 1831, the president of the U.S. central bank, Nicholas Biddle, brushed aside President Andrew Jackson's promise to shutter the institution that allowed the existence of "a few Monied Capitalists, who are trading upon our revenue, and enjoy the benefit of it, to the exclusion of the many."

"Our political machine," Biddle told Alexis de Tocqueville, "is constructed in such a way as to run by itself. Right now, the president has lost the confidence of the Congress and the educated classes . . . Yet the public's business is proceeding as well as in the past, and no one fears for the future. For me, the most convincing proof of the goodness of our institutions is the ease with which we can do without government or carry on in spite of it."

As much as Benjamin Franklin might have been glad to hear this, his loan scheme still required active oversight. In 1831, Philadelphia's municipal bureaucrats turned their attention to managing a much larger gift, occasioned by the death of the country's richest man.

Stephen Girard had made his fortune as a shipowner. His $6 million bequest to Philadelphia—which honored him with the biggest public funeral since Benjamin Franklin's—was the largest to that point in American history. In his will, Girard apportioned the money among the Pennsylvania Hospital, trusts providing heating fuel to needy homes, and an endowment to fund and maintain a school for "poor white male orphans."

Although its construction had begun in 1833, nine years later Charles Dickens described seeing the "most splendid unfinished marble structure for the Girard College . . . which, if completed according to the original design, will be perhaps the richest edifice of modern times. But the bequest is involved in legal disputes, and pending them the work has stopped."

These challenges, from Girard's snubbed heirs, would occupy the Philadelphia civil servants who otherwise should have been keeping tabs on Franklin's loan scheme. The dispute would eventually reach the U.S. Supreme Court, where Daniel Webster, representing Girard's descendants, argued that the money given to the secular college did not meet a charitable purpose, since the benefactor's exclusion of clergy in its operation was "derogatory and hostile to the Christian religion."

The verdict cemented a foundational tenet of American philanthropy: "Donations," the court held, "for the establishment of colleges, schools, and seminaries of learning, and especially such as are for the education of orphans and poor scholars, are charities in the sense of the common law." The ruling also for the first time granted the right of a corporation to inherit property and hold it in trust. The

Supreme Court then said nothing about the racial redline that Girard had drawn to segregate the study body, which was legal at the time.

In his own will, Benjamin Franklin placed restrictions on loan applicants' sex, age, and marital status—but not on race, nativity, or creed. Because the ledgers do not record these details about each recipient, we regrettably cannot know if his loan scheme's managers shared his convictions.

Nineteenth-century Black tradesmen could have used his support. Even in free northern states, a de facto caste system reduced many minority skilled workers to economic peonage, especially in cities where they competed with a swelling population of European arrivals. After escaping captivity in Baltimore in 1838, Frederick Douglass fled north to New Bedford, Massachusetts, where an abolitionist whaling ship owner offered him work. When Douglass, a skilled caulker, arrived on deck, he heard the foreman announce that "every white man would leave the ship, in her unfinished condition," if a Black man joined their ranks. In the end, the shipowner paid Douglass $1 a day—half his trade's going rate—to perform menial tasks.

A visitor to Boston in 1833 noticed hardly any Black tradesmen. The exceptions were "one or two employed as printers, one blacksmith, and one shoemaker." Despite a color-blind law guaranteeing licenses to pushcart operators, few were granted to Black vendors.

A Philadelphia city report from this era found that less than two-thirds of skilled Black workers were employed in their fields. "The greater number were compelled to abandon their trades on account of the unrelenting prejudice against their color." Starting in 1834, a series of race riots scored the streets surrounding the Liberty Bell. In 1838, at a celebration held three blocks from Independence Hall, the Anti-Slavery Society opened its grand headquarters and auditorium, named Pennsylvania Hall. Three days later, in the nation's largest act of arson since the British torched the capital in 1814, a white mob burned the building to the ground.

Did Franklin's money help even one of the Americans on whose behalf he had submitted his final petition to Congress? Although the ledgers are frustratingly silent, an online genealogical search of each borrower recorded upon their pages makes this relief seem unlikely.

The man who managed Philadelphia's fund during the 1830s himself barely registers in the annals. In a short newspaper article, John Thomason is listed among the attendees of a Philadelphia meeting of the independent Working Men's Party, formed in 1828 to put tradesmen in office. (It folded after four years.) He next surfaces after his election to the city council, where, as chair of the Committee of Legacies and Trusts, he was tasked with overseeing Franklin's gift.

It was Thomason's 1836 letter to Boston to which William Minot had replied that Franklin's money was "now carefully attended to." Thomason next audited Philadelphia's account. What he discovered both disappointed and infuriated him.

The ledger showed 112 outstanding loans. Nineteen, Thomason reported, "have paid neither principal nor interest, although the accounts of some of them have been open for a period of thirty-four years." Ninety other borrowers were in arrears. Fifty-eight could reasonably claim they could not be sued, due to the expiry of the statute of limitations. "In this condition of the fund," he wrote, "it becomes difficult to estimate its present value."

After forty-five years of compound interest, Philadelphia's fund held $16,191. Thomason admitted that "had the fund been placed at simple interest" and not loaned out, its accrual would have neared the $39,933 that Franklin had predicted. Instead, it fell 60 percent short.

The former Working Men's Party supporter concluded his audit with a scathing indictment of how his predecessors had managed Franklin's legacy. "Had the requirements of the will been, in former years, fully complied with," Thomason wrote, "the operation of the fund at this day would be sensibly felt by the mechanics of Philadelphia . . . It would have increased the number of those who do business on their own stock. It would be a standing lesson on the immutable connection between capital and productive industry, thus constantly inciting to economy and prudence. It would have become the reward of every faithful apprentice, who could look forward to a participation in its benefit. It is deeply to be regretted that this state of things, which had so captivated the imagination of Franklin that he devoted a portion of his hard-earned wealth to realize it for the mechanics of Philadelphia, should, in the emphatic language of his will, prove 'a vain fancy'!"

In a bit of Beantown one-upmanship, the Harvard historian Jared Sparks made Thomason's censure the endpiece of the first volume of his ten-part book series, *The Works of Benjamin Franklin.* "By his statement," Sparks concluded, "it would seem that there had been at some time a remarkable want of fidelity in administering the trust, especially in allowing so large a number of bonds to become worthless by the statute of limitation, and neglecting to make seasonable demands upon the sureties."

Half the truth, again: Sparks did not reveal to readers what Boston's treasurer, William Minot, had been up to. "The absent are never without fault," said Poor Richard, "nor the present without excuse."

Yet in trying to right the course of Franklin's gift to Philadelphia, John Thomason inadvertently made matters worse.

Philadelphia granted only thirty-four loans in the 1830s. During that time, Thomason directed his energy to filing lawsuits against delinquent borrowers and to reinvesting the fund's unloaned principal. First, he purchased a $1,000 city bond that paid 5 percent over twenty years, followed by another that paid 6 percent. In 1838, he snapped up eighteen $100 shares of the initial public offering of the new Philadelphia Gas Works, a utility formed to realize Franklin Institute co-founder Samuel Vaughan Merrick's plan to light the city's streets. This scheme would further dim Franklin's legacy, through no fault of his own.

Initially, Thomason's investment seemed prudent. The 1841 ledger shows $178 earned interest from the bonds, and a $155 dividend on the Gas Works stock. But instead of diversifying his holdings, Thomason used his gains to purchase more of the same assets.

John Thomason was no William Minot, and freewheeling Philadelphia's sense of fiduciary responsibility contrasted with conservative, trustee-rich Boston. In 1836, after President Andrew Jackson had finally fulfilled his campaign pledge to shutter America's central bank, Philadelphia also lost its footing on the national stage.

Charles Dickens opened his Philadelphia hotel room curtains to see "a handsome building of white marble, which had a mournful ghost-like aspect, dreary to behold . . . It was the Tomb of many fortunes; the Great Catacomb of investment; the memorable United States Bank. The stoppage of this bank," Dickens wrote, "with its all ruinous consequences, had cast (as I was told on every side) a gloom on Philadelphia, under the depressing effect of which it yet labored. It certainly did seem rather dull and out of spirits."

The city was also nearly broke. Through a combination of negligence or malfeasance, Philadelphia's city council and its myriad commissions had for years operated in the red, issuing new bonds to cover the interest payments on old ones. The resulting shortfalls may explain the burst of posthumous trusts established during this era to provide indigent Philadelphians (of all origins) with necessities such as soup and heating fuel.

Even for a trustee and attorney such as William Minot, administering these motley pots of money would have demanded full attention, above and beyond the energy spent battling lawsuits contesting Stephen Girard's estate. These myriad endowments, moreover, were overseen by civil servants working within administrations that steadily bled Philadelphia's coffers dry.

Slipshod accounting snowballed into venality. The Gas Works, created to illuminate Philadelphia, morphed into a shady political machine. In 1841, control of the utility passed to a board of appointed trustees. Soon this "Gas Ring," as it became known, fell under the thumb of Philadelphia's answer to Tammany Hall's Boss Tweed.

What would Benjamin Franklin have made of the fact that the city he had shaped to serve the public good had become a one-man spoils system, ruled by a man nicknamed "King"? For all of his contempt for aristocratic Boston, Franklin may actually have been more disgusted by the perfidy of the Republican Party boss, James McManes.

"King James," as he was known, controlled the Philadelphia Gas Works' $4 million annual budget, an estimated half of which went to kickbacks. He also sent his employees out canvassing for his hand-picked candidates, who packed the city government.

His authority became absolute. "Political caucuses," reported the *Public Ledger,* then Philadelphia's largest newspaper, "were held in the Board Room. Appointments to the local, state, and national offices emanated from its walls and inspiring politicians looked to its sacred precincts for inspiration."

McManes next gained control of the tax department, a source of even greater graft, and then the local Republican caucus, proving Poor Richard's notion that "Party is the madness of the many, for the gain of a few."

To add further insult, Philadelphia's gas was often of poor quality, prone to shutoffs, and more expensive compared with other cities'. But three times the courts struck down good-governance crusaders' attempts to topple King James. His reign lasted eighteen years, until 1883. By then, the Franklin ledger showed that its sizable stake in his utility was all but worthless.

Poor Richard had also warned, "Sell not virtue to purchase wealth, nor Liberty to purchase power." By trusting Franklin's money to a profligate city council and a corrupt cartel, Philadelphia's well-meaning treasurer had unwittingly managed to do both.

Philadelphia even let its benefactor's final resting place sink into obscurity. "So well hidden is this grave," one newspaper reported in 1853, "and so little frequented, that we have known many native Philadelphians . . . who could not direct one to the locality where it may be found." Franklin and his family remained interred in the Christ Church Burial Ground, in the heart of central Philadelphia.

The story was reprinted across the country. At a Boston town meeting, Robert Charles Winthrop, former Speaker of the U.S. House of Representatives, read the outrage aloud. Winthrop compared Franklin's grave to that of Archimedes, which Cicero finally found, overgrown with brush, in Syracuse, 137 years after the mathematician's death. Philadelphians, Winthrop taunted, had forgotten Benjamin Franklin in less than half that time. He urged Bostonians to reclaim Franklin as their own. It would be Winthrop who, capping the public holiday's festivities in 1856, unveiled Boston's bronze likeness of him.

But then, what was a statue compared with Franklin's actual remains? After the publicity generated by Boston's celebration, a trickle of pilgrims carried stools to peer over Philadelphia's Christ Church cemetery wall. One elderly minister, upon finding the gates locked, borrowed a ladder from a nearby store and scaled the barrier. "The grave of Franklin was discovered," a newspaper reported, "and kneeling upon the sod, the ardent admirer of the dead philosopher spent an hour in rapt meditation upon his hero's life and character." Only then did the minister realize that he was trapped. The shopkeeper had recovered his ladder. The minister managed to scale the wall, then perch on top in his long black coat and white clerical cravat, considering the way down.

A procession of passing Quaker Friends stopped to ask if he was insane. "'Insane!'" the preacher thundered. "Then he was to be regarded as a madman for his devotion to Franklin! He stretched forth his hand, concentrated upon himself all eyes, and then — astride the wall as he was — commenced an eloquent address upon the neglect of Franklin's memory. His success upon this occasion was triumphant. From the accused he had become the accuser. A ladder was brought him, and ceasing his oration, he descended from his perch. He was greeted as he reached the ground by hearty applause, and retired followed by an ovation."

Readers wrote to Philadelphia's newspapers, suggesting that the cemetery gate remain unlocked. Another letter proposed inserting "a railed aperture in the wall opposite the grave, in order that the universally felt and laudable desire of strangers and citizens to view the resting-place of the statesman, philanthropist, and sage, may be gratified."

If that proposal sounded technically specific, it was because staff at the Franklin Institute had submitted it, unsigned, hoping to gather support for their idea.

The next year, in 1858, America celebrated the laying of the first transatlantic telegraph cable. Philadelphia held a parade, and speeches connected Franklin's charged kite string to the ribbon of wire pulsing with electrical bursts sent between Europe and North America.

That autumn, thousands flocked to Arch Street to view Franklin's burial place through the newly installed fence of iron bars. "From present indications," one newspaper predicted, "the pavement near the aperture in the wall will require renewing frequently, so incessant is now the shuffling of feet in that hitherto rather neglected spot."

The improved view of Franklin's grave.

• • •

Did any of these grave spotters spare a thought for Franklin's living legacy? In 1853, the treasurer of his gift to Philadelphia's tradesmen wrote off sixty-one delinquent loans. One 1855 entry can stand for many: after the treasurer had received payment for a municipal note purchased twenty years earlier (earning $102 on $1,000, or 0.5 percent annually), he parked the cash in a new note at the same sluggish terms, redeemable in another twenty years.

In Boston, meanwhile, William Minot's deposit in Nathaniel Bowditch's life insurance company earned a steady 5 to 6 percent interest. Franklin calculated that in 1855, his funds would first reach six figures, or $100,910 (equivalent to approximately $3.2 million at the time of this writing). That year, Boston's total stood at $57,286. Philadelphia's had fallen to $20,600. The last time it had been worth less was thirty years earlier, after the Panic of 1819.

In 1866, the year William Minot retired from managing Boston's fund after fifty-five years, Philadelphia newspapers suddenly took notice of the widening gulf between the two cities' balances. A King James–controlled paper reported that Philadelphia trailed Boston by a score of $110,167 to $34,139. Instead of faulting the city's slapdash management, the reporter blamed its incorrigible tradesmen.

"The most distinguished instances of success in life," the *Philadelphia Daily Evening Telegraph* lectured, "are those who depended upon themselves alone for the means of pushing their fortunes. The ill success attending the practical working of the Franklin fund adds one more to the many instances which prove that all efforts to promote the welfare of young men will be failures, so long as they do not encourage a spirit of self respect and self reliance."

Failing that, a dissenting reader might have thought, *they could always join the Gas Ring.* The *Telegraph,* like its competitors—and even Franklin's Philadelphia treasurers—seemed blind to the fact that his bequest did help launch the careers of tradesmen as diverse as the pearl jeweler Francis Prosper DuBosq (loan class of 1833), the wood planer

Peter Probasco (1823), and the three-term U.S. congressman John Test (1802). Test had run away to Philadelphia at age fourteen, after fleeing (like Franklin) a miserable indenture. Seven years later, after marrying an orphan named Lydia Dungan (later insisting, "I owe everything I am to my wife"), he received a $260 Franklin loan. Test repaid it over a ten-year period during which he and Lydia migrated to eastern Indiana, where he worked at a gristmill. After studying on his own to pass the new state's oral law exam, he became a judge and then won election to Congress, where in 1830 he spoke and voted against the Indian Removal Act. Test's district included Franklin County, where he and Lydia chose to settle down. Judge John Test died in 1849. A generation would pass before the Philadelphia press paid any attention to the loans, if not the successful men who owed their start to them.

In 1870, the city's largest newspaper, the *Inquirer,* exonerated Franklin for his scheme's apparent demise. Instead, it reproached "the dishonesty of borrowers, and the failure of sureties." The *Inquirer* was wrong, however, to claim that Franklin's money had been "swallowed up in that maelstrom of Philadelphia wealth, the Bank of the United States." In fact, his fund held only $2,000 in Treasury bills, which reliably paid 4 percent interest. The bulk of his gift had actually been swallowed up in the maelstrom of Philadelphia's own crooked government.

The newspaper most read by laborers split the blame between the testator and his executors. In 1870, Franklin had expected his Philadelphia legacy to grow to $220,273 (equivalent to $4.6 million at the time of this writing). Instead, it had staggered to less than one-fifth that amount: $40,167. "The reasons for this falling off are not difficult to ascertain," the *Philadelphia Daily Evening Bulletin* explained. "The conditions required of the borrower were too onerous; hence very few 'married artificers' availed themselves of the Franklin Fund, and the income was invested in worthless securities."

Poor Richard warned that "Blame-all and Praise-all are two blockheads." Only the *Bulletin* correctly noted that Franklin's stipulations had too narrowly restricted potential applicants, and that the city had irresponsibly handled his gift. In retrospect, the (slight) mention of the latter fact in print was itself newsworthy.

In 1871, Philadelphia's dissolute government broke ground on a city hall building whose Second Empire architectural style was named for Napoleon III. Although planned to be the world's tallest structure—surpassed, by the time it was finished, by the Eiffel Tower and Washington Monument—Philadelphia's City Hall remains America's largest, with seven hundred rooms, topped by the tallest statue atop any building on earth. Ignoring its caster's instructions, workers installed the thirty-seven-foot bronze likeness of William Penn to face the wrong way. After sunrise, his face is cloaked in shadows.

This municipal castle rose throughout the "Great Depression," as the years following the Panic of 1873 were then called. In 1874, a judge approved the city's petition to raise the age of men eligible to receive Franklin's money by ten years, to thirty-five. The change had little effect. In 1881, only six Philadelphians applied for a Franklin loan. All were rejected, having been found by the Board of Directors of City Trusts "to be more impelled by misfortune to seek relief, than to be governed by the desire to advance their ability to do good work."

Even as the Progressive Era dawned in the 1880s, a group of Franklin's descendants suspected that Philadelphia's bureaucrats remained hapless. But what could they do?

"There is hardly a political question in the United States," Alexis de Tocqueville observed, "which does not sooner or later turn into a judicial one." The Declaration of Independence was an indictment of King George III. The Constitution is a contract. And so, as the centenary of his death approached, Benjamin Franklin's descendants did what affronted Americans have long felt compelled to do. They decided to sue.

9

They Rowed.
And Also They Rowed.

The year is 1889, and the scrupulous Samuel McCleary remains where we last left him—in his mansard-roofed Boston office, seated at his desk, whose drawer holds the supplies, including one-cent Franklin stamps, that he keeps separate for personal use. He reads the letter from his Philadelphia counterpart, who requests "any information concerning the use you propose to make of [Franklin's money] at the expiration of the first one hundred years."

The sixty-seven-year-old treasurer had become unwitting proof of Poor Richard's observation that "to serve the Publick faithfully, and at the same time please it entirely, is impracticable." After working thirty-one years as Boston's city clerk, McCleary had been sacked after Democrats finally won a majority on the city council. Their aldermen voted to replace him with an inexperienced colleague, who ineffectually protested that McCleary should keep the job. Supporters, and even former opponents, raised for him a testimonial of $12,500, equivalent to several years' salary. McCleary's honesty, one colleague said, had "saved the city from falling under the demoralizing influences which dominated New York and Philadelphia." McCleary continued to oversee Franklin's gift to Boston for free.

As the 1890 centenary of Franklin's death approached, newspapers suddenly remembered the founder's gift. But instead of revealing how his loan scheme had gone sideways, journalists turned his funds into a competition, similar to how Boston's and Philadelphia's baseball teams competed in the National League. Just as that season's Beaneaters would finish twenty games ahead of the Quakers, Boston's account balance also far outpaced its rival's.

In 1889, Philadelphia's fund totaled $89,058 (equivalent to $2.6 million at the time of this writing). Boston's held more than four times as much: $368,741 ($10.9 million). In that year alone, the interest on its deposit in the Massachusetts Hospital Life Insurance Company would add another $14,056 ($415,000)—more than Philadelphia's money had grown in the previous four years combined.

The manager responsible for Boston's winning streak did not live to see the final standings. William Minot, age eighty-nine, had died at Woodbourne in 1873.

"For sixty years," his son eulogized, "he went daily to the same office at the same hour. Luxury made no impression on him; fashion he ignored. Everything changed around him—habits, manners, material life and national character, but he moved on unaltered, unshaken, and faithful to his own convictions."

Minot Jr. did not mention the Franklin Fund, or the names of the many other trusts that his father had managed. A Boston trustee carried his discretion to the grave, leaving only the ledgers behind. And, in Minot's case, a sizable estate, passed wholly to his children, in a will devoid of charitable giving. (The manse named Woodbourne no longer stands. Its grounds are now ornamented with the tombstones of the Forest Hills Cemetery. The city of Minot, North Dakota, is not named for him, but for his grandson, Henry Davis Minot, a spirited Harvard dropout, ornithologist, and railroad scout killed in a train crash at the age of thirty-one.)

"His example and influence," Minot Jr. continued in his eulogy for his father, "tended very largely to establish and confirm the present admirable system under which trusts are managed in Boston, and of the millions of property that passed through his hands, it may be almost literally said that not a dollar was lost."

While that may have been true, William Minot's sheltering of Franklin's money had denied his intended recipients the opportunity to improve their lives through its use. The newspapers of 1889 reported Boston's win. They did not account for its cost.

Benjamin Franklin's face served as the backdrop for the string of celebrations marking the 1890 centennial of his death. At New York City's party, speakers stood onstage before his portrait, facing an audience of muttonchop-whiskered newspaper publishers and bow-tied politicians bouncing to the band playing the latest brassy John Philip Sousa march. Franklin's idea of a good speech, a minister announced, was to "first, go through your subject, then go around it, then go both ways, and when you've said what you've wanted to say, then stop." Thereupon the man sat down, to rapturous applause.

That Franklin never said such a thing (the tone was more Mark Twain's) didn't matter. Every generation discovers Benjamin Franklin for themselves.

"Benjamin Franklin had the best run of luck in being credited with pretty much everything which was done in his day that ever attended mortal man," the *Philadelphia Inquirer* noted in April 1890. "To his long list of reported achievements is now to be added the invention of the stove-pipe hat." Parisian milliners were attributing its design to a lid that Franklin wore upon his arrival there in 1776. "It is pretty clear," cautioned the *Inquirer,* "that Franklin doesn't deserve whatever credit there may be in originating the stove-pipe hat. He must have picked this up in Philadelphia, as he did a good many other things."

The newspaper also reported that at the Pennsylvania Hospital's annual meeting of contributors, attendees placed their hands on the uncovered cornerstone set by the man who had identified himself in its records as "Benjamin Franklin, clerk." His modesty belied his belief that quality health care should be made available to all citizens, regardless of income. In 1889 alone, the hospital had treated 8,000 patients, plus 25,000 more at home and in affiliated clinics—all free of charge.

To further set this era's scene, other *Inquirer* stories in 1890 included news of the admittance of Idaho and Wyoming as the forty-third and forty-fourth states, the opening of the London Underground, and Nellie Bly's completion of her around-the-world journey in seventy-two days. The paper did not report the suicide of a painter named Vincent van Gogh, the posthumous publication of Emily Dickinson's first book of poems, or a young Polish captain's journey up the Congo River, deep into colonial Belgium, upon which his novella *Heart of Darkness* would be based.

Also that year, Indian agency police shot and killed the Lakota leader Sitting Bull on the Standing Rock Reservation. Two weeks later, in what became known as the Wounded Knee Massacre, the U.S. Army gunned down an estimated two hundred to three hundred Lakota women and children.

"Do we come to America to learn and practice the Manners of *Barbarians*?" Franklin had roared in print in 1764, after a vigilante gang called the Paxton Boys had tomahawked unarmed Conestoga women and children in Pennsylvania. When the gang marched on Philadelphia, Franklin organized the city's defense, even carrying a musket himself.

After white settlers pushed into Cherokee territory in present-day Tennessee and proclaimed a state they called Franklin, its namesake rejected the dubious honor. In 1788, Franklin urged its ringleader to avoid "an Indian War by preventing Encroachments on their Lands." He then cut off correspondence with the group. "During the Course of a long Life in which I have made Observations on public Affairs," Franklin wrote, "it has appear'd to me that almost every War between the Indians and Whites has been occasion'd by some Injustice of the latter towards the former."

What would Franklin have made of the treatment of Native Americans in the ensuing century? The country that he had helped found inexorably pushed west. "At the end of a hundred years of life under the Constitution," pronounced the historian Frederick Jackson Turner, "the frontier has gone, and with its going has closed the first period of American history."

In an intimation of its second period, in 1890 were born Dwight Eisenhower, Charles de Gaulle, and Ho Chi Minh. The previous year saw the arrival of a baby named Adolphus Hitler. Tabulating machines for the first time added up the census, counting 63 million Americans. Railroads linked the country's coasts. Chicago — still in the future tense during Franklin's lifetime — passed Philadelphia to become the second most populous city, after New York. Jim Crow laws segregated the South. In Memphis, the elementary school teacher turned journalist Ida B. Wells watched the newspaper office where she worked get burned to the ground. Undaunted, she published her reporting on lynchings in a pamphlet titled *Southern Horrors*.

Two-thirds of Americans still lived in rural areas in 1890, but in the cities workers led by Samuel Gompers and his American Federation of Labor — formed, initially, to strengthen individual craft-and-trade unions — took up the cause of the eight-hour workday, down from the standard twelve, as employed at Andrew Carnegie's Pittsburgh steel mills. Two years later, a strike at the city's Homestead Works would end in bloodshed. An absent Carnegie pinned the blame on the company's chairman, Henry Frick. Two decades later, when he attempted a reconciliation, the latter allegedly replied, "Yes, you can tell Carnegie I'll meet him. Tell him I'll see him in Hell, where we both are going."

The fault lines widened. In a book published in Boston, one of William Minot's Brahmin grandsons defended corporations, without which "our railroads, our manufactories, our telegraphs, our steamboat lines, could never have been built." He did not mention the laborers who had made them. Congress, heeding calls to curb corporate monopolies, passed the Sherman Antitrust Act of 1890.

That spring, the *New York Times* decried the U.S. Post Office's botching of its new one-cent stamp. The printer had flipped Franklin's right-facing portrait so that he would look left at the letter's address, as was customary. "By no exertion of skill could his profile be changed," the newspaper fumed, "without entirely altering his expression and making him resemble the putty-faced personification of senility which now appears on the one-cent stamp." The result was a "libel upon Franklin."

That autumn, as the date of the first disbursement of his legacy to Boston and Philadelphia neared, more serious charges of discrediting and defaming the founder would be filed in court.

• • •

A SCHOOL BUILDING TO BE ERECTED
WITH MONEY LEFT BY BENJAMIN FRANKLIN

September 11, 1890, Philadelphia—An old legacy made by Benjamin Franklin turns up this year to help the board of education. The conditions of the fund were such that it was seldom loaned, and for several years there has been no demand for it. The Board of City Trusts proposes to use a proportion of it agreeing with Franklin's division for some public work, and it is proposed to devote $76,000 to the construction of a new normal school for girls. The matter has not been definitely determined, but the city has a site for such a school, and the amount named would about put up the building.

Two weeks later, a group of Franklin's descendants filed a petition in the Philadelphia Orphans' Court, as the probate bench that handled minors and estates was known. They claimed that Franklin's loan scheme violated the "rule of perpetuities," which forbade money to vest longer than twenty-one years after the benefactor's death, except when it was left to charity.

Because Franklin had stipulated that borrowers pay interest on his loans, the descendants argued, his gift could not be considered charitable. Furthermore, they charged that Philadelphia and Boston had failed to manage the scheme as he had directed. They asked the court to invalidate Franklin's bequests and return all of his money to the estate. In his will, he had decreed that Sally and her husband, Richard Bache, receive the "rest and residue" of any remaining assets. Legally, that meant the money should now pass down to the plaintiffs, since any living heir traced their lineage back to them.

POOR RICHARD'S MONEY, trumpeted the *Philadelphia Inquirer's* headline. To attract readers, the *Washington Post* totaled the combined balance of the Philadelphia and Boston funds: BEN FRANKLIN'S HEIRS. NEARLY $500,000 IS INVOLVED. Their claim, the *Washington Post* reported, "raised that the purpose of the testator has not been consummated owing to the apathy and negligence of the trustees, both in this city and Boston, but more especially in this city, where the principal sum has only attained about one-sixth of the proportion originally figured out."

The plaintiffs were not hard-up loafers seeking a handout. The group included Benny's grandson, then serving as paymaster of the U.S. Navy, and Sally's granddaughter, the widow of a U.S. congressman. That couple's son, Robert Walker Irwin, was serving as the Kingdom of Hawaii's first representative to Tokyo. (In 1885, it was Irwin who organized the first Japanese contract laborers to be sent to the islands, starting generations of immigration there, even as the Chinese Exclusion Act of 1882 barred Asians from moving to the United States.) His sister Agnes Irwin would become Radcliffe College's first dean.

A second petition was filed by Franklin's descendant Elizabeth Duane Gillespie, a feminist and social campaigner who in 1864 had organized Philadelphia's Great Central Fair to collect medical supplies for Union soldiers. In 1876, the city asked her to fundraise for the Centennial Exhibition, the first world's fair held in America, timed to celebrate the anniversary of the signing of the Declaration of Independence. Gillespie agreed, on the condition that Fairmount Park's two hundred buildings would include, for the first time at a world's fair, a pavilion showcasing women's achievements. When the promised structure did not materialize, Gillespie had it built herself.

She did not hide her connection to Franklin. In April 1890, Gillespie was a featured guest at the American Philosophical Society's centennial commemoration of his death. She also knew the law. Her father, William J. Duane — Sally's son-in-law and the former *Aurora* cub reporter whom Andrew Jackson had sacked as Treasury secretary for his refusal to withdraw federal deposits from the Second Bank of the United States — had also drawn up the extensive will of Philadelphia's richest man. After multiple challenges by his heirs, the $6 million that Stephen Girard had left to Philadelphia remained wholly in the city's hands.

But Franklin's descendants also knew that trusts could be punctured. The heirs of the former New York governor Samuel J. Tilden had successfully overturned his directive that upon his death, in 1886, half of his $10 million estate should be used to build a free library in New York City. After a series of lawsuits, the plaintiffs recouped all but $2 million, which the city added to existing bequests to form the New York Public Library.

In Philadelphia, Franklin's kin hoped for a total victory. Representing their combined claim was George Wharton Pepper, a callow University of Pennsylvania Law School graduate who had passed the bar only the previous year. Perhaps the family chose him for his own ancestral ties. He was descended from friends of Franklin, and also from Benny's widow. His father-figure uncle had founded Philadelphia's first free public library and named Pepper's brother–close cousin (later killed in the Argonne during the First World War) Benjamin Franklin Pepper.

But if they were anything like their forefather, Franklin's relatives would not have cared what George Wharton Pepper was, only what he could do. As an undergraduate, he had founded and edited Penn's student newspaper and starred in a Greek-language production of an Aristophanes comedy that earned a rave review in the *New York Times* after playing to a packed Manhattan opera house. Pepper went on to graduate at the top of his law class. His valedictory speech, titled

George Wharton Pepper prepares to step onstage.

"The Emancipation of Married Women," also could not have hurt his bid to be hired by Franklin's family.

In February 1890, Pepper served notice to Philadelphia, and through local council to Boston, to freeze any planned disbursements upon the April centennial of Franklin's death. "The heirs," reported the *New York Times,* "claim to be entitled to the fund which appears by the annual report of the Treasurer to have amounted to $368,741" (equivalent to $11 million at the time of this writing).

The *Times* sounded relieved that no gravediggers would play a part in this drama. It was pleasant to note, its correspondent wrote, "that no charge of 'undue influence' or weakness of mind is made against the famous testator, so that we are not likely to have the bones of the patriot, which have rested quietly for a hundred years, disturbed or his memory clouded by any sensational scandal, such as the ordinary will contest usually brings forth."

Pepper's injunction did, however, raise the specter of a scandal in Boston.

Its mayor, the decorated Union army surgeon Samuel Abbott Green, greatly admired Franklin, going so far as to publish an essay in the *Atlantic Monthly* urging people to read a new edition of his autobiography. In his first mayoral inaugural address, in 1882, Green reminded the audience that the centennial of Franklin's death was approaching. He suggested that the portion of the benefactor's money due to be released to Boston could build a new public park. "In no other way," Green argued, "could the bequest be made to subserve so well the convenience of the whole people."

Later that year, Boston's aldermen issued bonds to purchase 527 acres of West Roxbury land to be transformed into a common. "A large amount of these obligations," noted the treasurer Samuel McCleary, would "mature at the very time the city should have received its portion of the Franklin Fund."

The aldermen next passed a resolution specifying that because the park met Franklin's written requirement that the money be spent on "public works, which may be judged to be of most general utility to the inhabitants," the bonds would be repaid from Franklin's centennial disbursement. Furthermore, they resolved that the new common should be named Franklin Park, "in honor of the testator, who has so generously endowed his native town."

The lawsuit claiming municipal mismanagement of Franklin's money forced Boston to quietly repay the bonds from its own coffers, meaning taxpayers inadvertently footed the bill. "Fortunately, however," enthused Samuel McCleary, "the name of Franklin will always be associated with this popular park, though none of Franklin's money is invested there." Designed by Frederick Law Olmsted, Franklin Park remains Boston's largest green space.

Opposing the twenty-three-year-old George Wharton Pepper in Philadelphia was the city's counsel, sixty-five-year-old F. Carroll Brewster, "an able and adroit lawyer of long experience," in Pepper's estimation. The Brewster clan deserves their own book. The father, who descended from a *Mayflower* passenger, fathered F. Carroll with his mistress and favored this pair over his wife and legitimate children, the hard-living foreign correspondent Anne Hampton Brewster and her brother Benjamin, the U.S. attorney general. The three siblings avoided speaking to one another, although Anne could have used F. Carroll's help in court, where Benjamin would steal her inheritance.

Brewster argued that since Benjamin Franklin had barred Sally and Richard Bache from collecting the funds that staked his loan scheme, their descendants held no stronger claim to the money. "In a way that was maddening to youthful opponents," George Wharton Pepper recounted in his memoir, Brewster "cleverly pictured the case as an attempt by greedy and ungrateful relatives to defeat a worthy charity."

Brewster won this round. The judge, Pepper wrote, "decided the case against us on the somewhat remarkable ground that the City of Philadelphia, being both trustee and beneficiary, had by accepting the trust and administering it over a long period of years entered into a contract with the testator which was binding."

The loquacious Pepper then tried to have Franklin's will voided in its entirety. The unconvinced judge brushed him aside by quoting Poor Richard: "Smooth words butter no parsnips." Had Franklin been a lawyer, the judge wrote, and "not merely a great statesman and profound philosopher," he would have in his will explicitly established a charity. Regardless, his intentions were clear. Thus, his descendants had no right to the money.

At this point, Pepper might have heeded Poor Richard's bit of dog-gerel, published in 1750, that warned, "If any Rogue vexatious Suits advance / Against you for your known Inheritance," one should expect "So many Rubs [to] appear, the Time is gone / For Hearing, and the tedious Suit goes on."

"Not a bit discouraged," Pepper continued, "we appealed to the Supreme Court of Pennsylvania." He traveled to Boston to consult a Harvard professor whom he deemed "the greatest living authority on this branch of the law." The man agreed with Pepper's arguments but cautioned him that due to public sentiment, they "could not possibly win." Nevertheless, he accepted a reduced retainer and "threw himself into the case with vigor."

Another year elapsed. "The [Pennsylvania] Supreme Court treated us with great consideration," Pepper recorded. "In due time, however, an adverse decision was announced." That was strike three, but Pepper refused to sit down. In 1892, he tried arguing to the county court of common pleas that Franklin's codicil had not established a charity. "Again we were defeated." The judge ruled that "the whole scheme was charitable and that charity covers a multitude of sins." His (rather ten-dentious) opinion stated that Franklin "was sagacious enough to see that the days of apprenticeship (one of the best systems of education ever known to the people) would pass away, and this fund would in time be without demands upon it."

Franklin certainly had not foreseen the demise of apprentices. The judge "failed to convince us that we were wrong," George Wharton Pepper insisted in his memoir, "but by this time it had dawned upon us that we had attempted the impossible. We had sense enough not to ap-peal." Pepper added that every attorney "knows the sinking of heart that comes when an anticipated victory is turned into a defeat. My young heart," he admitted, "had been wrung by losing the Franklin will case."

Pepper would enjoy a long and distinguished career, but the Frank-lin case remained a thorn in his paw until the end. "I shall never forget my bitter disappointment," Pepper wrote at the age of seventy-seven. However, "half a century later, the Orphans' Court appointed me Master to determine a question arising under the provisions of Franklin's will. Thus I was called upon as a judge to facilitate the administration of the trust which as a youthful advocate I had tried to set aside."

He was being modest. After losing the lawsuits, George Wharton Pepper would go on to do more than any modern Philadelphian to perpetuate Franklin's legacy, down to the present day.

• • •

FRANKLIN'S HEIRS DEFEATED

May 26, 1893, Boston—The decision of the case of the Franklin heirs against the city of Philadelphia means that this city will get $414,700. It is understood that no further legal steps will be taken.

Three further challenges would be filed in Boston before a single cent of Franklin's centennial money was disbursed.

On July 1, 1893, the seventy-one-year-old Samuel McCleary recorded in the ledger that Boston was due to receive $322,490 (equivalent to $9.7 million at the time of this writing). "As soon as this sum was fixed," McCleary wrote, "applications for its expenditure poured in upon the Trustees."

In his will, Franklin had directed his gift to be spent on infrastructure "such as fortifications, bridges, aqueducts, public buildings, baths, pavements, or whatever may make living in the town more convenient to its people, and render it more agreeable to strangers resorting thither for health or a temporary residence."

In a public hearing, Bostonians stood to recommend that the money be used to repay the debt incurred by overeagerly purchasing the land for Franklin Park, to buy machinery for the city's Mechanic Arts High School, to build a surgical ward for Boston City Hospital, or to be given to the Franklin Typographical Society for the relief of poor printers. Other residents argued that Franklin would have wanted his gift to establish free public baths, to care for and propagate the city's trees, to build a monument to firemen, to erect playgrounds, to build a labor exchange and employment bureau, to construct a library, to create a pension fund for wage earners, or to build a trades school.

"A secret ballot was taken on the various items," McCleary recorded. As a result, the board resolved to spend the money on "the erection of a 'Franklin Trades School.'"

At the hearing, master mechanics had testified about the difficulty of finding skilled workers to hire. The trades school would provide the modern equivalent of the defunct apprentice system and provide an alternative to Boston's universities. "Many boys who do not cultivate their heads may become proficient with their hands," McCleary wrote, "and handicraft, when well directed and applied, is in turn a stimulus to brain power." (Workmen without tools, said Poor Richard in 1742, were like lawyers without fools.)

From the second portion of Franklin's bequest, each of the school's graduates would be eligible to receive a $300 loan to start their career. At a time when an average American worker earned around $400 a year, Franklin's money could still make a difference. Yet Boston's plan failed to broaden the pool of those he could help by loosening his stringent requirements. Judging by his notes, the only objection that Samuel McCleary had to the proposal was the fact that Boston officials traveling to inspect other cities' trades schools had asked him to reimburse their expenses with Franklin's money.

The profligacy struck a nerve. A decade earlier, as he had neared the end of his long term as Boston's city clerk, "the junketing was a sore trial to Mr. McCleary," a friend observed. "He had a great deal of influence with the City government on most questions, but on this one he was powerless to secure reform." After McCleary had regularly refused invitations to join bureaucrats for "meals at all hours" on the taxpayers' dime, the men had "laughed over his sarcastic remarks as those of a well-meaning but narrow-minded and rather cranky individual."

No one, it seemed, appreciated the fact that for over one hundred years, Benjamin Franklin's Boston treasurers had, at least, protected his money from spendthrift politicians.

"Under a solemn sense of duty," McCleary wrote in his letter reject-ing the expense report, "the undersigned declines to pay any portion of the Franklin Fund for the purpose indicated unless ordered so to do by a judicial order." No such mandate came. The cranky individual had prevailed.

In January 1894, McCleary transferred Boston's portion of Frank-lin's centenary gift to the city treasurer, keeping the remainder of the $102,455.70 on deposit with the Massachusetts Hospital Life Insur-ance Company. Per Franklin's instructions, after another hundred years, its accumulated amount would be divided between Boston and the State of Massachusetts, "and the Fund will then cease to exist."

McCleary, ever the optimist, predicted that on that date in 1991, "it will at once be seen what a superb bequest this is, not alone in a pecu-niary point of view, but vastly better, as an educational factor of great promise and value." The gift would also prove, as Franklin allegedly said, that an investment in knowledge pays the best interest.

In December 1895, McCleary received a second letter from his Philadelphia counterpart asking how Boston intended to use its cen-tennial money. Philadelphia had spent only $1,600 of its $110,000 (approximately only one-third of Boston's purse) to fund a series of free public lectures on electricity.

But for once Philadelphia seemingly surpassed Boston in municipal efficiency. "An offer has been made," the letter said, "to apply [the money] toward the cost of the erection of a museum or art gallery in Fairmount Park." Franklin's litigious descendants supported the idea, so long as the museum was named for him. Yet because the project's cost would require the city to match Franklin's donation, his gift re-mained unopened.

Like the castaway oarsmen of that era's popular Stephen Crane story "The Open Boat," who surmount one wave, only to discover another one rising behind it, the custodians of Franklin's money in both cities seemed to make no forward progress. To borrow Crane's disconsolate phrasing: *They rowed. And also they rowed.*

In Boston, the argument pitted the Franklin Fund against the city government. After inspecting two dozen land parcels, Franklin's trustees finally voted to spend $87,120 to purchase five acres in Roxbury. Franklin's gift no longer seemed adrift. His vision would at last be realized in the form of the trades school that had been decided upon in the previous year.

And then Boston's city treasurer refused to disburse the cash.

Alfred Turner was a career civil servant, rising, after four decades in Boston government, to become its treasurer. Turner believed that only Franklin's intended beneficiaries—the people of Boston—could spend the money. Alfred Turner worked for the people, and so Alfred Turner held tight. The sum might well purchase land and construct a school, but taxpayers, he argued, would have to fund the building's annual operating expenses, contravening Franklin's stated intention of leaving Boston a one-off gift.

Across an entire year, Turner refused to relent. Boston's mayor finally petitioned the Suffolk County probate court to force his treasurer's hand. The judge instead appointed ministers from the three churches Franklin had specified in his will, plus four laymen (retaining McCleary as treasurer), to manage the gift, as its testator had wished. Another year passed. In 1897, two years after the Roxbury lot had been selected as the site of the trades school, this reconstituted board of trustees again asked the Boston city treasurer to transfer Franklin's money. Turner preferred not to. The stalemate dragged on.

"If the social and legal complications increase in the same proportion as the fund," the *Boston Journal* sardonically observed in 1896, "we may well congratulate ourselves that a kind Providence will permit us to leave to the citizens of a century hence the problems which the Franklin millions will then give rise."

In 1897, the Franklin Fund trustees sued Turner, demanding that the treasurer return the money to their control. The benefactor would likely have been dismayed to learn that his legacy had become the plaything of a profession for which he held little respect. In 1733, the year Franklin chose Deborah to hold his power of attorney, Poor Richard fired several darts, including, "God works wonders now and then; Behold! a *Lawyer*, an honest Man!" Four years later, he quipped, "A countryman between two Lawyers is like a fish between two cats."

Yet another year expired before the Massachusetts Supreme Judicial Court ruled that the trustees could spend Franklin's centennial gift as they saw fit. However, the judge also ordered the current board to be dissolved and replaced with one made up of clergy and aldermen, as Franklin's will had instructed. Samuel McCleary remained the treasurer. In 1898, the new board supported the existing plan to build a trades school.

Seven years had elapsed since the money had become available — a period in which the United States fought and won the Spanish-American War, Thomas Edison invented the kinetoscope and built a film studio, Boston opened the nation's first subway, and Mark Twain assured the world that the report of his death was an exaggeration. Franklin's gift remained moribund.

The Boston mayor, Josiah Quincy VI (descended from the first, the friend to whom Franklin had written in 1783, "May we never see another War! for in my Opinion, *there never was a good War, or a bad Peace*"), argued that because Franklin desired "to make his benefaction of most general utility to the inhabitants," his money should not build a school to serve only a fraction of the population. Instead, it could pay for five or six free public bathhouses, with attached gymnasiums, open to everyone, 365 days a year. Boston then had but one public bath, used by up to a thousand people daily. Would Benjamin Franklin not be shocked to learn that, as in his time, cholera and typhoid remained among Boston's leading causes of death?

The baths, each of which would be named for him, would also fulfill Franklin's wish to make the city more agreeable to strangers, showing Boston's "earnest desire to carry out conscientiously the exact intentions of Franklin." Perhaps any leftover funds, the mayor added, could finance the construction of a meeting hall for labor unions.

It was a politically cagey postscript. During the stalemate, Boston's union bosses had backed the city treasurer's refusal to disburse the money to build a trades school, fearing that it would produce an annual supply of young skilled workers and undermine their demands for higher pay.

Whose side would Franklin have been on? Unlike his acquaintance Adam Smith, who in *The Wealth of Nations* criticized business owners who colluded to deflate wages but called for the magistrates if their workers organized, the entrepreneurial Franklin's sympathies often lay with management—to a point. He had chafed while apprenticing with his brother and repudiated the miserly Penns. Yet for six decades, he had remained a loyal British subject. In 1766, after Parliament debated to repeal the Stamp Act despite the "*illegal and hostile* combination of the people of America," Franklin wrote in his transcript's margin, "Surely there is nothing illegal in People's resolving to work for themselves. Every Man in Britain may do it." As relations between the Crown and the colonies frayed, Franklin recognized that there was power in a union.

Collectivization could topple a king, but the laws of the market economy appeared to him immutable. Eight years prior to the 1776 publication of Adam Smith's seminal book, Franklin in a London magazine argued against the idea that government should compel business owners to raise the pay of their workers. "If it be said that their wages are too low," he wrote, "and that they ought to be better paid for their labour, I heartily wish any means could be fallen upon to do it, consistent with their interest and happiness; but as the cheapness of other things is owing to the plenty of those things, so the cheapness of labour is, in most cases, owing to the multitude of labourers, and to their underworking one another in order to obtain employment."

Franklin offered no solutions in this essay. He did not even suggest the formation of guilds. His final words on lifting those he dubbed the "labouring poor" came in his last will and testament, where he shared his own escape route to independence and freedom: become your own boss.

In November 1898, the trustees of Franklin's bequest to Boston convened a pair of public hearings to consider spending his money on public baths or other proposed ideas, including the school. The Central Labor Union, fresh off its success lobbying for the new national holiday called Labor Day, packed the hearing with its members.

The union's representative, the fifty-eight-year-old George McNeill, looked like a slimmer version of Karl Marx, replete with the magnificent beard. McNeill had started working in a textile mill at age fifteen, only to be fired after he joined a strike demanding a shorter workday. The strike had failed, but a decade later McNeill's tireless advocacy convinced Massachusetts lawmakers to restrict shifts to ten hours.

In 1892 — six years before speaking at the public hearing on Franklin's gift — McNeill wrote one of the first histories of the American labor movement. Eight years after this hearing, the American Federation of Labor founder Samuel Gompers would deliver George McNeill's eulogy.

Did Franklin's Boston trustees realize, the animated McNeill asked the packed room, "that it takes eighty-six men, women and children to make a boot now?" He had apprenticed as a cordwainer, trained to fabricate a pair of boots alone, just as they had been crafted in Franklin's time. Now production had sped up. The division of labor saw "cutters" cut, "stitchers" stitch, and "buzzers" craft heels. A factory owner had recently told McNeill that if he had to choose between hiring a skilled shoemaker and hiring someone who had only worked as a logger, he would take the logger, "because the other man would have to unlearn all that he had learned."

McNeill implored his audience to acknowledge the realities of the modern economy. "The day of small manufacturers has gone," he announced. "And goodbye to it. We want no revival of the antediluvian methods. Machinery has come. You cannot legislate men back to homespun. We cannot legislate them back to the spinning-wheel. You cannot legislate them back to the shoemaker's bench. Your trades school is simply a reactionary process, an attempt to get back to the good old times of master and servant."

The entire hearing's transcript ran eighty-seven single-spaced pages. George McNeill's testimony filled ten of them, punctuated by his audience's reactions. Although many speakers—including civic leaders, laborers, and even the usually apolitical Samuel McCleary—stood to support the school, the Boston newspapers prominently featured McNeill. He ended his speech by suggesting a compromise: instead of a traditional trades school, Franklin's money could be used to build an institute modeled on the one Peter Cooper had given to New York City, which taught academic subjects alongside vocational training. The Cooper Union for the Advancement of Science and Art also included a bath, gymnasium, and forum. The school, McNeill said, was fulfilling Franklin's desire to help the "rising generation" upon which democracy depended. It charged no tuition and welcomed qualified students independent of race, religion, sex, or social status.

"The great demand of the United States," McNeill declared, "is for qualified citizenship (cries of 'Hear! Hear!'), men qualified to deal with the great problems that are confronting us. You may fill the streets of Boston with men who know how to handle the hammer or the saw or the plumbers' tools, or anything else, and you haven't raised the level of citizenship. You want blacksmiths who are capable of being Congressmen (applause)—capable, even if not able to be elected there (laughter); but when we get the mass of the people capable of serving us in Congress, the tone of Congress will be levelled upward."

The trustees withdrew to cast their votes. If a crystal ball had allowed them to see ahead to the 2020s, when less than 2 percent of Congress members had ever held a working-class job, would they have supported McNeill's proposal? That evening's edition of the *Boston Journal* announced:

RESCINDED

MAYOR WINS PARTIAL VICTORY AT LAST

NO TRADES SCHOOL IS TO BE ESTABLISHED

The vote really had only overturned the resolution to buy a building plot. The owner of those five Roxbury acres promptly announced that he would sue the city for breaking its purchase agreement.

More lawyers, more briefs, more courts. (*They rowed. And also they rowed.*) That case took another three years to resolve—a period in which the United States fought and won the Philippine-American War, Carrie Nation swung her ax inside saloons, the Wright brothers perfected their glider design, Andrew Carnegie sold his steel empire to begin a life of philanthropy, and Vice President Theodore Roosevelt defined his ideal foreign policy as "Speak softly, and carry a big stick." Twelve days after Roosevelt's September 1901 speech, he became president following the assassination of William McKinley.

That year, Massachusetts's highest court finally dismissed the Roxbury lot owner's suit. But still, no baths, and no trades school. Franklin's money sat idle at a time when large projects could be built quickly and comparatively cheaply. That spring, it took only two months and $35,000 to build the Huntington Avenue Grounds, the new home of the Boston Americans baseball team, later known as the Red Sox.

In April 1901, Samuel McCleary died at his Harvard Street home, at the age of seventy-nine. While he did not live to see how the money he had so assiduously guarded would at last be spent, he had been present at the meeting where its trustees unanimously passed a resolution "to testify [to] their appreciation of Mr. McCleary's ability, integrity, and trustworthy actions in the management of this sacred trust."

At his funeral, McCleary was described as "one of the very few men who emerge from City Hall and municipal life as fine morally as when they went in."

A few weeks later, the city treasurer, Alfred Turner, died, too, never releasing his grip on Franklin's centennial gift. The Boston City Council voted to lower City Hall's flag to half-mast, to send flowers to his family, and also to pay for his funeral. The men resolved to charge their respects to the municipal account called Incidental Expenses.

McCleary left a tribute to himself, of a sort, on a shelf. In 1897, his self-published monograph *A Sketch of the Franklin Fund* had been printed with a single error on its scant fifteen pages. McCleary nevertheless carefully hand-corrected the mistake—crossing out "July" and inking "February" above it—and sent a copy to the Harvard Library.

Opening this time capsule reveals McCleary's graceful cursive handwriting on its endpapers. "This sketch," he inscribed, "of which only 75 copies are printed, will be in demand as time goes on and I desire to have it absolutely correct." Bound in unlettered brown cloth, the slim volume appears to have hibernated, untouched, since leaving Samuel McCleary's dependable hands.

Boston's Franklin Fund managers continued to meet, to propose, to resolve. In the spring of 1902, its subcommittee, revisiting the labor leader George McNeill's suggestion to build a school along the lines of the Cooper Union, recommended a pared-down version of his plan, without a bathhouse and gymnasium. The board also agreed to purchase a lot in Roxbury costing 50 percent more than the previous choice, a price that smelled of kickbacks.

Boston's city treasurer balked: a real estate transaction was a purpose neither contemplated nor declared by Franklin in his will. The trustees threatened to buy the land anyway, and then sue the city for its failure to pay.

The newly elected mayor, Patrick A. Collins—who had apprenticed as an upholsterer—struck upon a novel solution to end this vicious cycle for good. Previous lawsuits had shown that the mayor could not force the city treasurer to take orders from an unelected committee whose designs would force taxpayers to maintain a trades school. So instead, he sued the managers of Franklin's money.

In his will, Franklin had designated town selectmen to oversee his loan scheme. Incorporation had apportioned their powers to an elected mayor and city council. The court, overturning a previous ruling, agreed that Franklin would want the mayor to serve among his trustees.

The judge appointed him, ex officio, as part of a new board of civic boosters who would not have looked out of place at a Boston branch meeting of Franklin's Junto. Joining Collins were two men who had served in President Grover Cleveland's cabinet, a four-term Boston mayor, and two state legislators. The court also appointed James J. Storrow—a lawyer active in the city's charities—along with the dean of Harvard Medical School, who happened to be a grandson of Nathaniel Bowditch. Finally, the judge added the astronomer and president of the Massachusetts Institute of Technology, Henry S. Pritchett.

Due to his constellation of prominent colleagues, Pritchett would play a key role in the next act of Benjamin Franklin's afterlife. One famous (and infamous) friend would be particularly crucial in rekindling Franklin's legacy.

In 1903, someone cut out and pasted a final news article into the late Samuel McCleary's scrapbook. This coda was headlined:

WITH CLEAN HANDS — FRANKLIN FUND CAN BE USED
FOR BENEFIT OF THE PEOPLE

The appointment of the new trustees, reported the *Boston Journal,* "means a great deal to Boston. It means that a fund will no longer be a magnet for politicians and grafters, and that it will be put to some good and worthy use in accordance with the will of the founder and without the intervention of land bonders or other professional schemers. Had some other mayor done what Mayor Collins did, already the people would be reaping the benefit of the fund."

The newspaper had spoken too soon. Its reporting omitted that in its ruling, the court had reminded the trustees that they "could not compel the city to assume any burden of maintenance or otherwise involving the use of money to be raised by taxation."

Fourteen years after the centennial of Franklin's death, compound interest had increased his still-unopened gift by 20 percent, to approximately $408,000 (equivalent to $12.5 million at the time of this writing). In December 1904, a new round of hearings asked Bostonians how they wanted to spend it. Many of the same speakers repeated the same proposals they had made six years before. Again the board was urged to follow the template of New York City's Cooper Union.

The hearings, Henry S. Pritchett wrote, evinced that building such a school in Boston serving "the practical needs of working men and women met the popular ideal for the use of Franklin's money. The difficulty in such a plan was to have means of support for such an institution once established."

But he was being coy, abiding by Poor Richard's advice to "speak little, do much." Pritchett had already secured that support, after paying a visit to a castle in the Scottish Highlands.

Act III
REBIRTH

1904 and Beyond

10

"My teacher, Franklin"

My dear Mr. Carnegie," Henry S. Pritchett wrote to Skibo Castle three months before the Boston public hearing. "I have taken occasion to look up Franklin's Will, and send you a copy of it so far as it relates to the bequests to the City of Boston and to the City of Philadelphia. This document is so full of the shrewd common sense and kindly spirit of Franklin that I am sure you will be interested in reading it."

Pritchett sought to continue a discussion that the close friends had started that summer of 1904 at Andrew Carnegie's Scottish castle, overlooking the Dornoch Firth. Pritchett told the industrialist that after thirteen years of disputes, Boston's centennial share of Franklin's gift had grown to approximately $408,000. A consensus supported using the money to build for Boston an institute modeled on the Cooper Union, and also—Pritchett shrewdly added—New York City's General Society of Mechanics and Tradesmen's school. Carnegie was a trustee at both institutions; his donation had helped the latter move into its building on West Forty-Fourth Street, where it remains.

Boston, Pritchett continued, faced a hurdle: Franklin's money would cover the cost of the school's construction, but not its operating expenses. Again, Carnegie could commiserate. For the same reason, Pittsburgh had initially refused his offer to build a public library. (Lawmakers added an annual levy to residents' property tax bills — still charged today — for its upkeep.) After Pritchett explained the obstacles that had delayed Boston from opening Franklin's gift, Andrew Carnegie struck upon a solution: "I'll match Ben Franklin."

One of Franklin's favorite inventions had built the Pennsylvania Hospital. Now a matching grant would carry his public-mindedness into the twentieth century. Carnegie said that if the trustees convinced the City of Boston to purchase the land and Franklin's centennial sum funded its construction, his contribution would stake the school's endowment.

After reading the copy of Franklin's will sent to him that autumn of 1904, Carnegie replied to Pritchett: "We are here helping only those who show an intense desire, and strong determination, to help themselves — the only class worth helping, the only class that it is possible to help to any great extent."

Carnegie's pledge matched Franklin's money to the penny: $408,396.48 (equivalent to $12.5 million at the time of this writing). It was a substantial amount to build a single school. In 1890, John D. Rockefeller had spent $600,000 to establish the entire University of Chicago. After Carnegie's contribution, Franklin's centenary gift to Boston would total $816,792.96.

Although generous, Carnegie's gift barely dented the vaults of cash that the sixty-five-year-old raced to empty before he died. Charles-Joseph Mathon's Fortunate Richard had calculated that it would take three hundred years of compound interest for his own legacy to build libraries and museums and to establish a fund to support "the unfortunate." In the mere three years following his 1901 retirement, Carnegie had spent $30 million creating libraries, The Hague's Peace Palace, the Central American Court of Justice, steelworker pensions, and benevolent organizations, such as the Hero Fund, which continues to reward people who have saved lives.

Earlier in 1904, after a New York City reporter asked if he had any unfulfilled ambitions, Andrew Carnegie admitted that ever since Horace Greeley had published a piece of his writing when he was seventeen, he had wanted to become a journalist. At which point, the reporter wrote, Carnegie turned to his friend Charles M. Schwab — the broker of Carnegie Steel's sale to J. P. Morgan for $480 million — and, shaking with merriment, said, "Say, Schwab, will you contract to buy up and consolidate six of the biggest New York dailies for me?"

Although Carnegie's wealth far exceeded Franklin's, his matching gift to Boston demonstrated his admiration for the man whose early American philanthropy proved foundational to his own enormous giving. Beyond their shared affinity for journalism, Carnegie's remarkable rise from an uneducated Scottish immigrant to the world's richest man paralleled Franklin's own story.

Both men had been born British subjects and became naturalized Americans. Both had fathers who had mastered a trade as skilled fabric workers. In London, Josiah Franklin had been a dyer. On a hand-loom in Dunfermline, William Carnegie had woven fine damask. Steam-powered looms produced linen faster and cheaper, and in 1848 William put his family on a boat to the United States. Andrew Carnegie would never have helped forge America's industrial revolution had his father not been a casualty of the British one.

Benjamin Franklin and Andrew Carnegie both left school before reaching puberty, and as teenagers both loathed their first apprenticeships. Both became entrepreneurs after mastering the communications technology of the day — Franklin with his printing press and horse-driven postal routes, Carnegie with the telegraph and railroad. Franklin dashed off an inspiring speech dotted with dozens of Poor Richard's sayings in an *Almanack* entry that became known as "The Way to Wealth." Carnegie's own widely read essay was called "The Gospel of Wealth." In it, he instructed scions to give away their money, and called for the formation of an estate tax to punish "selfish millionaires" who left their hoard to heirs instead of for the common good. "The man who dies thus rich," Carnegie wrote, "dies disgraced." Both men treasured libraries. Franklin raised a few hundred pounds to open the first one in America, operating on subscription, while Carnegie spent $56 million to build 2,509 libraries worldwide that were free to the public.

Carnegie modeled his autobiography on Franklin's. His foundation myth also begins on a boat journey to an uncertain future in a Pennsylvania town. Instead of buying loaves of bread upon landing, Carnegie's family purchased steamboat tickets to Pittsburgh. Passing slowly through the 137 locks linking the Erie Canal to the Ohio River in 1848, the thirteen-year-old watched from the deck as workers laid railroad tracks beside the water. This three-week journey from New York City was about to be cut to ten hours. Carnegie would improve at an equally rapid clip.

The young immigrant found work as a bobbin boy in a small factory, earning $2 a week to run a small steam engine that fired the boiler. "It was too much for me," Carnegie recalled. Fearing the boiler might burst, he spent sleepless nights checking the steam gauges. A reprieve came when the owner—who had poor penmanship—asked if Carnegie could write. He moved out of the basement and became a clerk, but after finishing the paperwork, he was tasked with bathing newly made cotton spools in oil vats. The nauseating smell drove him to learn bookkeeping at a night school. When he returned home one evening, his uncle told him that the telegraph office was looking for a messenger boy.

"Upon such trifles," Carnegie wrote in a passage that the Boston treasurer Samuel McCleary might have underlined, "do the most momentous consequences hang. A word, a look, an accent may affect the destiny not only of individuals, but of nations. I was wild with delight. No bird that was ever confined to a cage longed for freedom more than I."

The job lifted Carnegie into a heaven, he wrote, of "newspapers, pencils, and sunshine," plus a raise, to $2.50 a week. At the midpoint of the nineteenth century, Carnegie dreamed of earning $300 a year

—about the same amount that a Franklin loan provided young trades-men to open their own business.

As a messenger boy, Carnegie entered the orbit of the industrialist and power broker William "General" Robinson. Carnegie watched the first telegraph line stretch into downtown Pittsburgh, and witnessed the first locomotive to arrive there, too. On his rounds to Robinson's office, he heard that the region held America's most valuable deposit of coking coal. Yet Pittsburgh barely made any steel, which, Carnegie learned by listening, was stronger than iron, and better for building train tracks and bridges.

After sweeping up the office, Carnegie began to play with the tele-graph machine. He became adept enough with the technology to en-tertain his peers by transcribing messages by ear. After filling in for an absent operator one day, Carnegie kept the job, and rose, at age eigh-teen, to the post of private telegrapher for the president of the Penn-sylvania Railroad. Again echoing the credit Franklin gave to the early assistance he had received from patrons—and dispelling the myth of the unprivileged, self-made man—Carnegie observed, "The battle of life is already half won by the young man who is brought personally in contact with high officials."

On a piece of hotel stationery in 1868, a thirty-three-year-old Car-negie scribbled a memo to himself that hinted at his future philan-thropy, but also his ruthlessness. "The amassing of wealth," he wrote, "is one of the worst species of idolatry. Whatever I engage in I must push inordinately."

In 1875, Carnegie's first steelworks produced rails on the site where the 1755 British expedition outfitted by Franklin had met its inglo-rious end in the French and Indian War. "There, on the very field of Braddock's defeat," Carnegie recalled, "we began the erection of our steel-rail mills. In excavating for the foundations many relics of the battle were found—bayonets, swords, and the like."

In 1892, Carnegie Steel's own fight on Pittsburgh's outskirts re-sulted in the deaths of ten striking workers and Pinkerton agents. Critics charged that Carnegie's turn to philanthropy was motivated not by a desire to do good, but to scrub the bloodstains from his name. He would not have been the first to be so motivated. In 1744, Poor Richard chronicled in verse:

> Virtue was reckon'd the chief Thing of Old;
> Now lies all Merit in Silver and Gold:
> Virtue has lost its Regard in these Times,
> While Money, like Charity, covers all Crimes.

It is true that many southern cities refused a Carnegie library because he insisted on equal access for all. The Washington, D.C., branch that opened in 1903 was the capital's first desegregated public building. But more often, towns rebuffed Carnegie's largesse because it came from him. After voters in Wheeling, West Virginia, rejected a proposed library, a local union leader exulted, "There will be one place on this great green earth where Andrew Carnegie can't get a monument with his money."

Another detractor, whose father had helped establish the New York Public Library system with a Carnegie cash gift, observed, "Never before in the history of plutocratic America had any one man purchased by mere money so much social advertising and flattery. He had no ears for any charity unless labelled with his name. He would have given millions to Greece had she labelled the Parthenon Carnegopolis."

Carnegie was not deaf to this perception. John D. Rockefeller, after all, had refused to brand the University of Chicago after himself and named Spelman College for his abolitionist in-laws (although later, New York City's Rockefeller University would bear his name, and his son would develop Rockefeller Center). Regardless, Rockefeller's comparable humility did not fool all. At their final meeting, Rockefeller purportedly told Henry Ford that he would see him in heaven. Ford derisively replied, "You will if you get in."

• • •

At the December 1904 Boston public hearing chaired by Henry S. Pritchett, speakers urged trustees to use Franklin's money to build a trades school. Pritchett listened impassively and then announced that Andrew Carnegie had pledged to make this wish come true.

After newspapers reported the matching gift, Pritchett sent Carnegie a *Boston Herald* editorial cartoon showing Franklin and Carnegie shaking hands, linking America's founding philanthropist with his present-day counterpart.

The positive press was short-lived. Four days later, the *New-York Tribune* reported the rumor that Carnegie had made his donation conditional on his name being appended to Franklin's money. In the story, headlined DR. ELIOT AGAINST CARNEGIE GIFT, Harvard's president, Charles Eliot, declared the fund's name sacrosanct. "It should not be a Carnegie-Franklin Fund on any account," Eliot insisted. "It should be the 'Ben' Franklin Fund simply. Carnegie's reported conditions are impossible, at least according to my way of thinking."

Carnegie fired off a telegram clarifying that "Mr. Carnegie's <u>conditions</u> do not touch any change of name— It would be sacrilege in my opinion."

Henry S. Pritchett raced to assuage his prized donor. Among his papers, held at the Library of Congress, is a letter that begins, "I regret more than I can tell you if you have been caused any annoyance by the announcement of your generous offer." Pritchett blamed the "irrepressible yellow press" for the mix-up. "There are journals of the objectionable sort with whom the facts will make no difference, and whose attitude has been most discouraging to me. You are older in this kind of experience, and have doubtless had so much of it in your time that you are able to preserve a clear vision in the face of such unfair suspicions and unjust treatment."

But Andrew Carnegie did feel the stings. Among his collected papers, also held at the Library of Congress, is a letter, written shortly after Eliot had publicly rebuked him, addressed to "My Dear President." Carnegie assured Eliot that "the idea of tampering with Franklin's name never entered my mind any more than when I duplicated

Peter Cooper's gift of six hundred thousand [for the Cooper Union]. When Pritchett told me of the Boston fund, I volunteered to duplicate it, glad to do something for Boston, for which it isn't easy to do, much blessed as she is with a very rich and gift getting University and Public Libraries."

Carnegie claimed to dislike seeing his name attached to his philanthropy. "I find it difficult to avoid having gifts for new things called after donors," he told Eliot. "Carnegie Hall New York was called by me The Music Hall, a la Boston. Foreign artists refused to appear in 'A Music Hall.' The board changed it in my absence in Europe without consulting me . . . 'The way of the Philanthropist is hard,' but as I don't do anything for popularity and just 'please myself,' do what I think is useful, I never reply to any attacks. Altho I confess I was surprised that you should have for a moment imagined there was a man living who could dream of coupling his name with Franklin."

Boston's trustees voted to name the trades school Franklin Union, brushing aside a letter from Philadelphia's mayor, who warned that it would be confused with his city's scientific society, the Franklin Institute. The school would be built on a plot of land in Boston's South End. After fourteen years of intransigence and indecision, Franklin's centennial gift was about to be opened at last.

With his will, Benjamin Franklin had hoped to manufacture good citizens. In his lifetime, Andrew Carnegie strove to support their teachers. In early 1905, after learning that the longest-tenured college professors still earned less than the clerks at his steel mills, Carnegie announced that he was giving $10 million to establish a pension system for instructors at any university or trades school.

"I hope this fund may do much for the cause of higher education," Carnegie said, "and to remove a source of deep and constant anxiety to the poorest paid and yet one of the highest of all professions." After reading the news, Mark Twain dubbed the tycoon "Saint Andrew," and told Carnegie, "You can take my halo."

Like Franklin in his last will and testament, Carnegie attached conditions to his gift. In order to receive the money, a school first had to secularize, forbidding any imposition of religious belief upon its faculty. Of the 627 schools to which Carnegie initially offered his "Pension Fund for University Professors," only 52 accepted.

Nine years after delivering his "Cross of Gold" speech at the Democratic National Convention, William Jennings Bryan urged his fellow Illinois College trustees to reject Carnegie's offer. "Our college cannot serve God and Mammon," Bryan insisted. "It cannot be a college for the people and at the same time commend itself to the commercial highwaymen who are now subsidizing the colleges to prevent the teaching of economical truth. It grieves me to have my alma mater converted into any ally of plutocracy." The college accepted Carnegie's money anyway. Bryan resigned from its board.

What would he make of contemporary campuses, where donors' names adorn chairs, plazas, labs, buildings, schools, stadiums, and hospitals? If Charles Eliot rebuked Carnegie for his purported payment to have his name appended to Franklin's fund, imagine his reaction to Harvard Medical School's "Leadership Giving" webpage, which lists the prices to self-brand a bit of Harvard. A named professorship costs $4 million. A research center begins at $10 million.

Under Henry S. Pritchett's management, Carnegie's pension scheme grew into the Teachers Insurance and Annuity Association of America. Today TIAA administers retirement plans for faculty at over 15,000 tertiary schools. Because its benefactor did not name the scheme after himself, few academics realize that the program originated with a mogul who, during this period of his life, often resembled the top-hatted Monopoly man.

In July 1905, Boston's mayor informed Andrew Carnegie that—as the state legislature debated the city's plan to issue bonds to fund the purchase of the Franklin Union's building site—Franklin's centennial bequest had earned another $11,000 in interest, increasing its balance to $419,581.93.

Carnegie ignored the mayor's hint to top up his matching contribution, instead transferring the amount he had pledged via $408,000 in U.S. Steel bonds, plus a check for $396.48. The Massachusetts legislature finally approved the bond sale, and the city paid $79,000 for an irregular wedge of the South End bordered by Berkeley and Appleton Streets. Boston was, at last, fulfilling Benjamin Franklin's "earnest desire to be useful," as written in his will.

His wish to help Philadelphia remained unfulfilled. By the end of 1905, the city's centennial gift totaled two-thirds less than Boston's, with a balance of about $159,000 (equivalent to $4.9 million at the time of this writing). Plans to build an art museum named for Franklin in Fairmount Park had stalled after the city had balked at splitting the cost. "Nothing further has been done in this direction," an auditor reported. "No money has been expended, and the funds still remain in the hands of the Board of Directors of City Trusts." The auditor suggested that "it may become proper to reconsider the previous resolution, and to transfer this Fund to some other of the purposes named in Franklin's will. A Disposition of this kind would be very appropriate in connection with the celebration of the bicentennial of Franklin's birth."

Franklin had been born on January 17, 1706. In inimitable Philadelphia fashion, the city launched its celebration on April 17, the anniversary of his death.

The festivities kicked off with Andrew Carnegie, as Lord Rector of the University of St. Andrews, conferring an honorary doctor of laws degree upon Agnes Irwin, the first dean of Radcliffe College. Franklin had received the award 147 years before. Now it was Carnegie's honor to place the mantel on Franklin's great-great-granddaughter. "We can imagine with what feelings he would look down upon all this," Carnegie told the assembled dignitaries. "It is all to me so delightful, so graciously beautiful, that I bless the kind fate that has made me a humble instrument in the ceremony."

The program's notes do not record what Agnes Irwin had to say. Nor did anyone set down the speech Carnegie delivered to close Franklin's bicentennial celebration. It is not included in the event's two-hundred-page commemorative book. In his memoir, Carnegie, too, omitted this talk, which also escaped notice in his many biographies, each about as thick as a rail tie. The typed homily—heavily annotated with the unsharpened pencil Carnegie often used, an instrument as blunt as he was—lies buried in a sheaf of speeches among his archived papers.

Carnegie sounded, on this final night, like a man who had tired of the party. The events had included a parade down Broad Street, the placing of wreaths at Franklin's grave (while a Delaware-anchored battleship fired a salute), and a series of dinner speeches that added nothing new to Franklin's story. The speakers, all men, painted new coats of purple over the same old prose. One line can stand for many: "That rough diamond sparkled and shone." No one mentioned Deborah or how Benny had made use of his inheritance. Not a word was said about the loan scheme or Franklin's role as a progenitor of American philanthropy.

At least not until the last speaker took the stage. Carnegie started by admitting that he had never before addressed such a formidable gathering. "The educational institutions which upon this occasion have honored Franklin are legion," Carnegie said from the dais. "As address after address from various countries was [read aloud] for several hours, one was disposed to exclaim, 'Will the line stretch until the crack of doom?'"

Carnegie quickly catalogued Franklin's achievements in science and diplomacy, before slowing to highlight Franklin's charitable contributions to Philadelphia. "In this whole range of history," Carnegie challenged the audience, "where is there a parallel to this record of civic service by one who had held high place in the councils of the nation? I know of none."

The Scottish immigrant devoted the final two-thirds of his speech to credit Franklin's influence upon his own giving. "I beg you to consider for a few minutes," he told the self-satisfied room, a side of Franklin "which as far as I have seen has passed unnoticed."

Carnegie would have surmised that most of the audience, even if

The Gift of Benjamin Franklin

they were not regular churchgoers, called themselves Christians. This did not deter him. "Can I be deemed so bold," he continued, "if I venture to say to Americans, 'Find your theology in Franklin!' I was fortunately in my youth led at a critical time in a state of theological rebellion to my teacher, Franklin. Tonight from personal experience I speak of him in this domain, claiming that he is the greatest religious teacher among all his contemporaries and successors."

Carnegie quoted a line from Franklin's autobiography that had stuck with him when he had read the book as a child. "The message he gave to me was this: 'I have never doubted that the most acceptable worship of God is doing good to man.' . . .

"Imagine Jonathan Edwards," Carnegie continued, invoking the eighteenth-century Puritan revivalist, "preaching in Philadelphia today the dogmas of his time, and Franklin preaching 'Do good to man.' One would be the teacher of the past, the other of the present and the future.

"This has been ignored in all that has been said during this commemoration," Carnegie concluded. "No life of Franklin can be considered complete which does not place him in the foremost rank of religious teachers. The whole trend of Christian thought is in the direction of his doctrine. We are going more and more to him for our theology. Pardon a humble disciple for making this claim on behalf of his teacher."

Two years later, in 1908, Boston's Franklin Union finally opened its doors. One of its benefactors had died 118 years earlier. The other had declared himself to be Franklin's student. The souvenir postcard sold at the school's opening was captioned, simply, THE GIFT OF BENJAMIN FRANKLIN.

As he neared death in 1788, Franklin wrote to a Boston minister, "I have sometimes almost wish'd it had been my Destiny to be born two or three Centuries hence." Had he arrived in the early twentieth century, Franklin would have seen, in 1908, a series of events marking the arrival of the modern age.

That year, the first Model T, costing $850, rolled out of Henry Ford's factory. A company named Hoover bought the manufacturing rights to an invention called the vacuum cleaner. Mother's Day was celebrated for the first time. The Boy Scouts were founded. At the London Olympics, the track star John Baxter Taylor became the first Black American to win a gold medal. Ernest Shackleton sailed for Antarctica. A two-year-old boy named Puyi became the last emperor to take the imperial Chinese throne. The Young Turk Revolution spelled the end of the Ottoman Empire. After the revelation of atrocities, Belgium's King Leopold II relinquished his personal control over the misnamed Congo Free State. In the U.S. presidential campaign, William Jennings Bryan promised to ban politicians from receiving corporate donations. He lost, handily, to William Taft.

In Philadelphia, the city finally turned over the first part of Franklin's centennial gift to the scientific Franklin Institute, which planned to build a larger, modern home. As in Boston, Philadelphia agreed to purchase the building site—a plot beside what would become a wide boulevard modeled on the Champs-Élysées. The institute would have to raise an endowment for its maintenance. Andrew Carnegie had already ignored its request. "Franklin Institute has applied twice to me for funds," he wrote to a colleague, "but as I am spending a million there in Libraries I did not respond."

In Boston, 533 students enrolled in the Franklin Union's first class. Over the next five years, the number would triple. Demand for courses such as Principles of Telephone Operation and (fittingly) Electricity outstripped supply, even as MIT faculty voluntarily taught night classes. The course in gasoline engines was so popular that the line to sign up for its waiting list stretched around the block.

Although the interest earned on Andrew Carnegie's matching gift annually added around $20,000 to the school's endowment, in 1913 the Franklin Union's director cautioned that expenses were already outpacing revenue. "It is inevitable," he wrote—unaware that his successors for the next century would repeat his warning—"that in the near future Franklin Union will outgrow its present facilities and will need a further endowment."

The task of asking for money fell to the newly created Franklin Foundation, a charitable corporation created by legislative act, making it a board of the City of Boston. Its purpose was both to operate the Franklin Union and to manage the portion of Franklin's money due to Boston and Massachusetts in 1991, on the bicentennial of his bequest. That second sum had more than doubled since 1891, rising to $208,898 (equivalent to $5.7 million at the time of this writing). Disregarding Franklin's wishes that this money be loaned to young skilled workers for another hundred years, the cash remained on deposit at the Massachusetts Hospital Life Insurance Company.

The Franklin Foundation retained the same board members as the Franklin Fund, including Henry S. Pritchett. After a court had blocked his proposal to merge MIT with Harvard, the astronomer resigned as MIT's president to manage Carnegie's giving. Carnegie wanted his philanthropy to be run as a formal business, unlike Franklin's loan scheme, which had rested its hopes of survival on unpaid "benevolent citizens" operating with little oversight.

Belying its benefactor's supposed modesty, the organization was called the Carnegie Corporation. Placing its headquarters in Manhattan took advantage of the Tilden Act, passed in the aftermath of Samuel Tilden's bequest to establish a free library in New York City. The law gave trustees the power—previously reserved for a judge— to change how a philanthropic organization made use of its money. It also allowed a foundation to enlarge, and obfuscate, its declared mission. In 1911, the seventy-six-year-old Carnegie transferred $125 million (equivalent to $3.6 billion at the time of this writing) to create the world's largest charitable trust, for the "advancement and diffusion of knowledge and understanding."

Had he returned to early-twentieth-century America, Benjamin Franklin—after first wrapping his polymathic mind around, among other things, the abolition of slavery, the suffrage movement, a U.S. population of 100 million, and the invention of the light bulb, typewriter, postage meter, mousetrap, zipper, and fortune cookie—would likely have been intrigued by Carnegie's innovation of philanthropy. While he would have been staggered by Carnegie's wealth, Franklin also may have smiled at the entreaties flooding the mogul's mailbox, proof of his observation that a person who donated to a cause would soon be asked to give an even larger amount.

"The work is so excellent," a Franklin Union director beseeched Carnegie, via a letter to Henry S. Pritchett, "and the results so good, that perhaps Mr. Carnegie will carry his gift up to one million dollars. I remember that you [earn] nearly half a million a month from your large fund." The request also included a rather tone-deaf aside: "The Franklin Fund is really monumental; perhaps Mr. Carnegie would like to ally his name in large measure with it. Personally, I should be very glad to ally my name with that of Franklin."

"He that lives upon Hope," said Poor Richard, "dies farting." Pritchett later told another Franklin Union head, "The fact that you need additional funds to carry on the work is extremely interesting. Such funds would naturally be furnished by citizens of Boston interested in the type of education which the Union carries on."

The school's fortunes turned unexpectedly in 1917, when the United States entered the First World War. The Franklin Union was transformed into a National Army Training Detachment base. Male mechanics learned how to repair engines, and female recruits trained as field hospital nurses. The women also learned how to teach knitting, basket weaving, and wood carving to veterans suffering from the newly recognized affliction called "shell shock."

The war had a percussive effect on American philanthropy, too, one that resonated across the next century. The ratification of the Sixteenth Amendment in 1913 permitted the federal government to collect an income tax. To protect charities from declining contributions during mobilization, in 1917 Congress passed the War Revenue Act. Its key provision would have looked familiar to Benjamin Franklin.

In 1736, Franklin borrowed Daniel Defoe's suggestion from *An Essay upon Projects* to form America's first fire insurance company, as well as organize its first firefighters, a bucket brigade he called the Union Fire Company. To attract volunteers to the project, Franklin persuaded Philadelphia to grant a property tax abatement to households that joined. Nearly two centuries later, the War Revenue Act enshrined the idea in the tax code, allowing Americans to deduct charitable contributions from their assessed income.

The 1917 provision also exempted a philanthropic foundation's entire endowment from taxation. Philanthropies became an amalgamation of giving and investment, tasked with increasing their holdings while giving a portion away. It was a uniquely American invention.

The law also provided a massive tax dodge. Inland Revenue agents told the Rockefeller Foundation's London office that the United Kingdom did not recognize, as a charitable purpose, "the well-being of mankind." But the United States did, just as the law allowed Henry and Edsel Ford to spare their heirs from paying crippling estate taxes on $321 million worth of their car company's stock. Selling shares to cover the bill would have caused them to lose control of the business, and so the stock instead staked the Ford Foundation, devoted to "scientific, educational and charitable purposes, all for the public welfare."

Andrew Mellon, scion of the banking empire built by his Franklin-worshipping father, helped his heirs avoid taxes by donating his sizable art collection—purchased, in part, from Joseph Stalin, who in 1930 secretly sold Rembrandt, Velázquez, Botticelli, and Raphael paintings from Russia's Hermitage museum—to form the National Gallery in Washington, D.C.

At its opening, President Franklin Roosevelt praised Mellon "as a giver who had stipulated that the gallery shall be known not by his name but by the nation's." While Benjamin Franklin may well have applauded that act, he likely would have been critical of the snowballing effect of tax avoidance, especially by the wealthiest Americans.

"The Remissness of our People in Paying Taxes," Franklin wrote shortly after signing the Treaty of Paris in 1783, "is highly blameable, the Unwillingness to pay them is still more so . . . He that does not like civil Society on these Terms, let him retire & live among Savages. He can have no right to the Benefits of Society who will not pay his Club towards the Support of it."

Just as a lung ailment had killed Franklin, a bout of pneumonia took Andrew Carnegie. His life span nearly matched Franklin's; Carnegie died in 1919, six months before reaching his eighty-fourth birthday. He had wanted his epitaph to read "Here lies a man who knew how to enlist in his service better men than himself." Instead, a slab showing only his name rests under a Celtic cross in New York's Sleepy Hollow Cemetery. Ironically, his neighbor in death turned out to be the labor union leader Samuel Gompers, whose even more austere tombstone stands a few feet away.

In the months before Carnegie's passing, Henry S. Pritchett sent a letter of condolence to Theodore Roosevelt, whose youngest son,

Quentin, had been killed when his plane was shot down behind German lines. Pritchett himself had lost one son to an artillery accident; another, whom Roosevelt had appointed into the Army, was an infantryman on the western front. Roosevelt replied to Pritchett, "May your son be spared to you."

Pritchett's son returned safely to the United States and later collected and donated his father's papers to the Library of Congress. In the archive is the story of yet another lawsuit. "Tis easy to see, hard to foresee," Poor Richard wrote in 1736, but Henry S. Pritchett and his fellow trustees could not have been surprised in 1930 when Boston again sued for control of Franklin's money. Because the city, along with the State of Massachusetts, was due to receive the second portion of its benefactor's gift in 1991, it wanted a say in how the money was being invested. Adding a new level of legal absurdity, Boston's mayor, serving as an ex officio member of the Franklin Fund board of trustees, was named as a defendant in the action, which he had instructed his treasurer to file. The mayor was suing himself.

He won (naturally), but the outcome was not the one he wanted. The 1931 ruling said that Franklin's trustees could continue managing his bequest at their own discretion. "I can't help feeling," the Franklin Union director wrote to Henry S. Pritchett, "that the real issue was whether the Franklin Funds were to be kept out of political control." The decision ensured the money's "complete freedom from political interference."

But as Poor Richard wrote, "In Rivers and bad Governments, the lightest Things swim at [the] top."

In 1938, a magazine interested in the history of Franklin's loan scheme located Pritchett, then retired to a large mission-style home in Santa Barbara, California. "You must have many reminiscences of historical interest and value," the editor wrote, "and I wonder if you would some time feel like jotting them down and sending them to us."

Pritchett maintained the tight-lipped discretion of a Boston trustee. "I have gone through my files," he replied. "I find very little information bearing on this subject." He died the next year, at the age of eighty-two.

Every generation discovers Benjamin Franklin for themselves. Amid the excesses of the Jazz Age, the man who had once been branded as the impious, licentious father and grandfather of illegitimate sons became the emblem of wholesome conservatism. The admiring editor of the saccharine *Saturday Evening Post*—published in the same Market Street location where Franklin had begun the *Pennsylvania Gazette*—added Franklin to the masthead as its founder.

Franklin's name also became synonymous with frugality. In 1927, when the proprietor of a five-and-dime store wanted to promote its low prices, he invoked the man known for saving pennies. (Although Franklin never wrote "A penny saved is a penny earned," as Celia Single he promised, "A penny sav'd is a penny got.") Ben Franklin retail stores mushroomed across the country; among the franchisees was a young Arkansan named Sam Walton, who would go on to found Walmart.

In 1916, organizers including the Young Men's Christian Association chose Franklin's birth date as the start of Thrift Week, a nationwide drive that continued after the end of the First World War, drawing support from Presidents Calvin Coolidge and Herbert Hoover. As the Depression beginning in 1929 dragged Americans into de facto Thrift Months and then Thrift Years, Hoover told the *New York Times,* "The ideal today has shifted from the self-made man toward the government-coddled man. When the spirit of Franklin decays the sun of America will have begun to set." Hoover, apparently, did not know that Franklin had found his early success via government posts and printing contracts.

Gilded Age writers such as Horatio Alger had celebrated the Franklinian rags-to-riches rise in their stories. The postwar Lost Generation singled Franklin out as the archetype of the self-serving middle class.

Their Franklin sounded nothing like a man who believed that American prosperity depended on its working class. This Franklin sounded like John Adams.

His voice was "frightened and horribly smug," the poet William Carlos Williams wrote in his 1925 book *In the American Grain*. "His mighty answer to the New World's offer of a great embrace was THRIFT. Work night and day, build up, penny by penny, a wall against that which is threatening, the terror of life, poverty. Make a fort to be secure in . . . He is our wise prophet of chicanery, the great buffoon, the face on the penny stamp."

In 1923's *Studies in Classic American Literature,* D. H. Lawrence ordered American mythmakers to lower the "dry little snuff-coloured" Franklin, and elevate the ignored, out-of-print Herman Melville, whose commercial flop of a novel *Moby Dick* "moves awe in the soul." In contrast, "Benjamin overlooked NATURE."

Lawrence did not mention the fact that in *Moby Dick*'s fateful wake, a broke Melville turned to writing Franklin fan fiction. The serialized novel *Israel Potter* imagined its titular character escaping from his British captors after a Revolutionary War sea battle and then sheltering with Franklin in Paris. The story's one inspired bit sees Franklin loan Israel a livre to pay a bootblack. Moments later, Israel realizes that his pocket holds the French coin, and he hands Franklin's back, adding, "No interest, Doctor, I hope." Melville has Franklin reply, "My good friend, never permit yourself to be jocose upon pecuniary matters. Never joke at funerals, or during business transactions. The affair between us two, you perhaps deem very trivial, but trifles may involve momentous principles."

For all of his animated novels, poems, and letters, D. H. Lawrence never sounds more alive on the page than when throwing a tantrum. He was downright ecstatic when attacking Benjamin Franklin. "I do not like him . . . I haven't got over those Poor Richard tags yet. I rankle still with them. They are thorns in young flesh . . . I just utter a long loud curse against Benjamin and the American corral. Moral America! Most moral Benjamin. Sound, satisfied Ben!" Perhaps most damningly, Lawrence added, "If Andrew Carnegie, or any other millionaire, had wished to invent a God to suit his ends, he could not have done it better."

The do-good Franklin also poisoned Midwestern kids such as Jay Gatsby, whose ascent to greatness, readers learn at the end of F. Scott Fitzgerald's 1925 novel, had started with a Franklinian self-improvement schedule. At Gatsby's funeral, his father shows Nick Carraway the timetable. Young Gatsby rose at 6 a.m., exercised, and then for an hour sat to "study electricity, etc." After a day of work and sports, he practiced "elocution, poise and how to obtain it," followed by an hour to "study needed inventions." This was followed by a list of "General Resolves" that included reading one improving book per week and treating his parents better. (Franklin's own daily plan began with "The Morning Question: What Good shall I do this Day?" and ended with "Evening Question: What Good have I done to-day?")

Gatsby's father, Nick relates, "was reluctant to close the book, reading each item and then looking eagerly at me. I think he rather expected me to copy down the list for my own use." The two men are the only people who show up for Gatsby's funeral.

Even after Gatsby's machinations end in tragedy, the narrator admits there was "something gorgeous about him, some heightened sensitivity to the promises of life." Nick felt that Gatsby turned out all right in the end.

And so, surprisingly, did Philadelphia, at least in its attempts to honor its benefactor's dying wish. In the 1920s, the Board of Directors of City Trusts publicized Franklin's loan scheme. The cause of this sudden, and overdue, promotion is unclear. Was it to one-up Boston, which had last made a loan in 1886? Or was it an attempt by Philadelphia's new mayor to set things right?

J. Hampton Moore had served as clerk to the city treasurer in the 1890s, when Franklin's centennial gift sat untouched. Moore had also worked as a reporter at the *Public Ledger,* the first Philadelphia newspaper to expose "King James" McManes's grip on local government. Moore had passed beneath Benjamin Franklin every day. The paper's publisher—an illegitimate son who had risen from obscurity to buy his press—had installed a two-story statue of Franklin over the *Ledger*'s main entrance.

A court allowed Philadelphia to loosen Franklin's requirements; two guarantors were no longer needed if an applicant could put up property as collateral. The city sent Franklin loan applications to the American Federation of Labor. Its bosses told members not to apply, and so none of them did. An exasperated City Trusts board member finally asked a judge to allow Franklin's money to be spent on—to quote his will—"whatever may make living in the town more convenient." The court rejected the request, scolding the legacy's managers for their fatalism. But what more could they do?

Next, Franklin's money was offered as loans to the graduates of the Pennsylvania Institution for the Instruction of the Blind. It found no takers. Even as the Depression felled banks and dried up credit, Philadelphia did not make a single Franklin loan during the 1930s.

A child born in 1891—when Franklin had intended his money to build something useful for the city—had become, by 1931, a middle-aged adult. In Boston, this person and even their own child could learn a trade at the Franklin Union. In Philadelphia, this person could stare at an empty lot that promised, one day, to become the new Franklin Institute.

Cue the return of George Wharton Pepper, his brown hair since frosted by age into the color of snow. "As I had when a young lawyer attempted unsuccessfully to break Franklin's will," Pepper said, "it was no more than fair that in maturer life I should help preserve his memory."

After losing that first lawsuit (four times) four decades before, Pepper had embarked on a distinguished career whose victories included the decision exempting professional baseball from the Sherman Antitrust Act. In 1922, the Pennsylvania governor called Pepper from the bench, appointing him to fill a U.S. Senate seat after its incumbent had died.

"The simple fact is that never in my life have I felt the itch for public office," Pepper said, "impossible as it may be to make people believe this." That sentiment was not unusual for upper-crust Philadelphians. In his drive to serve the colony, commonwealth, and country, the Boston-raised Franklin had been an exception. George Wharton Pepper became the first Penn graduate since 1801 to represent Pennsylvania in the Senate.

As a senator, Pepper carried a soft stick. He peacefully arbitrated a coal strike and argued against the blight of billboards along rural roads. Pepper next stood for reelection against the Republican congressman William S. Vare, a notorious machine operative who — continuing the lineage descending from King James — was known as one of the Dukes of South Philadelphia.

The machine won, and then lost: Pennsylvania's governor refused to certify the election. The Senate, also suspecting a rigged vote, declined to seat Vare. After another Republican was appointed to the seat, Pepper returned to Philadelphia, co-founding the law firm that in 2020 merged with another to become Troutman Pepper.

In 1929, the sixty-two-year-old volunteered to lead the effort to finally make use of Benjamin Franklin's centennial gift. For thirty-eight years, Franklin's money had remained unspent. More than two decades had passed since the city had promised to give the $175,000 to the Franklin Institute to build its new science museum. But first it had to raise a matching amount.

No one else wanted the job, Pepper recalled, especially after the New York Stock Exchange plummeted that October. Fundraising in the aftermath of the Great Crash seemed hopeless. But George Wharton Pepper took his swing. In twelve days, he raised $5.1 million.

The building site was moved to a larger, square-block lot bordered by Twentieth Street and the boulevard that would be christened Benjamin Franklin Parkway. The neoclassical enormity of the Franklin Institute science museum opened in 1934. "Although the architect lost an opportunity to do a great piece of work," Pepper wrote (voicing a bit of Philly fatalism), "he at any rate did a good one."

Four years later, at the start of a three-day ceremony held in May

1938, Pepper unveiled, a massive statue of Franklin seated in the institute's rotunda. An eight-story vaulted ceiling modeled on Rome's Pan-
theon allowed sunlight to halo the benefactor's head. Its sculptor said
he drew inspiration from his subject's "all-pervading curiosity," and
carved Franklin looking "ready to turn the full force of his keen mind
on any problem that concerned life." This also proved easier than chis-
eling a kite and string. (In 1972, Congress designated the twenty-foot-
tall white marble likeness the Benjamin Franklin National Memorial.)

"As my life has spanned half the space that separates us from Franklin's century," Pepper later recalled, "it was appropriate enough that on
these various occasions I should figure as a sort of liaison man between
the ancient and modern worlds."

After dedicating Franklin's memorial, a man handed Pepper a check
for $100,000, asking him to kick-start the stalled project to build the
National Cathedral. But the capital moved even slower than Philadelphia. George Wharton Pepper did not live to see the church's completion in 1990. He died in 1961, at the age of ninety-four.

In 1976, Philadelphia named a new middle school in his honor.
The brutalist concrete building looked more like a prison to hold students sentenced to adolescence. Due to shoddy construction, it was
shuttered in 2013.

At the Franklin Institute, the only mention of the man crucial to
its construction is seen over the entrance to the original reading room.
The cavernous Pepper Hall features a hand-stained ceiling, an antique
wood floor, and built-in mahogany shelves that sit completely empty
of books. The space is now a for-hire event venue, perfect — the institute's website enthuses — to captivate guests with a "cocktail reception
or dining experience surrounded by historical significance." But this
description does not explain, or even hint at, what that significance
might be.

11

Turning the Tap

President Franklin D. Roosevelt canceled plans to attend the dedication of Benjamin Franklin's Philadelphia memorial. Instead, he sent a letter, read aloud at the ceremony, that explained he was detained in Washington, D.C., monitoring the multinational crisis over Adolf Hitler's threat to seize the Sudetenland.

In the run-up to the Second World War, Germany enlisted Benjamin Franklin. Nazi propagandists printed and distributed a translation of a pamphlet titled *Franklin's Prophecy*. First published by a bigoted North Carolina press, the tract falsely claimed that the founder had attempted to add a line to the Constitution banning Jewish immigration to the United States. The bigger the lie, Joseph Goebbels presumed, the more people will believe it.

In New York, supporters of the 1938 gubernatorial candidate Thomas Dewey mailed out handbills quoting Franklin's supposed anti-Semitism. In the annals of racist campaign tactics, this was less of a dog whistle and more of a Klaxon. Dewey was running against a Jewish man, the incumbent Herbert H. Lehman. Historians such as Carl Van Doren — whose landmark Franklin biography would win the 1939 Pulitzer Prize — raced to declare *Franklin's Prophecy* to be fake. The popular Lehman won a fourth term, but by a margin of only 1 percent.

In May 1938, as George Wharton Pepper unveiled Philadelphia's Franklin Memorial, across the Atlantic Ocean a thirteen-year-old boy named Walter Alphons Lyon finished his school year in Berlin. "I was the only Jewish student in the school," Lyon remembered. "I looked different. I had black hair; most of the other kids had blond hair. And yet I was completely accepted."

In America, 1938 was the year that saw the debuts of Superman, *Our Town*, a nascent Bugs Bunny, and the radio broadcast "The War of the Worlds." In Germany, the terror was real. "Everybody in my class said, 'Heil Hitler,' when the teacher came in," Lyon recalled. "I didn't, and I didn't have to. But in the marketplace on the Prinzenstrasse where I lived, there was an exhibit of the *Der Stürmer* paper which was one of the Nazi publications designed to generate hatred and anti-Semitism against Jews."

In September, the British prime minister, Neville Chamberlain, met Hitler in Munich. On his return to England, Chamberlain declared that he had achieved "peace for our time." The following week, Germany formally annexed the Sudetenland. Within months, it would occupy the rest of Czechoslovakia. In October, the Reich Ministry of the Interior declared all German passports held by Jews to be invalid unless stamped with a red *J*.

On November 9, 1938, Walter Lyon took the train into central Berlin to attend a night class. "My father had wanted me to learn English," Lyon recounted. "That was an evening school, and as the train pulled into the station at the Fasanenstrasse, I saw the big synagogue burning." It was the start of Kristallnacht, the Night of Broken Glass, when mobs smashed and burned approximately 300 synagogues and 7,500 Jewish businesses.

"I went out into the street," Lyon continued, "and I saw the storm troopers smashing the windows of Jewish stores, and I decided that wasn't a very healthy place to be, and I got back on the train and went home."

In front of his house, Lyon watched two men in civilian clothes exit a car. They had come to arrest his dad. The widower had served as an officer during World War I, fighting in fifty-six battles and receiving the Iron Cross. Two Nazis did not scare him. After asking for a private moment with his son, he told Lyon where in their garden he had buried the family jewels. "He said not to worry, that he would be back." After a few tense days, he returned. Suddenly Lyon understood why he had been enrolled in a night class to learn English. Earlier that year, his father had secured visas to the United States. In 1939, the pair made a fraught journey via Switzerland to a ship departing from Le Havre to freedom in America.

That fall, as Americans flocked to cinemas to see *The Wizard of Oz* and *Gone with the Wind,* Germany invaded Poland, sparking World War II.

Although President Roosevelt initially declared America's neutrality, the war transformed Philadelphia and other industrial cities into arsenals. Its Depression-shuttered factories cranked to life, pumping out armaments, supplies, and transports. Some 350,000 Philadelphians, out of a total population of 2 million, worked in the defense industry, including 150,000 in the Delaware River shipyards alone.

In 1944, at the age of twenty, Walter Lyon left his studies in civil engineering at Johns Hopkins University and enlisted in the U.S. Army. After Japan's surrender, Lyon was sent to oversee the unloading of rebuilding materials in Yokohama Harbor. When longshoremen went on strike along America's West Coast, their Japanese counterparts staged a sympathy action. Lyon traveled to Tokyo to ask the new shogun, the American general Douglas MacArthur, what to do. MacArthur listened to the young Lyon and barked, "'Strike? Union strikes are the American way, and if they want to strike, let them strike.'"

Three decades later, as the bicentennial of Franklin's death approached, a chance reading of his last will and testament would spur Walter Lyon to stand for his own cause, and enlist Benjamin Franklin's money to pay for it.

• • •

Just as the war brought changes to Philadelphia, including an influx of new workers, it also caused alterations to Franklin's loan scheme. In 1939, George Wharton Pepper, serving as master for the city's Orphans' Court, allowed the fund's managers to broaden the applicant pool to finally include women. Pepper also permitted a sixfold increase in the loan amount to keep pace with inflation. Borrowers could now request $3,000.

Alternatively, the managers could follow their Boston brethren and abandon the loan scheme altogether. He ventured "to suggest for future consideration the possibility that, for the sake of attaining the testator's primary purpose, it may at some time become necessary to substitute for the loan scheme a simple program of productive investment."

The managers struck upon a creative way of redrawing Franklin's blueprint for prosperity. In his will, he had written that "good apprentices are most likely to make good citizens." With the war over, a baby boom under way, and the GI Bill providing benefits for self-betterment, the manifestation of the American Dream now meant owning a home.

Starting in 1948, notices began appearing in the largest Philadelphia newspapers announcing:

> The City of Philadelphia, trustee under the will of Benjamin Franklin, deceased, has mortgage funds to lend at 4% to workers, skilled, unskilled or clerical on homes in Philadelphia in amounts not in excess of $3,000, loans to be repaid in ten years.

A Philadelphia starter home then cost around $5,000. A Franklin loan, when matched by one from the still-solvent legacy of the Edinburgh pharmacist John Scott, would allow a first-time, working-class home buyer to bypass banks completely.

Benjamin Franklin might well have approved of this new use of his money. In a sense, his success had been built on a mortgaged foundation. In 1729, a twenty-three-year-old Franklin was granted the chance to print the Pennsylvania General Loan Office Mortgage Register. After delivering a near-flawless job, he next was awarded a commission to print paper currency. That, too, proved superior to his competitors'. In his memoir, Franklin called it "a very profitable Job, and a great Help to me." It was (literally) a license to print money. In early 1730, the Pennsylvania Assembly chose Franklin to print its laws. His shop became, in effect, the government press, a lucrative account that he held for the next thirty-six years.

Franklin and Deborah favored real estate over other speculations. In addition to their Philadelphia portfolio, Franklin bought property to help friends and family in Boston. Unlike lending cash, which could be gambled away or otherwise squandered, this form of charity doubled as an investment. "When you're good to others," Poor Richard knew, "you are best to yourself."

In 1754, Franklin guaranteed a friend's £200 mortgage on a Berks County, Pennsylvania, farm purchased from Daniel Boone, who was setting out for the wilds of Kentucky. Eight years later, as the farm failed, Franklin personally underwrote a second mortgage for £258. The man died without repaying much beyond "the beste of the flower that I ever saw," Deborah wrote to her husband in London. She turned the flour into "the beste Buckwheat Kakes that ever I maid." Deborah was no pushover, however. She held power of attorney and directed the lawyer Thomas Wharton—whose descendants would include George Wharton Pepper—to collect from the borrower's wife, who eventually repaid the Franklins in full.

In 1948, Philadelphia's Franklin ledger showed a balance of $204,559 (equivalent to $2.3 million at the time of this writing), less than one-third of what Boston held, but still enough to help around seventy working-class Philadelphians purchase homes. Yet that year the board rejected all but two of the fifty applicants without recording why.

In 1949, Philadelphia's trustees successfully petitioned to have Franklin's loan restrictions loosened further. In addition to demonstrating an uncommonly modern use of pronouns, the judge overwrote Franklin's order that his money could only benefit married tradesmen who had trained in town. The new guidelines permitted loans of up to $6,000, repaid over fifteen years, to unmarried workers "without regard to the place where or the mode whereby he or she has obtained his or her qualifications."

The 1949 election of a clean-government-crusading city controller, or chief financial officer, led to a review of the municipal books. Joseph S. Clark Jr.'s investigation of the embezzlement of $40 million in public funds resulted in the indictment or resignation of dozens of officials. Nine committed suicide. In 1952, Clark became the city's first Democratic mayor in sixty-eight years.

The German refugee Walter Lyon—who after returning from Japan earned degrees in civil and sanitary engineering at Johns Hopkins—joined Philadelphia's Environmental Health Section. "The 1950s," Lyon recalled, "were the beginnings of the government and the people of the United States recognizing that there was serious air and water problems." He soon would discover that Benjamin Franklin had presciently warned his fellow citizens about the latter during the expansion of colonial Philadelphia.

Mayor Clark's administration reorganized the city's government under a new charter that, among other improvements, ended the patronage system for civil servants that had been entrenched since King James's Gas Ring. In 1954, Clark demonstrated the new spirit of transparency by lending Franklin's will and his legacy's ledgers to the American Philosophical Society, hopeful that they would attract the attention of reporters and scholars.

Riding this wave of municipal reform, the Board of Directors of City Trusts again attempted to revive Franklin's wish for his money to help tradespeople. It asked the Metal Manufacturers Association to encourage members to apply. Its leaders candidly admitted that they wanted their young members to remain in unionized shops, not independently competing with them. They also said that the maximum loan amount of $6,000 was insufficient to start a business.

Was that true? For the first time in either of his hometowns, Franklin's money managers sought to find out. Philadelphia commissioned a study that estimated start-up costs in twenty-three of the city's most popular trades. Benjamin Franklin would have recognized most of them. Twelve were among the skilled positions that his earliest loans had supported: cabinetmaking, carpentry, drapery, dressmaking, hairdressing, house painting, millinery, printing, shoe repair, tailoring, upholstery, and watch repair.

The newer trades—including auto repair, electrical wiring, and welding—were among the most popular courses offered at Boston's Franklin school. Not only was there a demand for skilled workers to fill these jobs, Philadelphia's study reported, but a $6,000 loan would cover the equipment and space required to open an independent shop for all of them, save for optical mechanics.

But this encouraging news did not translate into action. Philadelphia's Board of Directors of City Trusts, perhaps fearing the same run of defaults by workers who had gutted the fund in the nineteenth century, opted to lend his money only to home buyers. By 1957, however, only thirty-three applicants had been approved.

In 1789, Thomas Jefferson wrote to James Madison from Paris, wondering if "one generation of men has a right to bind another," either in laws or in debts. Jefferson concluded that since "the earth belongs to the living and not to the dead," it followed that "no society can make a perpetual constitution, or even a perpetual law."

In 1957, three years after *Brown v. Board of Education* outlawed segregation in public schools, Philadelphia refused to comply with the U.S. Supreme Court's decree to desegregate Girard College. The city argued that the benefactor and slave owner Stephen Girard's stipulation that restricted enrollment to "poor, white orphans" did not violate the Fourteenth Amendment's Equal Protection Clause because the amendment had been ratified after Girard's 1831 bequest. The court battles lasted until 1968, when the boarding school admitted its first Black students. Sixteen years passed before the first girls joined the student body, which is today drawn from single-parent families who live below the poverty line. (On its website, the school proudly touts a college acceptance rate of 100 percent.)

Franklin's last bet had originated in the embers of the American Revolution and remained in play at the dawn of the Cold War. While it took court orders and public demonstrations to bring Stephen Girard's bequest in line with the times (and the Constitution), Franklin's custodians continued to work largely without attracting oversight or outside attention.

Philadelphia, at least, put his money back in play—if cautiously —via home mortgages. In Boston, Franklin's trustees divided his ledger into two columns. The first tabulated the portion of his wager still on ever-increasing deposit with the Massachusetts Hospital Life Insurance Company, to be paid out in 1991. "It may be of interest," a New York–based reporter wrote admiringly in 1956, "that several of the people now serving on its board of directors are descendants of those originally identified with the concern. They don't seem to go much for outsiders up Boston way." That account totaled $1.4 million (equivalent to $14 million at the time of this writing), or nearly six times more than Philadelphia's balance.

The second column charted Boston's cash-bleeding Franklin Union, which had since changed its name to the Franklin Technical Institute. Uncharacteristically, the rebranding did not result in a lawsuit, or even a peep of protest from Philadelphia's Franklin Institute science museum. But the trades school would find itself back in court before long.

Its annual shortfall averaged $182,000. The trustees replaced the school's director. Next they appealed to the public for donations, and then to Boston businesses. Sinking further, they attempted to use Andrew Carnegie's endowment—earmarked for the building's upkeep —to make payroll. The city refused. No prizes for guessing what happened next. Massachusetts's highest court finally ruled that "the principal of the Carnegie donation cannot be used in payment of payrolls or other current expenses, or to repay money borrowed for the benefit of the institution."

And then in 1957, a trifle—shiny, Soviet, and the size of a beach ball—zoomed across the October sky.

In a symbol of diplomacy, American officials had ceremoniously planted flowering Franklinia trees in the ashes of Hiroshima the year before. After Sputnik launched the space race, politicians opportunistically pressed Franklin's legacy onto a new front. "There is a great need," said a Massachusetts state senator, "to expand our available supply of skilled technicians in the current race between Soviet Russia and our own nation."

This "practical-minded" Boston Democrat, reported the *New York Times* in 1958, "has made known his intention of wielding a legislative knife on the legal bands tied around a codicil of Benjamin Franklin's will." The threat of nuclear war compelled his bicentennial gift to be immediately given to Boston's trades school, so it could "get on with its work, instead of waiting thirty-three years."

"Between now and 1991," the senator warned, "someone may push a button and none of us will never know what might have been done with the money."

Seven months later, the state approved an act to immediately cash out Franklin's bet. The Massachusetts Supreme Judicial Court struck it down. "We observe in the codicil," the justices explained, "an intent to provide substantial gifts to future generations in the two cities. We shall not defeat that intent by destroying the trust now. Franklin's codicil is unique."

The court also admonished his money's managers past and present who had claimed Franklin's loan scheme to be inoperable. "There need be no sterile accumulation," of his money, the ruling urged. "Some charitable outlet . . . could be found for use of the income until 1991."

An attorney for two college students subsequently applied for Franklin loans to help fund their mechanical arts courses at Boston's

Wentworth Institute. The attempt failed but planted the seed of an idea. The court had wanted Franklin's money to be made useful to the "rising generation." While indebted apprentices no longer worked Boston's streets, a surfeit of overdrawn graduate students did fill its sidewalks. Many wore scrubs.

Medical students completing their residencies might not seem analogous to Franklin's leather apron class—although, in his time, a surgeon often wielded the same tools as a carpenter or blacksmith. But medical residents were young apprentices, many of whom needed financial assistance to open their own practices. And, Boston's Franklin trustees agreed, the future earning potential of white-coated physicians made them less likely to default than their blue-collar brethren. Furthermore, Franklin had been proudest of his fundraising that built the Pennsylvania Hospital. He also once wrote that medical students learning from old practitioners "must be upon the whole most for the Publick Welfare."

FRANKLIN'S FUND FREED BY COURT, announced the *New York Times* in 1962. "The Massachusetts Supreme Court released today a loan fund of $1,735,549 in Benjamin Franklin's will." The story also half-correctly reported that "the last loan was made in 1886. Since then legal entanglements have discouraged applicants."

The loosening of Franklin's restrictions allowed his Boston trustees to make loans of up to $8,000 (equivalent to $72,000 at the time of this writing) to residents at area hospitals, as well as to fourth-year students at local medical schools, including Harvard, Tufts, and Boston University. Enrolled students would pay an interest rate of 2 percent, increasing to 5 percent upon graduation, with the total due within five years.

Ignoring Poor Richard's warning that "He's a Fool that makes his Doctor his Heir," the trustees at first did not require guarantors. In 1974, a rising default rate required the medical schools to back the loans themselves. By 1976, 1,749 Boston medical students had funded a portion of their studies with Benjamin Franklin's money. One-quarter of the Tufts University School of Medicine's class of 1979 — nearly half of them women — received a Franklin loan.

Demand impelled his trustees to finally liquidate the fund's account at the Massachusetts Hospital Life Insurance Company, opened by William Minot 152 years before. "Since it was an important feature of the testator's [will] that his bequest be invested in young citizens," Franklin's current managers recognized at last, "it is arguable that no part should be withheld from the loan program."

After losing its Sputnik-launched attempt to divert all of Franklin's money to its empty coffers, the Franklin Institute of Boston (as the trades school had rebranded itself) limped through the Vietnam War era, bleeding enrollment. In a newsletter, its director lamented that he had not better publicized the fact that Selective Service draft boards would grant deferrals to Franklin students. In other news, a judge had approved the school's plan to add its first dormitory.

"Hopefully," its director reported, "we shall see some clearing of the site in the beginning of the spring of 1969. If so, construction could start in the spring of 1970." He then thought to mention that the school could not fund the project.

After Boston banks refused the school's application for a $250,000 mortgage just to meet payroll, a lifeline was thrown from the banks of the Charles. In 1974, Boston University agreed to underwrite the loan in exchange for a merger that would create the Franklin School of Boston University. The combined class of "artisanry" majors could make use of both campuses, including BU's library and dorms. "We stand," its director promised, "at the threshold of a great new era."

The schools actually were about to step into years of litigation. The marriage hinged on a dowry: legislation would first have to hand the university the entirety of Franklin's money, immediately. More acts, more judges: City council members demanded to know why state lawmakers were approving the transfer of Franklin's money, a portion of which belonged to Boston. Massachusetts's highest court agreed, ruling that Franklin's intended beneficiaries were the citizens of 1991, not 1977.

The union was called off, and Boston University eliminated its program in artisanry. Its newly built studios were eventually razed to make way for life science and engineering labs, whose shiny building bears another donor's name.

The redundant faculty moved their materials to a school in New Bedford, the town from which the protagonist sets off in *Moby Dick*. Sounding like a young Franklin, Ishmael realizes there are times that make a person take the whole universe for a practical joke, "though the wit thereof he but dimly discerns, and more than suspects that the joke is at nobody's expense but his own."

The 1962 publication of a different classic book propelled the German exile Walter Lyon to a new post, created after Rachel Carson's *Silent Spring* had compelled her home state to protect its watersheds. "Anything related to water in Pennsylvania was my responsibility," Lyon said of his promotion to the state's newly formed Department of Environmental Resources.

"It was pretty rough going initially," he remembered. "I was hired in August, and by Christmas time, my door was surrounded by gifts from people who wanted to influence me because I had a lot of regulatory power. To their disappointment, all that stuff had to be shipped back. And that's how they found out that there was a new regime in Harrisburg."

Lyon shocked his fellow bureaucrats by telling the *Wall Street Journal* that he would not drink the capital's water himself because it was not safe. That made lawmakers move. A new filtration plant opened in 1969.

And then, another trifle: five years later, a fifty-year-old Walter Lyon

Walter Lyon.

happened to read, in the *Harrisburg Patriot,* a 1974 wire service story
headlined FRANKLIN TRUST FUND $16 MILLION SHORT OF BEN'S
VISION. Rather than reporting Franklin's hoped-for role in shaping
public discourse from beyond the grave, the article focused on his
wager's final payout. At its current rate of growth, the total would
amount to 88 percent less than what he had envisioned.

A member of Philadelphia's Board of Directors of City Trusts
blamed the benefactor. "He didn't foresee that young people going
into business didn't always make a success."

The same could have been said about older bureaucrats attempting to manage a public trust. In 1963, when Philadelphia's fund held
roughly $326,000, its trustees made twenty-eight home loans total-
ing $76,000, or a little less than a quarter of Franklin's money. After
three further court-approved adjustments loosened his restrictions,
twenty-year home loans of up to $10,000 were made available to any
worker of any trade, single or married, under the age of thirty-nine. "I
believe," the board's secretary (incorrectly) told an inquirer, "this is the
first time in the history of the fund, that almost all of it is being used
in accordance with the terms of the trust."

In fact, Philadelphia was only lending out a little over half of Franklin's money. It could have been working overtime to disburse the entire
amount. In an era when commercial interest rates reached 11 percent,
Franklin's money provided home loans charging 5 percent. His gift

helped keep nurses and firefighters close to the neighborhoods they served, disavowed redlining, and underwrote first-time buyers rejected by banks.

After seeing an ad in a local alternative newspaper, a custodian at the American Philosophical Society told its librarian to check out the scheme. "All of the banks had turned me away," the man recalled (as a bust of Franklin watched us from atop a bookshelf). "And then I saw the ad in the *Welcomat,* saying these funds were available to people who were buying downtown. It was an incentive to repopulate the historic neighborhood and fix up the row houses. I never could have bought down here if not for Franklin's will. I think assistance like this is what the founders meant by the freedom to pursue life, liberty and happiness."

After escaping from Nazi Germany, Walter Lyon could personally attest to those inalienable American rights. In 1974, after reading about Franklin's bequest for the first time, Lyon was struck by his own thunderbolt of inspiration.

Four years earlier, 45,000 people had gathered in Philadelphia's Fairmount Park to celebrate the first Earth Day. Lyon realized that the observance fell only a few days after the April 17 anniversary of Franklin's death. In his will, Franklin had directed his money to be spent on a project "judged of most general utility to the inhabitants." What could be of greater use, Lyon thought, than the freedom to breathe clean air and drink clean water? After reading the will, Lyon believed that Franklin would agree.

On a copy of the document — which Lyon labeled "Exhibit A" in a folder of his papers deposited at the Pennsylvania State Archives — he marked Franklin's suggestion for the "public works" that Philadelphia might build with its centennial gift, including the laying of new pipes to bring in fresh water from Wissahickon Creek. The Fairmount Park reservoir built after Franklin's death had mooted this proposal. But Walter Lyon wondered if he could instead direct Franklin's money toward environmental conservation as a whole.

Lyon sent the will to the Department of Environmental Resources' chief counsel. After reading Franklin's autobiography, he also asked the lawyer if they could pursue payment for Franklin's Paris expenses, for which he had never been reimbursed. The lawyer looked into it and replied that "there was doubt as to whether or not Congress legally owed Franklin anything, and that, in any event, Franklin himself chose to let the matter drop. I do not recommend that we pursue this route further."

"I am indeed dismayed," Lyon responded, sounding as if they were discussing a contemporary colleague's expense report, "that Mr. Franklin forfeited his right to the funds to which he appears to have been entitled as a result of his work in France."

In 1979, after the partial meltdown of the Three Mile Island nuclear reactor, Lyon personally monitored radiation levels in the waters around the facility, thirteen miles downstream from Harrisburg. He steered an environmental journalist to ask him instead about Franklin's will, praising the founder's "sensitivity to the problems of storm management."

Next, Lyon wrote to the U.S. Environmental Protection Agency, crediting Franklin with anticipating metropolitan "non-point source pollution problems." In his will, Franklin had warned that urbanization prevented rainwater from "soaking into the Earth and renewing and purifying the Springs, whence the water of wells must gradually grow worse, and in time be unfit for use." Walter Lyon felt that Benjamin Franklin should be credited as a forefather of American environmental engineering. As his bet's final payout drew near, no other person so passionately promoted "Ben's vision."

In 1982, while Boston's and Philadelphia's trustees wondered whether they should stop making medical school and mortgage loans whose final payments would come due after 1991, Walter Lyon mailed photocopies of Franklin's will to Pennsylvania lawmakers. Under the founder's terms, a 100/131 portion (76 percent) of his money would be

given to the State of Pennsylvania. The remainder would go to Philadelphia. Pooling the cash and putting it all toward conservation, Lyon
argued, would fulfill Franklin's "earnest desire to be useful" in an era
when budget cuts were gutting the state's environmental bureaus.

Following this course could also publicize Franklin's public-spirited
problem-solving, and perhaps dampen public criticism of the final
amount.

"Benjamin Franklin may not have been thinking of the Parable of
the Talents," commented a 1987 *Philadelphia Inquirer* editorial, "but
ensuing events have followed the script of that biblical tale. Boston has
managed its fund aggressively, leaving it with $4 million today; Phila-
delphia buried its money in the backyard, so to speak."

Even though the city that—in the decades immediately after
Franklin's death—had been first would indeed finish last, its decision
to lend his money as interest-paying mortgages had more than doubled its balance, to $1.5 million.

In 1989, after state senators had proposed a bill that would hand
Pennsylvania's share to Philadelphia's Franklin Institute science museum, Walter Lyon sent legislators his own idea, one that had been
fifteen years in the making. The founder's far-seeing bequest could instead build a public archive that preserved the records of government
agencies, private groups, and individuals who worked to conserve the
state's environment. Lyon called it the Benjamin Franklin Center for
the History of Pennsylvania's Natural Resources.

Although its acronym—BFCHPNR—looked like a terrible starting rack of Scrabble tiles, Lyon's proposal attracted immediate support.
The state's Department of Agriculture, its Historical and Museum
Commission, the Nature Conservancy, and the mayor of Harrisburg
(where the center would be built) all endorsed his idea. "It does not
seem presumptuous," lobbied the mayor, "to suggest that Benjamin
Franklin would be pleased to see his willed monies expended in the
pursuit of his goal of natural resource preservation and awareness."

Fortuitously for Lyon's one-man campaign, Earth Day's twenti-
eth-anniversary celebrations in April 1990 would take place during the

same week as the bicentennial of Franklin's death. Although the Senate voted unanimously to give the state's portion of money to the Franklin Institute, the House refused to consider the bill. Instead, thirty-five legislators added their names to the one supporting Lyon's idea. In awfully arid prose, its author averred that the act "closely aligned with the purpose intended by Mr. Franklin in his bequest and will best serve the Commonwealth's environmental concerns."

Perhaps the lawmaker should instead have emulated Franklin's pithy wit. "When the Well's dry," Poor Richard quipped in 1746, "we know the Worth of Water." For all of his talents, Benjamin Franklin was also a charismatic pitchman for his country, his state, his city, and himself.

His successors in the Pennsylvania Assembly weighed Walter Lyon's vision of what the founder's money could build. The bill died in committee.

"I am dismayed with the failure of the House regarding the Franklin will," Lyon wrote to a state senator. Still, he refused to give up. "Is there any chance of getting that changed in the Senate? We need an archive regarding Pennsylvania's unique environmental history. No state has shown as much leadership in this field as Pennsylvania."

In 1758, Poor Richard famously observed that "there are no Gains, without Pains," but a lesser-known saying written five years earlier can serve as a more fitting coda to Lyon's dogged odyssey through the halls of political power: "He that best understands the World, least likes it."

"We finally got it away from those bastards"

The state senator did not know why Walter Lyon's proposal had fallen short in the Pennsylvania House of Representatives. "I must admit," he told Lyon, "I have only been following the house debate on Franklin's will in a general way." The founder's gift had not seized the legislative spotlight. That same week, the Pennsylvania Assembly also debated measures to reform judicial sentencing, provide better health care for Vietnam veterans, freeze property taxes for the elderly, reduce elementary school classroom sizes, curb unsolicited sales phone calls, and regulate the dry-cleaning industry.

It turned out that the bill rivaling Lyon's had garnered renewed interest, even after it emerged that the chairman of Philadelphia's Franklin Institute had lobbied the Senate majority leader to sponsor it. The fight over the founder's last big payout continued.

FRANKLIN'S WILL SPLITS LEGISLATURE announced a *Philadelphia Inquirer* headline. Franklin had hoped his money would build "public works, which may be judged of most general utility to the inhabitants." But his gift would cover only 2 percent of the estimated cost of the Franklin Institute's new wing.

"If I were the Franklin Institute and had the ability to get my hands on some of that money, I probably would," the ranking member of the Pennsylvania House Appropriations Committee told a reporter. "But, we need a vision, similar to the vision of the people of Boston. We need to build lives, not buildings."

By 1990, the *Inquirer* noted, Boston's $4.5 million fund not only was worth nearly three times as much as Philadelphia's, but in recent years had made loans to over 1,400 medical students. In contrast, Philadelphia had backed just 95 mortgages. Boston's mayor also had already set up a committee to brainstorm uses for the city's $1.2 million share of the disbursement, following two guidelines: "One, that it should not be spent as a one-shot deal . . . Second, that it try to follow the original intent of Franklin's will." The mayor hoped the money would go toward helping "people who work with their hands, in a broad sense."

Boston's "1890 distribution took 14 years to settle," cautioned a *New York Times* editorial. "Now starts the scrapping over [what] remains today."

The bicentennial of Benjamin Franklin's death arrived in an era when news reports decried government waste, including a military contract that paid $640 for a plastic toilet seat and $37 for a screw. A Manhattan real estate developer hung a digital clock in Midtown that displayed the national debt ticking upward. Soon its circuits had to be upgraded to keep pace with the speed of the increase. States and cities, too, incautiously ran into the red. Poor Richard's maxim "If you'd know the Value of Money, go and borrow some" seemingly applied only to those who expected to pay it back.

In 1990, Massachusetts's deficit topped $1 billion for the first time. "It's a wonderful irony," its attorney general said, "that eighteenth-century money should become available just when we need it for our problems today." He had a worrying premonition of what lawmakers intended to do with Franklin's bequest. "I would hate to have it just end up funding the debt."

Behind closed doors, Philadelphia's deputy solicitor wrote a memo to his superior stating that Franklin's money would soon "go into the City Treasury general fund, and may be considered a revenue source to balance future appropriations." Yet he hoped that it would be used in a way that satisfied the benefactor's intent. "As Franklin stated in his Will," the deputy explained, "'it has been an opinion that he who receives an Estate from his Ancestors, is under some kind of obligation to transmit the same to their posterity.'"

At that time, the only public proposal to use Philadelphia's share of the bicentennial disbursement had come from the rather covetous Franklin Institute, which wanted to spend the approximately half a million dollars to create the Benjamin Franklin National Memorial Awards, given to those who had "distinguished themselves in diplomacy and communications."

When informed of the plan, a renowned Franklin scholar exclaimed, "Oh, Lord!"

"I should explain why I used that exclamation," the longtime American Philosophical Society librarian continued. "Medals and awards don't do very much good. It ought to be possible to carry on some Franklinian idea, like public education."

That was a tall order in 1990, when Philadelphia's city government faced both bankruptcy and a transit strike that brought public transportation to a halt. Five years earlier, its police had bombed the row house commandeered by the Black liberation group MOVE, killing eleven people, including five children. With the city's reputation in tatters, the mayor's office decided how best to spend Benjamin Franklin's gift.

"As a presiding genius of the 18th century," the *Inquirer* reported, "Franklin was smart enough to know he could not predict a future that distant. Two hundred years after his death—which turns out to be this year in April—his precious legacy might urgently be needed for something even the founder of the nation's first fire department, library and university could not dream of. Some unfilled need that in the wildest flights of fancy, even he could not imagine. Something like . . . Tourist Promotion."

Until the veteran city news correspondent Thomas Ferrick Jr.'s shoe-leather reporting broke the story, the cash-strapped City Hall had quietly earmarked the founder's money to cover the cost of image-repairing events it was calling the Freedom Festival, the Festival of Firsts, and Music in Museums. The concerts would be Franklin-themed, in a manner of speaking. On the Fourth of July, the city planned performances by the dancer Ben Vereen and the singer Aretha Franklin.

"Get it?" Ferrick wrote. "*Ben* Vereen, Aretha *Franklin.*"

"It took us a long time to come up with those two names," admitted a city official.

"When they learned of the city's decision," Ferrick reported, "those interested in the fund had two reactions: First, slack-jawed disbelief. Then, anger." *Distressing,* said one local politician. *Terrible,* said another. *Crass,* added a third. The librarian emeritus of the Franklin-founded Library Company asked if it was a joke. "This is the old Roman bread and circuses," he grumbled. "You have a circus to get people's mind off the awful state of the city administration. It is inexcusable."

Yet the patron saint of printers would likely have been cheered by the enduring power of the Fourth Estate. Only four days later, an *Inquirer* headline announced: CITY RETHINKING ITS USE OF $500,000 FRANKLIN FUND.

Letters poured in to the mayor's office, urging the city to find a solution that perpetuated Franklin's ideals, instead of blowing his legacy on a one-off wingding. At the very least, one citizen suggested, a portion of the money could buy and distribute smoke alarms to low-income residents across Philadelphia.

Compelled by an act of the city council, the mayor appointed a committee of seven historians to "offer some insight as to how Dr. Franklin would dispose of the trust given the current problems of illiteracy, teenage pregnancy, homelessness, and high drop-out rates."

The group sorted through three hundred proposals. Franklin's money could go toward filling potholes, funding bookmobiles, or building a replica of the Goddess of Democracy statue pulled down the previous year in the bloody crackdown at Tiananmen Square. From London came a surprising bid to use the money to restore the Craven Street town house where Franklin had lodged for nearly sixteen years. The building had survived the Blitz but now sat derelict on a quiet lane between the Thames and Trafalgar Square. The most popular idea, floated in a quarter of the submissions, called for spending Franklin's money to create more green spaces, like the pasture where he and William had flown his famous kite.

At a public forum, a builder pitched a construction training program he called Girl Renovators in Training, or GRIT. A Temple University graduate student suggested searching for donors willing to match Franklin, and then use the increased principal to create a protected sinking fund, with its annual interest donated to community groups. The fundraising would begin now, the student said, handing a $20 check to the startled chair, who said, "I don't quite know what to do with this."

A twenty-two-year-old dance studio owner suggested putting the entire sum in a hundred-year bond. "Use it as a sign to the future to show what we were in 1990," he urged. "Maybe they'll need it more than we do." An elderly gentleman reminded the room that Philadelphia once had not one but two municipal bands. They had no connection to Franklin. He just thought it would be nice to start one up again.

The committee winnowed the proposals down to two finalists: The City Parks Association hoped to create a perpetual endowment to acquire and maintain green spaces. The Philadelphia Foundation instead wanted to pair high school graduates interested in crafts and trades with job training programs.

Although the Philadelphia Foundation had been founded in the age of Carnegie and Rockefeller, few people remembered its benefactor, since William Purves Gest had not named the philanthropy for himself. In 1990, its diverse board managed 130 individual trusts, matching donors with community causes that met their goals for giving.

A Philadelphia judge appointed a lawyer to ensure that handing Franklin's money to either finalist would meet the donor's original intentions. "It was a pain in the butt at first," the attorney told the *Inquirer,* "but after a while I got caught up in it. What astonished me in reading his will was how much energy, intelligence and vigor came through after 200 years. I began to have a greater appreciation for Franklin's place in history."

On the bicentennial of his death, Philadelphia decided that its share of Franklin's gift should help train the "rising generation" of tradesmen and -women. The Philadelphia Foundation announced that it would raise funds to match Franklin's $589,741 and continue his legacy in perpetuity.

"I thought it would be a wonderful thing if it could continue for more than two hundred years," said the judge. "And I thought it would be unfortunate if this money was just thrown into the pot and its special nature was lost. The fact that it will continue [as a trust] will attract more contributions from corporations and individuals who will want to be a part of that history."

Franklin's gift to his beloved city would be everlasting. But the fate of Pennsylvania's share of his bet remained undecided.

After Walter Lyon's plan for an environmental archive died in a house committee, legislators refused to consider the Senate's plan to hand $1.5 million to the Franklin Institute science museum. "Unless or until the two chambers reach a compromise," the *Inquirer* reported in the autumn of 1990, "the money will go nowhere, just sit as it has for 200 1/2 years in a trust in Philadelphia."

The impasse, one Democratic lawmaker said, was that the science museum had been the sole recipient of the centennial portion of Franklin's gift. "It's more important to me that the money go to people," he explained. "I think that's more consistent with Franklin's will than to let the money go to brick and mortar."

The legislator instead proposed that the sum—plus the $228,000 in the Edinburgh pharmacist John Scott's trust, set to expire alongside Franklin's—be given to Commonwealth Community Foundations, a consortium of twenty nonprofit organizations that managed trusts, raised matching grants, and paired donors with causes. He suggested that local program offices could apply to receive up to $200,000 to stake an endowment and distribute its earned interest to applicants in need. As in Philadelphia, through his money Franklin would remain present in the lives of contemporary Pennsylvanians.

This bill passed the House. For Franklin's wishes to finally be fulfilled, the state Senate would have to demonstrate the spirit of compromise that the benefactor had brought to the Constitutional Convention. "When a broad table is to be made," Franklin told its deadlocked delegates in 1787, "and the edges of planks do not fit, the artist takes a little from both, and makes a good joint. In like manner, here, both sides must part from some of their demands, in order that they may join in some accommodating proposition."

Pennsylvania's politicians struck a deal. The resulting bill, signed into law in December 1990, split the state's portion of Franklin's money between the community foundations and the Franklin Institute. Each received $833,605.24.

In the end, Franklin's $4,444.44 wager on Philadelphia netted $2,256,962.05—a 508-fold increase, but far short of the $17,868,400 that he had projected. Still, given his restrictive loan conditions, the onset of the industrial age, the defaults, the wars, the recessions, and municipal graft, the fact that even a penny of his money remained was remarkable. By providing loans to tradesmen and mortgages to first-time home buyers, and helping to build Philadelphia's cherished science museum, Franklin's bequest proved to be as enduring as the city he loved.

His legacy lives on. On its website, the Philadelphia Foundation heralds its continuing management of "Ben Franklin's civic gift of

1,000 pounds sterling." Its Franklin Trust Funds honor his conviction that "Labouring and Handicrafts" are the "chief Strength and Support of a People."

One share of his gift to the state circulates via the small grants that community foundations make annually from a "Ben Franklin Fund" for scholarships and projects that "increase the quality of life." Since receiving $25,000 of Franklin's money, Pennsylvania's Beaver County Foundation has annually awarded businesses that "provide a service or product that reflects pride in the county." The prize is not a medal or even a check. Instead, winners select their favorite charities, which receive a cash donation from the organization.

"There's a saying," its president said. "'People don't give to the Beaver County Foundation. They give through the Beaver County Foundation.'"

The charity disburses an average of $200,000 each year. In contemporary American giving, a donation of that amount barely warrants a press release—it wouldn't buy a university chair, let alone an ottoman. But a gift of $1,500 can go a long way in a small town. The modest grants also encourage lower- and middle-class residents to contribute. Most of the checks sent to Beaver County's scholarship fund are for amounts less than $100.

Echoing Franklin's ideal for public servants, the Beaver County Foundation's president does not accept a salary. "If I did it so I could have a paycheck," he said, "it would lose the philanthropic idea of it. Philanthropy is the love of humankind. If you can leave your community a little bit better off than what you found it, then that's good. You made a contribution."

After retiring from his government post, Walter Lyon taught a popular course at the Franklin-founded University of Pennsylvania on the environmental impact of engineering projects. He advised countries such as Brazil, Mexico, and China on clean water management and, among a dozen other advisory commissions, served on the Great Lakes Water Quality Board. If anyone could have written a biography of water, it would have been him.

Before he died in 2013, at age eighty-nine, Lyon was working on a book manuscript titled "Governing the Environment." In his collected papers, the final item in the Benjamin Franklin folder is the transcript of a 2002 speech in which he warned of the coming shortfall in funding to maintain infrastructure. The deterioration of stormwater systems would adversely affect aquifers, he wrote, and access to safe drinking water. For the talk's title, he borrowed not one of Poor Richard's optimistic quips, but Shakespeare's lament over wasted opportunities: "Lilies that fester smell far worse than weeds."

While Lyon did not succeed in his quixotic attempt to put Benjamin Franklin's bequest toward conservation, his own legacy lives on. The Pennsylvania Water Environment Association annually recognizes an individual's commitment to protecting the commonwealth's aquaculture with the Walter A. Lyon Purity of Water Award. The Pennsylvania Association of Environmental Professionals also gives a prize named for him, to an organization that makes a unique contribution to environmental management. Recent winners include the Suskie Bassmasters, anglers turned activists who protect the Susquehanna River watershed, and Allegheny CleanWays, which maps illegal dumping and organizes volunteer cleanup events along Pittsburgh's rivers.

Like Benjamin Franklin, Lyon was the son of an immigrant who fled to America to find freedom. He, too, was a forward-thinking applied scientist who wanted to be useful to the common good. He may have lost the battle to make use of Franklin's money, but of all the people drawn into the founder's orbit by his visionary last will and testament, Walter Lyon appears to be one of the few whom Benjamin Franklin would have enjoyed spending time with.

. . .

As the bicentennial of Franklin's death neared, a state bureaucrat told the *Boston Globe,* "It's fascinating the way he could foresee that Boston and Massachusetts would be needing this money."

"As you can imagine, everyone and his brother is after the money," said the head of the Benjamin Franklin Institute of Technology (as the trades school had been renamed yet again). Its attorney argued that "the money should stay with the institute. The likelihood of a kid out of the neighborhoods getting a skill that will last him the rest of his life is probably greater at Franklin than anywhere else." He invoked the 1958 act, passed after Sputnik's flight, granting the school the entirety of Franklin's money, which now totaled $4.5 million.

"From our point of view the legislation is moot," a Boston official replied. "It has no validity." The state attorney general's office agreed, noting that Massachusetts's highest court had struck down the Cold War–era bill that would have spent the money Benjamin Franklin had promised to future Bostonians. But now that future had arrived.

"It's a fascinating situation," said the state's attorney.

"There's going to be a scramble," added the trades school's president.

Silence followed. Because Boston's Franklin trustees had found no shortage of applicants for its medical student loans, they wondered when the program should end. A judge set the termination date as June 30, 1991. One week before that deadline, the *Boston Globe* printed a letter to the editor titled MUM'S THE WORD ON CODICIL TO BEN FRANKLIN'S WILL. "City Hall has said there will be no public discussion," the concerned citizen wrote, "that the mayor has already decided how the money is to be spent. Why? What is needed now is to hear the views of inhabitants of Boston before the money is spent without their knowledge."

Two weeks later, on Independence Day 1991, Boston's mayor announced the formation of the ten-person Committee for the Future of the Franklin Fund. The benefactor "might be the first example," the mayor said, "of a corporate leader giving back to his community by supporting the efforts of the future generation." Every generation discovers Franklin for themselves. The mayor hoped the money would underwrite his Safe Neighborhoods Plan, aimed at curbing gang violence.

The trades school created by Franklin's centennial gift, meanwhile, remained perched on the edge of insolvency. It held the dubious distinction, its exasperated president, Richard D'Onofrio, later told me, of being Boston's "only public institute that didn't receive public funds."

Years of budget cuts had left the once-impressive school filled with outdated equipment and underpaid faculty. Its deteriorating South End neighborhood compelled some teachers to carry a gun to class. Enrollment had been nearly halved. The annual $2 million operating budget depended entirely on the tuition the school had resorted to charging. Seventy percent of its students relied on aid to cover the $8,000 annual cost. The remainder of Benjamin Franklin's money, its leader pleaded, could go a long way here.

Richard D'Onofrio came from a working-class Boston family and knew firsthand the impact the school could make. D'Onofrio had skipped college to enlist in the military, only to find himself assigned to the Cold War's hottest American post, Colorado's Lowry Air Force Base, where he trained to become a nuclear weapons mechanic. (What was it like to work on these sensitive warheads? "I was scared to death!" D'Onofrio told me.) After being discharged, he enrolled at the Franklin school in 1961 to study electrical engineering.

The experience provided direction to his life. It also revealed the pleasure of learning a trade, of feeling not merely "handy" but useful. The school later passed that lesson on to his son, who after graduation was hired by a lab at MIT. The elder D'Onofrio moved into administration, rising to become the Franklin school's president.

"People choose to teach at Franklin," he told me, still sounding ardent in retirement, "because they want to nurture it. They understand its history, its purpose, its importance to the community. You do it for love, to perpetuate that."

That protective passion was hard for an outsider to feel, let alone un-derstand — especially in a city flush with so many famous (and flush) universities. To a stranger standing on Tremont Street, the Benjamin Franklin Institute of Technology looked like a drafty building from the slide rule era, whose classes trained poor kids to install HVAC systems. From this uninformed vantage point, these students did not represent Franklin's "rising generation." They represented the workers whom the white-collar class thought about only when their air-conditioning broke.

In 1990, as the school explored a merger with Suffolk University to stay afloat, D'Onofrio asked Massachusetts's highest court to revisit its Sputnik-era ruling. Could the statute that directed giving all of Franklin's money to the school now be declared valid?

In cases involving public trusts and charities, the state attorney general's office represents the donor, acting to ensure that trustees carry out their wishes. In this case, its lawyer, Richard Allen, would be standing up for a man whose will he had never read.

"I looked at a colleague and said, *'It's Ben Franklin,'*" Allen told me. "It was cool because of who he was, but it is also a very solemn role for an attorney, making sure that charitable funds are being used for the desired charitable purpose. You're upholding the way things are supposed to work."

Franklin had been far ahead of his time in creating a public trust. Massachusetts now had 23,000 of them. Subsequently, the Attorney General's Office Non-Profit Organizations/Public Charities Division was created to ensure that trustees followed benefactors' wishes. Imagine, Allen said, if you left behind money for a cause, but your descendants, or trustees, or politicians decided they wanted to spend it on something else. That's when his office stepped in.

"We didn't have any problem with the school," Allen continued. "But they wanted us to uphold the 1958 statute, and we said, 'This doesn't seem right.' You read the codicil, and see that Benjamin Franklin clearly intended that the money should go to the state and the city after two hundred years, and they would decide what to do with it. The legislation ran counter to that, and it was really couched in language that said, 'Terminate in 1958, and give it to the institute now.' One of the things we worried about was setting a precedent. We argued for preserving the court's prerogative to make adjustments to a will, not the legislature."

The proceeding, he remembered, was open to the public, but he didn't notice anyone from the press in attendance — a far cry from the contentious forums in Boston a century before. The hearing lasted only thirty minutes. "It was not my Daniel Webster moment," Allen admitted, with a self-deprecating laugh. "It was a tidy case."

The judge's ruling did not even count as front-page news. The *Boston Globe*'s story ran on page 22 in December 1993. "In a decision that would please Benjamin Franklin," the paper reported, "while threatening the survival of the technical school named for him, the state Supreme Judicial Court ruled yesterday that the city of Boston and the state, not the private Franklin Institute of Boston, are entitled to nearly $5 million in trust funds remaining from Benjamin Franklin's estate."

"We live hand to mouth every day, every semester," Richard D'Onofrio told the newspaper. "That is why this is such a blow to us. We've been waiting 34 years for this, thinking, 'This is our endowment.'"

In the same article, state attorney Richard Allen said the decision "enables the completion of the trust in accordance with the original words of Benjamin Franklin . . . It will show donors that their wishes will be carried out."

Allen recalled that a reporter asked him if the judgment was "a slap in the face" to the trades school. Although he was personally sympathetic to its mission, he told me, "Franklin would have loved this outcome. It proved that two centuries after his death, America is civil. Its organs of government work. The right people are getting his money."

In the end, perhaps they did. The school appealed to the court of public opinion. Within weeks, the president of the Massachusetts Senate added a clause deep within an appropriations bill that granted the state's $3.4 million share of Franklin's gift to the creation of a permanent endowment for the Franklin school's "maintenance, extension and use."

Four months later, Boston's mayor argued that the city should likewise donate its share of Franklin's money, given the school's "contributions to the community for more than a century." In truth, it had been open only eighty-six years. But the mayor was not the first person to fudge Franklin-related facts. In May 1994, the city council concurred.

In total, Boston's trades school received $4,646,613.48, 74 percent less than the $17,868,400 Franklin had anticipated, but more than double Philadelphia's final sum.

Although the two cities' rivalry had cooled across two centuries, Boston's fight had long been with itself: Puritans versus freethinkers, loyalists versus patriots, gown versus town, scrubs versus schlubs, the grubby boys versus the angel fish. "Having myself been bred to a manual art, printing, in my native town . . . ," Franklin wrote in his will's final codicil, "I wish to be useful even after my death." Now, at last, his money would wholly help his leather apron class, and not be pocketed by politicians or screened by a Boston trustee.

Upon learning that his beloved school would inherit the entirety of Benjamin Franklin's Boston legacy, a relieved Richard D'Onofrio said to himself: "We finally got it away from those bastards."

Benjamin Franklin's Return

In a letter written in 1773, Benjamin Franklin described the peculiar phenomenon of seeing several houseflies revived to life, although not by electricity. The insects had been "drowned in Madeira wine," Franklin wrote, "apparently as soon as they were bottled in Virginia to send here [to London]. When one of those bottles was opened at a friend's house, three drowned flies fell into the first glass we filled. They started with a few convulsive movements, . . . wiped their eyes with their front legs, flapped and brushed their wings with their hind legs, and flew away, being in ancient England without knowing how they got there."

Franklin wished that humans could be embalmed this way, "so that we could recall them to life when we would like." As he had "an extreme desire to see the state of America one hundred years from now," Franklin hoped that he could be so entombed, "to be then brought back to life by the warmth of the sun of my dear homeland."

If we uncorked a cask and poured out an embalmed Benjamin Franklin today, what would he make of the state of the country he helped found? Before we allowed him to watch cable news—imagine explaining all of *that* to him—we could ease Franklin back to consciousness by picking up where he left off: with his will.

He would likely be unsurprised to see that his hometowns remain hives of commerce and learning, enlivened by an admixture of natives, transplants, and immigrants. Would this reanimated Franklin be satisfied with the way his last bet paid out? After he learned how his heirs made use of their bequests, and how Boston and Philadelphia handled, and mishandled, his loan scheme, would he be surprised to learn that his example of civic virtue has been carried forward, as he had hoped, for two hundred years? Would he be cheered to hear about the rapid evolution of American philanthropy? Or would Franklin be stunned to discover that the nation's nonprofit organizations now employ more people than its manufacturers?

And how would this wine-stained Franklin react to the disparity of America's enormous wealth? A slight income gap would not be news to him. Franklin's self-improvement Junto counted sixteen members. Ten, including a carpenter and an ironmonger, were richer than he was then. Philadelphia's 1756 tax register recorded the property value held by the city's wealthiest man, William Allen—who would donate the land upon which Independence Hall would be built—at £600, or ten times the value of Franklin's assets.

But would Benjamin Franklin waggle the booze out of his ears after learning that the country's fifty richest people collectively hold as much wealth as the 165 million poorest Americans combined? "An enormous Proportion of Property vested in a few Individuals," Franklin wrote in his first draft of the Pennsylvania Constitution, "is dangerous to the Rights, and destructive of the Common Happiness, of Mankind; and therefore every State hath a right by its Laws to discourage the Possession of such property."

Franklin might ask if these modern—*what is the word,* billionaires?—rely on a workforce of tradesmen whose salaries anchor them securely within the middle class. We would have to explain to him the *new economy,* along with other additions to his friend Noah Webster's

English dictionary, including *unskilled labor,* a *living wage,* and *service sector,* where 71 percent of Americans earn their living. Franklin loved words, and I suspect he would notice that the terms *gig worker, self-employed,* and *independent contractor* sound liberating but obfuscate the fact that these positions—anticipated to comprise half the American workforce by 2028—free employers from paying benefits. I doubt that his reaction to this *new normal* would be as blithe as a laugh-cry emoji.

In 1784, Franklin explained to Europeans that America was a nation whose character was forged not through bloodlines, but through labor. Strangers were asked what they could do, and any arrival who worked a "useful art" would be welcomed and "respected by all."

Our decanted Franklin might wonder if that remains true. The reader's reply might match mine, shaped by my mother, whose hardware business installs locks and doors. She and my stepfather count themselves among the nearly two-thirds of Americans without a four-year college degree. Their skills and applied intelligence surpass most of the students and colleagues at the universities where I have spent much of my adult life. I've yet to meet an English major who can calculate payroll; decode ever-changing tax laws and health care plans; read blueprints; estimate a job's cost; and precisely cut and weld, deliver, and install at a building site an essential item that most people only ever notice when it needs repair.

My reply to Benjamin Franklin would not be scored by a Bruce Springsteen song celebrating the working class. Instead, I would have to admit that Franklin's "rising generation" is often looked down upon, and is all but absent from public life. Politicians and pundits rightfully raise their voices against sexism and racism, but they often remain silent on credentialism, perhaps the last accepted prejudice, discounting those without degrees. "The Boss," at least, has confessed that he has never worked an "honest job" in his entire life. Of his songs that have made him the bard of the blue collar, Springsteen has admitted: "I made it all up."

If I could, I would take our reawakened Benjamin Franklin to Boston's South End and lead him through the chipped, creaking wooden doors that open into the trades school that his money helped build. Upon seeing the portrait hanging next to his own, Franklin might wonder *who is Andrew Carnegie?* Looking up, he might smile at the series of friezes ringing the lobby's twenty-foot ceiling. Painted in 1908 by the same artist who created the stained glass windows in Harvard's Memorial Hall, the murals depict scenes from Franklin's life captioned with his words, including IT HAS EVER BEEN A PLEASURE TO ME TO SEE GOOD WORKMEN HANDLE THEIR TOOLS and WHEN MEN ARE EMPLOYED THEY ARE BEST CONTENTED.

On the first of my (solo) visits here, I squinted up at a painting that showed Franklin standing with his hand upon a table, watching a wigged man sign a parchment with a quill. I recognized that table. Putting my hand on the real one, where Franklin signed the Treaty of Paris, had touched off the idea for this book. The circle had closed.

This room's sentry paid me no attention at all. Glancing up from his phone, the security guard said that few pilgrims following Benjamin Franklin's Boston trail make their way down to the South End. Even most locals are unaware of the school's connection to the founder. Yet a visit here feels far more resonant than staring at the Shake Shack occupying the site of Franklin's birthplace on Milk Street. Even more than Franklin's London town house, now open as a rather sparse museum, the school is the space that, to me, best evokes his spirit.

Beside its Kite and Key bookstore, a notice board showed the schedule of the school's basketball team, named the Chargers (as in electricity). Other flyers advertised free math boot camps, a food drive competition between students and faculty called the Bensgiving Cup, and a reminder that the opticianry students made eyeglasses at wholesale cost. An enrollment poster promised HANDS-ON DEGREES FOR HIGH-DEMAND JOBS. In addition to associate's degrees, the Benjamin Franklin Institute of Technology offered bachelor's degrees in automotive management, health information and technology, mechanical engineering technology, and electrical engineering.

The school's president, Anthony Benoit, walked me through the building's four floors. Safety-goggled students were not passively sitting in classrooms, but actively wrenching, wiring, and welding. Over the din, Benoit said with proud enthusiasm, "We educate the old-fashioned way. We sit down with students and work beside them and make sure they learn." The school maintained a thirteen-to-one student-teacher ratio, even as enrollment had steadily increased to over five hundred. Seventy-four percent of the students were minorities, making it one of the region's most diverse colleges.

Annual tuition ran nearly $17,000, a sum that felt like $200,000 to the high school graduates he recruited, Benoit said. Most came from households whose median income totaled less than $25,000, at a time when the median U.S. household income was nearly three times higher. Ninety-three percent of Franklin students received federal aid, and over half of them were the first person in their family to attend college. In 2019, the Franklin school joined a city initiative that waived tuition for low-income public high school graduates.

Benoit, a Yale alum who went on to earn a graduate degree (like Walter Lyon) in environmental engineering, said that he told potential students that they could not afford *not* to enroll. The two, or even three, service sector jobs they were currently juggling might not exist in five years, let alone fifty. Why not learn a trade and gain a career?

"Businesses can't find people to fill jobs requiring the skills we teach," Benoit told me. "We will run out of graduates before companies run out of openings." The school boasted Massachusetts's highest graduation rate among two-year colleges, three times the state's average. It also enjoyed an 85 percent placement rate in full-time jobs within one year of graduation, at companies including Amazon Robotics, GE Aviation, Microsoft, Thermo Fisher Scientific, Warby Parker, and the Massachusetts General Hospital.

One of its recent commencement speakers had legally immigrated to Boston from Honduras at age five. "My favorite superhero was Iron Man," he told the assembly. "I watched with my older cousins and asked how Iron Man was able to create all these things. They explained that he was an engineer. If he could make all these practical things, I wanted to be able to do that." So at Franklin he earned a bachelor's degree in mechanical engineering technology and got a job at 3M.

I often dropped in on the school while researching this book. On my last visit, Anthony Benoit smiled when I asked how its curriculum would keep pace with the Fourth Industrial Revolution. "The fundamentals of engineering have not changed since Franklin's day," Benoit said, gesturing to a bust of Benjamin in his office. "Ohm's law, how to use a file to shave a part, how to listen to people describe a problem and then come up with a solution to make our lives better — all of that remains the same. Going forward, climate change means we need resilient infrastructure technology. We teach this. Automation means robot repair technology. People are losing their jobs to robots, but our students are gaining work. They're the ones fixing the robots."

Benoit had recently announced that the school would sell its historical building and create a new campus. "We have a responsibility to our students," he told me. "There's this excitement of building the school of our dreams, not this school that's retrofitted to the dreams of someone one hundred years ago."

The school planned to leave Franklin's endowment untouched, relying on the proceeds of the sale to finance construction of a smaller, modern campus. Its longtime location had never been more valuable. As Boston's tech boom brought an influx of new workers, the wave of gentrification reached the South End. Nannies pushed expensive Bugaboo strollers past Tremont Street bakeries and diners that called themselves "butteries" and "bistros." Other posh shop names employed two words where one used to suffice. On a walk around the school's block, I passed signs reading FLORAL DESIGN, GROOMING CENTER, DAY SPA, and TASTING ROOM.

The sale of the school was contingent on the buyer — Related Beal, the developer behind New York City's Hudson Yards and luxe condominiums in Boston's Back Bay — receiving planning agency approval. The filed designs included a new thirteen-story senior care building with ground-floor retail space, along with eighteen restricted-income apartments. The historic school building would be preserved by converting it into office space. The fate of the Franklin murals was not mentioned. Nor was the deal's price made public, although the new campus was expected to cost $40 million. Benoit said that the school had already paid $6 million for a one-acre lot a little over one mile away in Roxbury, closer to where many of its students lived and better served by public transportation.

The new site—at Harrison Avenue and Melnea Cass Boulevard, named for the Boston civil rights icon—resembles a "Before" picture of the Franklin school's current neighborhood. Working-class residents shop at the Daily Table nonprofit grocer, stop in at the Local 26 hospitality workers' union hall, and walk past an ophthalmologist whose eye charts show—in addition to the one topped by an *E*—tests in the Arabic and Hebrew alphabets, as well as in Chinese characters. At one corner, a small cemetery dating to 1630 holds the remains of one of the Massachusetts Bay Colony's first governors, Thomas Dudley.

In a novel attempt to curb gentrification, a community group in 2019 successfully lobbied the city government to change the predominantly Black neighborhood's name from Dudley Square to Nubian Square. "This is an area," Benoit said, "that a lot of people are thinking about as a critical location for attacking what I think of as one of Boston's primary issues: the tremendous gap between the rich and poor." The transition to the new campus would be overseen by Benoit's successor, Dr. Aisha Francis, who in 2021 became the first woman, and the first person of color, to be named president of the 113-year-old Franklin school.

As Benoit and I walked the old building's halls, stepping around a kite embossed on the floor and past a laser-printed sign reminding us that HEAT COSTS $$$$ CLOSE THE WINDOWS, I quoted a section of Franklin's will. In laying out his loan scheme, Franklin did not boast about his scientific or diplomatic credentials, but instead acknowledged the schooling and training that he had received in his birthplace, and his desire to pass that opportunity on.

As classes ended, we watched the hallway fill with young men and women who had decided to place a bet on themselves. Benoit turned to me and said, raising his voice above the din, "We are educating the poor to become middle-class." He sounded proud, and also defiant. Speaking louder, he added, "That's considered illegal by some people in this country." Now he was shouting: "It's a revolutionary act!"

Back at my desk, I regularly clipped articles from the *Wall Street Journal* and the *New York Times,* two large national newspapers whose editorial pages staked their political flags at opposing poles. In an era of increasingly partisan news coverage, however, the reporting around one particular topic was indistinguishable:

EMPLOYERS TRY BOOT CAMPS TO FILL JOBS

THE U.S. FURNITURE INDUSTRY IS BACK —
BUT THERE AREN'T ENOUGH WORKERS

SHORT OF WORKERS, U.S. BUILDERS AND FARMERS CRAVE
MORE IMMIGRANTS

The folder holding articles like these bulged to the size of a phone book. The phrases that I had highlighted in each story outlined a bigger one:

> The tightest labor market; 60 percent of contractors reported shortages — of bricklayers and masons, concrete workers and drywall installers, plumbers and roofers, painters and HVAC technicians; a shortage of immigrant workers; impacting housing and housing affordability; half of the kids in our carpentry program are DACA kids; more than 600,000 jobs remain open in manufacturing; electricians, pipe fitters, and radiology technicians are scarce; Americans continue to look down on those without college degrees; fewer than half of 25-to-34-year-olds nationwide earn an associate's or bachelor's degree; intense competition for skilled workers; em-

ployers are paying education costs and bonuses to move new hires across the country; the pool of skilled candidates is just not there; as we continue to be mesmerized by technology, we can't neglect the other makers; *no one wants to bust their butts anymore.*

While our revived Franklin might be gratified to hear the U.S. secretary of labor assert that "the apprenticeship model is one that is recognized by all as a successful model," his pride would be tempered by the fact that many employers are reluctant to sign on to existing apprenticeship programs, mostly run by trade unions such as the steamfitters, which they see as stalking horses for unionization. Although in the decade ending in 2019 the number of active apprentices had risen by a third, to 633,000, that figure was dwarfed by the 17 million Americans enrolled in college.

Were he able to peruse my stack of clippings (whose colored ink and photographs would likely fascinate him), our restored Franklin might even be amused, if also chagrined, to read about the land that had long enticed him. BEIJING INVESTS IN A NEW WORKFORCE announced a story describing the cluster of new vocational schools being opened across China to train workers in the automotive, aerospace, education, nursing, and logistics industries. "Everybody has a bachelor's degree," said one student who had enrolled after failing to land a white-collar job. Someone has to fix the air-conditioning, install energy-efficient windows, upgrade public infrastructure, and help to overtake a listing superpower in record time.

Pittsburgh, once the Carnegie-fired crucible of making things, commissioned a task force made up of political and business leaders, who concluded that by 2025, the region would be short eighty thousand workers, mostly in the trades. The Builders Guild of Western Pennsylvania said it would lose fifteen thousand carpenters to retirement. The group had begun a four-year apprenticeship program running on nights and weekends. Among the enrollees was a thirty-eight-year-old interior designer who fondly remembered the satisfaction of working with her hands as a child helping her father fix things.

The *New York Times* story that featured this apprentice — TIRED OF YOUR CUBICLE? TRY A TRADE — was unique for profiling a tradeswoman. She was also not the abstract "worker" that politicians and pundits, from champagne socialists to Ayn Rand acolytes, like to hail. (Would the five-figure salary class keep watching if the chyron below those talking heads showed their income instead of their affiliations?) She had a name, Hannah Grey. The accompanying photo showed Ms. Grey with her tools. She leaned against a wooden workbench that would not have looked unfamiliar to Benjamin Franklin, or to Deborah either.

As these stories filled one folder on my desk, another set of articles accumulated at its side. Over time, I had come to see them as a pair of trains rolling on parallel tracks that never cross. The headlines in the second folder included:

THE CASE FOR GIVING MONEY AWAY NOW

GIVING AWAY BILLIONS AS FAST AS THEY CAN

PLUTOCRATS AT WORK: HOW BIG PHILANTHROPY
UNDERMINES DEMOCRACY

The phrases that I highlighted in these articles told another story:

There are more billionaires on our planet than ever; Americans annually gave $450 billion; 100 million ordinary citizens donated an average of $3,000; your million-dollar gifts get you a letter saying, *Could you add an extra zero to that?*; the Giving Pledge — the new Gospel of Wealth; *Is charitable giving an elite charade?*; tax-exempt foundations exert their inordinate influence without public input or accountability; 40 percent of every foundation's wealth is diverted every year from the public treasury; this isn't a democratic process; this is a small group of people; deciding what issues they care about; anxiety in times of plenty; less than 6 percent of giving from major donors has gone to rural areas; organizations dedicated to helping girls and women receive only 1.6 percent of all donations; between 2018 and 2042, baby boomers will leave $61 trillion to millennials and their parents, the largest transfer of wealth in history.

This stack of stories did not mention faceless laborers, but familiar tycoons: Gates. Carnegie. Koch. Rockefeller. Soros. Ford. Zuckerberg. MacArthur. Buffett. Bezos. Bloomberg. Benjamin Franklin's name never appeared — not once, not even in contextual paragraphs that provided a potted history of American giving. But where would Silence Dogood fit into a culture of self-promoting philanthropy?

Uniquely, not all of the photos — and they were almost always flattering photos, showing rolled-up sleeves and bleached smiles — in these articles were of men. Prominent philanthropists included Priscilla Chan, Melinda French Gates, Agnes Gund, Laurene Powell Jobs, MacKenzie Scott, Liz Thompson, and Tracy DuVivier Gary, a Pillsbury relation known as "Janie Appleseed" for her forty-year career supporting women's charities.

Were Benjamin Franklin to leaf through these news clippings, he might be happy to see that most of the donors supported two of his favorite causes, education and health care. Institutionally, the fifty largest fundraising campaigns included nineteen universities and eighteen health-related nonprofit organizations, including the Mayo Clinic, St. Jude Children's Research Hospital, the American Cancer Society, the American Heart Association, and Planned Parenthood. The United Way outraised all of them, doubling what the Salvation Army and the American Red Cross received combined.

Only two of the top fifty charities worked for environmental conservation. Ranking far behind these groups, Teach for America received $195 million in outside contributions. That amount would barely make a dent in the $740 million shortfall facing Washington, D.C.'s public schools, let alone districts beyond the nation's capital.

Franklin believed that an elected government existed to improve the health and welfare of its citizens. He filled Philadelphia's vacuum of services with his philanthropic projects, but what would he make of the names appended to services today, including private grammar schools, health clinics, public parks, and bikeshares? Franklin may well conclude that the country has returned to its inequitable, colonial roots.

While American political candidates tout an "infrastructure of opportunity," the United States continues to crumble. "The problem is desire," one fed-up software tycoon wrote in a widely circulated 2020 blog post. "The problem is inertia. We need to want these things more than we want to prevent these things . . . And we need to separate the imperative to build these things from ideology and politics. Both sides need to contribute to building."

Benjamin Franklin would likely nod his assent to that. Given his lobbying and fundraising skills, he also would relish this challenge: "Demonstrate that the public sector can build better hospitals, better schools, better transportation, better cities, better housing. Stop trying to protect the old, the entrenched, the irrelevant; commit the public sector fully to the future. Milton Friedman once said the great public sector mistake is to judge policies and programs by their intentions rather than their results. Instead of taking that as an insult, take it as a challenge—build new things and show the results!"

Franklin (now sobering quickly) might ask why his Boston trades school continues to beg for donations, while his old bugbear Harvard has accrued an endowment of $53 billion. Or what he should make of the news clipping on my desk that profiles a wealthy Connecticut couple who annually hosts a weekend event that collects anonymous donations from attendees ranging from $1,000 to $10,000. Although puny by Silicon Valley or Ivy League standards, the gifts have an out-size impact when the couple pools them to send to budget-slashed, cash-strapped social service agencies.

In "The Way to Wealth," Poor Richard preached, "He that hath a Trade hath an Estate." But beyond that oft-quoted bit, Franklin's larger lesson is often forgotten. "And he that hath a Calling hath an Office of Profit and Honour; but then the Trade must be worked at, and the Calling well followed, or neither the Estate, nor the Office, will enable us to pay our Taxes."

Visitors won't find that quote at the Benjamin Franklin National Memorial inside Philadelphia's Franklin Institute. The plaques that line the base of his massive statue highlight his roles as citizen, statesman, and scientist. It would be so easy to add a panel titled Philanthropist.

The sculptor wanted to capture Franklin's curiosity in stone. On a recent visit, I found the trait effervescently emanating from the forty schoolchildren seated at Franklin's feet. The wide-eyed kids watched a museum guide demonstrate the shattering effect of liquid nitrogen on racquetballs. The domed chamber echoed with amazed delight. Franklin smirked in marble above them. When I asked one of the children if she knew whom the statue depicted, she confidently replied, "He's the dude who flew his kite into lightning!"

If Franklin were to reenact his arrival in Philadelphia, tracing his footsteps from the Delaware River docks up Market Street, he would recognize Christ Church and its steeple, but how would he react upon seeing the PHLASH bus passing by, sheathed in a decal of his face? Or seeing the same portrait, again, smirking on a sign over the Benjamin Franklin Beer Distributors?

Other changes might equally confound him: At the site of his first printshop now stands a sex toy shop named Kink. Next door, the Franklin Fountain makes floats with Franklin-brand ice cream. Would Franklin stop in at Silence Dogood's pub and tell the staff that he never actually said that God made beer because he loves us and wants us to be happy? If Franklin walked past the former location of his Union Fire Company, would he ask the shopkeeper the meaning of the logo on the T-shirt in the window?

~~THOUGHTS & PRAYERS~~

POLICY & CHANGE

And what would be his reaction to the answer?

Would Franklin be surprised that Market Street has retained its same footprint, still wide enough for horses pulling a wagon to make a U-turn? Lining this high street where Deborah first saw him carrying bread rolls, Franklin today would find a veritable melting pot of eateries, serving pizza, burritos, cheesesteaks, falafel, sushi, cheesesteaks again, biryani, pho, more cheesesteaks, and—imagine his delight— tofu.

Franklin would recognize the façade of his and Deborah's row houses between Fourth and Fifth Streets, where a post office still operates. He could look into the window of his, and later Benny's, press. Within Franklin Court, he could touch the ghostly outline of his house, marked by towering steel beams. Here, after returning from his eventful years in Paris, an elderly Franklin passed long winter evenings playing cards. He felt guilty about spending his hours so idly. "But another Reflection comes to relieve me," he wrote, "whispering, 'You know the Soul is immortal.'" Why should he be so miserly of time, when in his afterlife it would stretch for eternity? "So being easily convinc'd," Franklin continued, "and, like other reasonable Creatures, satisfy'd with a small Reason, when it is in favour of doing what I have a mind to do, I shuffle the Cards again, and begin another Game."

At the walled Christ Church Burial Ground, a crowd stands at the section of iron fencing that reveals his tombstone. Onlookers fish in their pockets for pennies, reach through the bars, and toss their money onto the epitaph uniting Benjamin and Deborah Franklin.

To me the copper-colored coins evoke the smallpox that killed their beloved Franky, resting here beside them. But still the pennies spread, tens of thousands of them, falling from the hands of 250,000 visitors each year, totaling around $4,000.

In 2016, the Christ Church Preservation Trust raised $66,000 to repair the tombstone, cracked by moisture and pitted by coins. (No visitors, apparently, toss less abrasive hundred-dollar bills.) After falling $10,000 short of its goal, the group started a GoFundMe campaign — imagine what Benjamin Franklin could have done with the internet — appealing to the public to donate one million pennies. The Philadelphia Eagles football team kicked in $1,000, and the rock musician Jon Bon Jovi added $5,000.

Those two donations grabbed local headlines, unlike the quiet $500 gift made by the Beaver County Foundation. Its president said it just wanted to give back a bit of Franklin's bicentennial gift that the organization had received two decades before.

I have some reason to wish," an elderly Franklin wrote, "that in a future State I may not only be *as well as I was,* but a little better." Just as water dissolves into air, and wood is transformed by fire, "I shall in some Shape or other always exist."

Visitors who pay the Christ Church Burial Ground's $5 entrance fee can sit on a comfortable wooden bench facing his grave. Parking yourself there brings the peculiar feeling of being on the other side of the bars at a zoo. A group of people stops outside the fence, stretches their hands through the bars, then leaves. The next group sidles up to take their turn. Smartphones simulate a shutter's click, Arch Street's traffic dopplers by, and pennies skitter *tink tink tink* across the tombstone.

But look closer. This family is visiting from Bangladesh. That man is from Buffalo. The Black woman holding her young daughter's hand has traveled from Chicago. The elderly couple standing beside them lives in Reno. The two backpackers have journeyed from Poland. A man who survived the war has come from Hanoi. You hear more hometowns: Shanghai, Dallas, Montreal, Berlin, Boston. "Philadelphia," a woman admits. "I never wanted to be a tourist in my own town. But this is Ben Franklin. He was quite a guy."

The woman kneels and gently places her coin on his grave. As at a shrine, the offering is an act of connection. Every generation discovers Benjamin Franklin for themselves. We can each of us choose to be his inheritor.

The tributary of small deposits flows throughout the day. Knowing what you now know, it looks like we have come to pay Benjamin Franklin back, one penny, one page, at a time.

Acknowledgments

This book would not have been possible without two of Benjamin Franklin's favorite things: libraries and philanthropy. After researching my previous books in China, I gained a new appreciation for the importance of conserving the past and the crucial role archivists and librarians play in preserving an open society. Thanks to the staff at the American Philosophical Society, the Philadelphia City Archives, the Pennsylvania State Archives, the University of Pittsburgh Barco Law Library, the Massachusetts Historical Society, and the City of Boston Archives, where the incomparable Marta Crilly and Meghan Pipp proved invaluable. I am also indebted to the Library of Congress and grateful for encouragement from David Ferriero, archivist of the United States. The National Archives Founders Online collection also proved instrumental, as did the astounding Papers of Benjamin Franklin website, produced by the American Philosophical Society, Yale University, and the Packard Humanities Institute.

Although I literally live in Mr. Rogers's neighborhood, a tight-knit corner of Pittsburgh imbued with his kindness, I also live in a place enriched by Andrew Carnegie's fortune. From my Squirrel Hill home, I can walk to two fantastic Carnegie libraries, whose staff deserve raises.

As do the faculty at Boston's Benjamin Franklin Institute of Technology, whose teaching perpetuates Franklin's desire to be useful. Thank you, Tony Benoit, for welcoming me into such an inspiring school.

I am also grateful that this research allowed me to come to know Boston and Philadelphia. Why Franklin felt such affection for his hometowns—along with London, where I teach each summer—is obvious to anyone who gets to explore and experience them. Thanks to Boston's Richard Allen and Richard D'Onofrio for generously sharing their time and memories, and to Tracey Gordon, Philadelphia's register of wills, who graciously allowed images of Franklin's will to be reproduced for the first time.

Like Franklin, my life has been indelibly shaped by public service, from teaching in urban elementary schools to volunteering with the Peace Corps. In 1995, it sent this Spanish speaker to China, a path that eventually (thanks to an invitation issued by Jeff Prescott and his wife, Susan Jakes) brought me to the State Department and that fateful table. Thank you, Susie and Jeff! Invite me to the White House or the United Nations, and let's see what I touch next.

Shortly after attending that first lunch, my research was informed by reading a 1995 dissertation by Bruce Yenawine at the University of Syracuse, describing Franklin as a forefather of microfinance. I am also indebted to the Highmark Blue Shield Living Legacy Series oral history project of Harrisburg, Pennsylvania, for which the late Ann Durr Lyon interviewed Walter Lyon. As a lifelong civil rights campaigner, she, too, would have fit into Franklin's orbit.

My many trips to archives were funded by the National Endowment for the Humanities Public Scholars program, as well as the University of Pittsburgh's Special Initiatives to Promote Scholarly Activities in the Humanities. MacDowell provided seclusion in its Barnard studio. Edward and Marian MacDowell's conservators have ensured that residents receive the greatest gift of all: time. The great food and ample firewood fueled me, too.

Thanks to Georges Borchardt, Peter Hessler, William Lychack, and Stephen Platt for critical readings of early drafts. I am also indebted to Michael Goettig for sharing his legal knowledge, along with Prince and Replacements bootlegs, and our usual Vikings misery.

Adam Hochschild asks his Berkeley writing students how many of them have ever read a nonfiction book that they wished were longer. No one ever raises their hand. Adam's comments greatly trimmed down this book's manuscript. If it still felt long, then spare a thought for its incomparable editor, Alexander Littlefield, who had to slog through its first iterations. Thank you, Alex, on behalf of us all. In Zach Phillips I found a trusty Sentence Guy, and in Barbara Jatkola a copy editor extraordinaire. The three of you are credits to your (often thankless) trade.

Like Franklin, I, too, enjoyed the good fortune of having a partner who did not write me off at first ridiculous sight. (Instead of bread, I carried lesson plans.) Frances, you remain my everything. Thank you for reading an early draft, and for putting up with these years of research. Although, it was you who first told me to read Franklin's will. 活该. 嘿！我爱你.

Benji, here is more proof that the man whose name you share was more than the dude who flew his kite into lightning. He was multilingual, at home on both sides of the ocean, and a diplomat, scientist, and writer who, in addition to his great works, once penned an essay on farts, as well as an epitaph for a squirrel: "Here Skugg / Lies snug / As a Bug / In a Rug." Like you, he was the son of a first-generation immigrant. Already you share his insatiable curiosity, his empathy for others, a quick wit, and the ability to laugh at yourself. Your mother and I cannot wait to see what you will contribute to the common good. You remain our lightning rod of pride and affection.

Time Line of Benjamin Franklin's Life and Afterlife

LIFE

1706: Born in Boston on January 17

1716: Ends formal schooling to begin work at his father Josiah's candle shop

1718: Starts as an apprentice printer under his brother James

1722: Writes Silence Dogood essays

1723: Runs away to Philadelphia and meets Deborah Read

1724: Sent to London on an errand by the Pennsylvania colonial governor; marooned; works there as a printer

1728: Opens his own printshop in Philadelphia

1730: William born; common-law marriage with Deborah

1732: Begins publishing *Poor Richard's Almanack;* Francis (Franky) born

1736: Organizes the first fire department and the first American tax abatement for charitable work; made clerk of the Pennsylvania Assembly; Franky dies of smallpox

1737: Appointed postmaster of Philadelphia

1741: Designs fuel-efficient stove

1743: Founds the American Philosophical Society; Sarah (Sally) born

1748: Retires from printing

1749: Appointed president of the Philadelphia Academy, which becomes the University of Pennsylvania

1751: Elected to the Pennsylvania Assembly; invents the matching grant to build the Pennsylvania Hospital

1752: Invents the lightning rod; with William, performs the famous kite experiment

1753: Appointed joint postmaster for the American colonies

1755: Outfits British general Edward Braddock for his campaign to present-day Pittsburgh in the French and Indian War

1757: Final edition of *Poor Richard's Almanack;* arrives in London for the second time, as the agent of the Pennsylvania Assembly; lodges at 36 Craven Street, the only Franklin home standing today

1759: Receives honorary doctorate from the University of St. Andrews; becomes known as "Dr. Franklin"

1760: Illegitimate grandson William Temple Franklin (Temple) born in London

1762: Leaves London for Philadelphia; son William appointed royal governor of New Jersey

1764: Loses reelection to the Pennsylvania Assembly; returns to London for the third and final time, representing colonial interests before the Crown

1765: Opposes the Stamp Act, leading to its repeal in 1766

1769: Grandson Benjamin Franklin Bache (Benny) born in Philadelphia

1771: Begins writing his autobiography

1774: A year after the Boston Tea Party, admits in London to releasing the letters of Massachusetts colonial governor Thomas Hutchinson; publicly censured and stripped of his job as colonial joint postmaster general; Deborah dies, in Philadelphia

1775: Leaves London for Philadelphia; elected to the Second Continental Congress; helps draft the first Articles of Confederation

1776: Signs the Declaration of Independence; son William imprisoned; sails to France as American commissioner

1777: Settles in Passy (in today's 16th arrondissement) with grandsons Temple and Benny

1778: Negotiates and signs the Treaty of Alliance with France

1782–1783: Negotiates and signs the Treaty of Paris with Britain

1785: Reads Charles-Joseph Mathon de la Cour's *Testament de M. Fortuné Ricard;* sees William, briefly, for the last time, when his ship calls at an English port on his return to Philadelphia

1787: Participates in the Constitutional Convention; elected president of the Pennsylvania Society for Promoting the Abolition of Slavery

1790: Submits the first petition to Congress calling for an end to slavery; dies in Philadelphia on April 17 at the age of eighty-four

AFTERLIFE

1790: Senate refuses to grieve for Franklin; France declares three days of mourning

1791: Franklin's American eulogy finally delivered; Boston and Philadelphia each accept $4,444.44 to establish his loan scheme; first Franklin loans disbursed; Benny uses his inheritance to begin his career as a newspaper publisher

1792: Sally auctions off items at Franklin Court, sells diamonds from Louis XVI's portrait, and travels to London

1798: Benny becomes first American charged under the Alien and Sedition Acts; dies during yellow fever epidemic in Philadelphia

1808: Daughter Sally dies, in Philadelphia

1811: William Minot begins his fifty-five-year reign as treasurer of Boston's Franklin Fund

1813: Son William dies, in London; Edinburgh chemist John Scott's bequest to Philadelphia doubles the amount of money available to Franklin borrowers

1816: Temple finally begins publishing his edited volumes of Franklin's papers

1823: Grandson Temple dies, in Paris

1824: Franklin Institute for the Promotion of the Mechanic Arts founded in Philadelphia

1827: Minot makes first deposit of Franklin's money into Nathaniel Bowditch's Massachusetts Hospital Life Insurance Company

1828: Boston's Franklin Fund balance passes Philadelphia's for the first time, never to trail it again

1830: *Harvard College v. Amory* establishes the "Prudent Person Rule" concerning trusts

1831: Historian Jared Sparks, hunting for the originals of Franklin's papers, finds caches in a Philadelphia stable and being cut into patterns in a London tailor's shop; America's richest man, the shipbuilder Stephen Girard, dies, leaving most of his estate to Philadelphia

1838: Philadelphia's Franklin Legacy treasurer John Thomason purchases Philadelphia Gas Works stock, further impeding the money's growth when the company becomes a tool of corruption and patronage

1856: Boston celebrates the sesquicentennial of Franklin's birth with a public holiday and parade

1858: A fence of iron bars installed in a portion of Philadelphia's Christ Church Burial Ground's wall; tourists flock to see Franklin's grave

1890: Franklin's descendants file suit claiming his bequests to Boston and Philadelphia should revert to their control

1893: Boston publicly debates how to spend Franklin's centennial gift

1895: Boston's city treasurer refuses to relinquish Franklin's money to build a trades school

1898: In another round of public hearings, Bostonians argue that the school should be modeled on New York City's Cooper Union

1904: Andrew Carnegie agrees to match Franklin's gift to Boston

1908: The Boston trades school, Franklin Union, finally opens

1934: Franklin's centennial gift to Philadelphia at last used, to build the new Franklin Institute science museum

1938: In Philadelphia, George Wharton Pepper dedicates what will become the Benjamin Franklin National Memorial

1939: Philadelphia court adjusts Franklin's loan requirements, allowing women to apply for the first time

1948: Philadelphia permits Franklin loans to help fund first-time home buyers

1958: Sputnik-induced frenzy leads to attempt to disburse Franklin's bicentennial gift early to Boston's Franklin school to train mechanics and engineers

1962: Boston's Franklin Fund begins approving loans to medical students

1974: Walter Lyon begins his quixotic attempt to steer Philadelphia's Franklin Legacy to build an archive cataloguing records related to the preservation of Pennsylvania's environment

1990: Philadelphia proposes spending Franklin's money on a series of concerts and celebrations; after a public outcry, his legacy is divided between local and state philanthropic foundations and the Franklin Institute

1994: After losing a court ruling, Boston's Franklin school nonetheless receives the entirety of his bicentennial gift

2019: Boston's Franklin school announces plans to sell its historic South End campus and construct a larger, modern one in Roxbury

Notes

ABBREVIATIONS

APS: American Philosophical Society, Philadelphia.
BCA: Boston City Archives.
BFP: Benjamin Franklin Papers.
LOC: Library of Congress.
MHS: Massachusetts Historical Society, Boston.
NA: National Archives.
PCA: Philadelphia City Archives.
PSA: Pennsylvania State Archives.

Most of the Franklin citations can be found in *The Papers of Benjamin Franklin,* a series of forty-three volumes published since 1959 by Yale University Press. Its invaluable website, FranklinPapers.org, allows users to search the massive haystacks of Franklin's correspondence by date, name, or phrase. I found many sought-for needles there and discovered more that I did not know existed. Documents found in this archive that were written by Franklin, including his wills, are cited in the notes without his name. References to letters to and from Franklin include only the correspondent's name, not Franklin's. Other letters include both correspondents' names.

Another trove of correspondence can be found at Founders Online—Founders. Archives.gov. In addition to listing all the published and unpublished materials that I mined, the bibliography includes a list of newspapers, along with the full names of court cases involving Franklin's will, as well as collections of papers.

Introduction: All About the Benjamins

PAGE

xiii   *"account of the universal":* Letter to John Bartram, Jan. 11, 1770, BFP.

Packets of Chinese rice: Letter to John Bartram, Oct. 17, 1772, BFP.

scored the margins: "Notes on Reading an Account of Travel in China," 1762, BFP.

xv   *"the Wise and Brave":* Poor Richard Improved, 1751, BFP.

xvii   *"Benjamins":* The term appears on the 1994 Notorious B.I.G. album *Ready to Die;* Puff Daddy and the Family popularized it further in their 1997 song "It's All About the Benjamins."

xviii   *From London in 1774:* Letter to Richard Bache, Sept. 30, 1774, BFP.

"Intrigues with low Women": Franklin, *Autobiography,* p. 52.

selling enslaved men and women: One such notice read: "A likely young Negro Fellow, about 19 or 20 Years of Age, to be disposed of: He is very fit for Labour, being us'd to Plantation Work, and has had the Small-Pox. Enquire of the Printer hereof." May 11, 1732, BFP.

"the Mother": The author was the cave-dwelling dwarf Benjamin Lay. Lay, p. 106.

xix   *at the time:* Rather than obfuscating his grandfather's slave owning, Temple Franklin placed on the first page of a volume of Benjamin's collected papers a letter from Franklin to his mother about an incident involving two slaves at his home. "We conclude to sell them both," the letter ended, "for we do not like Negro Servants. We got again about half what we lost." Letter to Abiah Franklin, Apr. 12, 1750, BFP.

"a King of England": Letter to James Lovell, Oct. 17, 1779, BFP.

submitted the first petition: For the original document, see "Benjamin Franklin's Anti-Slavery Petitions to Congress," Center for Legislative Archives, NA, https://www.archives.gov/legislative/features/franklin. Franklin did not write the text, but he signed it. See Letter from James Pemberton, Feb. 5, 1790, BFP.

"In order to secure": Franklin, *Autobiography,* p. 50.

"I have frequently": Poor Richard Improved, 1758, BFP.

xx   *"Do not make it":* Letter to [John Franklin], Dec. 25, 1750, BFP.

"Silk," he wrote: Pennsylvania Gazette, Oct. 19, 1752. The experiment took place in June. Joseph Priestley's book *The History and Present State of Electricity* was published in 1767.

"I Sopose you See": Letter from Jane Mecom, Nov. 11, 1788, BFP.

xxi   *"sacred and undeniable":* For the draft, see "Thomas Jefferson: Declaration of Independence," LOC, https://www.loc.gov/exhibits/jefferson/jeffdec.html. For a pithy account of the Declaration's editing process, see Isaacson, pp. 309–313.

"A republic": The exchange may be apocryphal. See "Creating the United States: 'Monarchy or a Republic?,'" LOC, http://www.loc.gov/exhibits/creating-the-united-states/convention-and-ratification.html#obj8.

"an appearance that promises": Letter to the French scientist Jean-Baptiste LeRoy, Nov. 13, 1789, BFP. Franklin did not, in fact, coin the famous phrase, which perhaps originated in Daniel Defoe's *The Political History of the Devil* (1726).

xxii *"Sense being preferable"*: Letter to Richard Price, Mar. 18, 1785, BFP.

"My timepiece": Will and Codicil, June 23, 1789, BFP. All quotations from Franklin's will are from this source unless otherwise noted.

"Bad Commentators": Poor Richard's Almanack, 1735, BFP.

xxiii *"The slightest events"*: Abbé Martin Lefebvre de la Roche to C. Pierre Didot, n.d., BFP.

1. *"My earnest desire to be useful"*

4 *"It is impossible"*: Federal Gazette, Apr. 19, 1790.

"to need any attempt": Massachusetts Centinal, Apr. 28, 1790.

"discharged a great quantity": Pennsylvania Gazette, Apr. 21, 1790. The physician was John Jones.

5 *twice as long*: Demographers place the average American life span in 1790 between thirty-five and thirty-eight years, a number skewed by an infant mortality rate estimated between 40 and 50 percent. If an American man made it to age sixty-five, he lived an average of another ten years. Franklin made it an additional nineteen.

dabbled in vegetarianism: Franklin, *Autobiography,* p. 27.

book-filled suitcase: Abbé Martin Lefebvre de la Roche to C. Pierre Didot, n.d., BFP.

"the Water-American": Franklin, *Autobiography,* p. 34.

"I rise early": Letter to Jacques Barbeu-Dubourg, July 28, 1768, BFP.

the common cold: "Notes on Colds," 1773, BFP.

"I was afraid": Adams, vol. 3, p. 75.

6 *Adams resented*: "From John Adams to Benjamin Rush, 4 April 1790," Founders Online, NA.

"Congress yesterday": "From James Madison to Thomas Jefferson, 11 February 1783," NA.

"The History of our Revolution": "From John Adams to Benjamin Rush, 4 April 1790," NA.

7 *dangerous tonic*: Letter to Jan Ingenhousz, Apr. 29, 1785, BFP.

former Parisian neighbors: Letter to Rodolphe-Ferdinand Grand, June 7, 1788, BFP.

8 *"Ambition and Avarice"*: Convention Speech on Salaries, June 2, 1787, BFP.

"was treated with great respect": Madison, p. 55.

refusing to be paid: From David Redick: Order to Pay Benjamin Franklin's Final Salary, Oct. 27, 1788, BFP.

"£2250 paper money": "Executor's Papers of Benjamin Franklin's Estate," APS.

accounting for inflation: "Inflation Calculator," U.S. Official Inflation Data, Alioth Finance, http://www.officialdata.org/us/inflation. I used this website, which calculates monetary equivalency based on the U.S. Department of Labor's records of inflation, for all equivalencies. Calculations made in August 2021.

"the Truth": Franklin, *Autobiography,* p. 85.

he overturned: "Benjamin Franklin," U.S. Postal Service, https://about.usps .com/who-we-are/postal-history/pmg-franklin.pdf.

9   *"diligently employed"*: Letter to Benjamin Vaughan, Oct. 24, 1788, BFP.

"I grew convinc'd": Franklin, *Autobiography,* pp. 43–44.

"all facts": Ibid.

"the youngest Son": Franklin, *Autobiography,* p. 3.

"Whereby I find": Letter to Mary Fisher, July 31, 1758, BFP.

"were so covered": Letters to Deborah Franklin, Feb. 19 and Sept. 6, 1758, BFP.

10   *"a practice which"*: Letter to John Langdon, Apr. 4, 1788, BFP.

run away, unpursued: King absconded in England. An unbothered Franklin wrote Deborah that the man was sheltered by a woman in Suffolk, who converted him to Christianity, "sent him to School, [had] him taught to read and write, [and] to play on the Violin and French Horn." Letter to Deborah Franklin, June 27, 1760, BFP.

It would not: Waldstreicher, p. 239. Bob may have been the "Negro Man" listed on Franklin's son-in-law's 1779 state tax roll (held at the Philadelphia City Archives) whose value was sickeningly assessed at £7.80.

"My Constitution": Letter to Joseph Priestley, May 31, 1789, BFP.

"My Friends drop off": Letter to Richard Price, May 31, 1789, BFP.

An invoice: "Executor's Papers of Benjamin Franklin's Estate," APS.

11   *"It has taken away"*: Letter to Louis-Guillaume Le Veillard, Sept. 5, 1789, BFP.

12   *Franklin's ethical lending scheme:* Yenawine, p. 2. The concepts of microcredit and microfinance are commonly credited to the 2006 Nobel Prize–winning economist Muhammad Yunus, who pioneered the use of small loans in rural Bangladesh.

13   *"Blessed is he"*: *Poor Richard's Almanack,* 1739, BFP.

"Remember that Time": "Advice to a Young Tradesman, Written by an Old One," July 21, 1748, BFP.

"As to the Pain": Letter to Jane Mecom, July 1, 1789, BFP.

14   *"You know you were"*: Letter to Jane Franklin, Jan. 6, 1727, BFP.

"I have lately": Letter to Jane Mecom, Dec. 17, 1789, BFP.

curmudgeonly complained: Letter to Noah Webster, Dec. 26, 1789, BFP.

"This Day": Letter from Jane Mecom, Jan. 17, 1790, BFP.

his signed petition: Its text was nearly identical to the statement of principle Franklin had intended to deliver at the Constitutional Convention. The

Pennsylvania Society for Promoting the Abolition of Slavery, along with northern delegates, had urged Franklin to stand down there. Ellis, p. 110. The day before Franklin's action, two separate Quaker-penned petitions called on Congress to open an inquiry on the "licentious wickedness" of the slave trade. *"consent to the Federal Compact":* Waldstreicher, p. 236. The senator was Pierce Butler. For an account of the congressional debate, see Ohline.

15   *"blow the trumpet":* Nash, *Race and Revolution,* p. 39, quoting James Jackson.
a constitutional clause: Article 1, section 9, clause 1: "The Migration or Importation of such Persons as any of the States now existing shall think proper to admit, shall not be prohibited by the Congress prior to the Year one thousand eight hundred and eight, but a Tax or duty may be imposed on such Importation, not exceeding ten dollars for each Person."
"The firmness": Waldstreicher, p. 237.
"Even great men": Ellis, p. 112.
"Reading last night": Benjamin Franklin to the *Federal Gazette,* Mar. 23, 1790, BFP.

16   *"Tho' at the time":* Benjamin Franklin Bache to Margaret H. Markoe, May 2, 1790, APS.
"perfectly clear": Letter to Thomas Jefferson, Apr. 8, 1790, BFP.
"his conversation": Rush, *Letters of Benjamin Rush,* p. 564.
"I hope not": Ibid.
"From that day": Benjamin Franklin Bache to Margaret H. Markoe, May 2, 1790, APS.

17   *"A dying man":* Rush, *Letters of Benjamin Rush,* p. 564.
"Whenever I approached": Benjamin Franklin Bache to Margaret H. Markoe, May 2, 1790, APS.
"My duty calls": Richard Bache to Jane Mecom, Apr. 19, 1790, BFP.
"He while living": Jane Mecom to Sarah Bache, Sept. 6, 1790, in Van Doren, *Letters,* p. 342. Van Doren's compendium includes correspondence in its original form, along with letters—like this one—whose spelling and punctuation had been corrected by other historians.
"I think there is": Benjamin Franklin Bache to Margaret H. Markoe, May 2, 1790, APS.

2. The Foundation of His Fortune

18   *"It is recommended":* Pennsylvania Gazette, Apr. 21, 1790.
An estimated 20,000: Pennsylvania Gazette, Apr. 28, 1790.
minute guns: The noise must have been cacophonous: "There is among the State papers at Harrisburg, a bill for £22 9s 8d paid for the powder, etc. employed by the artillery on this occasion." *Philadelphia Press,* Aug. 25, 1859, p. 1.

"*Clergy of the city*": Pennsylvania Gazette, Apr. 28, 1790.

Franklin had helped save: Green, "This Day in Jewish History."

19   *using a kite:* Lemay, vol. 3, p. 104.

"*Were I*": Letter to Deborah Franklin, July 17, 1757, BFP.

"*It is the first*": Letter to Ezra Stiles, Mar. 9, 1790, BFP.

20   "*His Sermons*": Franklin, *Autobiography*, p. 77.

"*that Faith*": Pennsylvania Gazette, Apr. 10, 1735.

"*Serving God*": Poor Richard's Almanack, 1753, BFP.

"*I stuck by him*": Franklin, *Autobiography*, p. 77.

"*Don't throw stones*": Poor Richard's Almanack, 1736, BFP.

"*The frequent*": Poor Richard Improved, 1758, BFP.

21   "*My child*": Price, p. 133.

22   "*It is full*": Letter from Benjamin Vaughan, Feb. 23, 1785, BFP.

"*the* Testament": Letter to Benjamin Vaughan, Mar. 5, 1785, BFP.

"*I am glad*": Letter to Benjamin Vaughan, Apr. 21, 1785, BFP.

23   "*During the last*": Letter from Charles-Joseph Mathon de la Cour, June 30, 1785, BFP.

"*Reading it*": Letter to Charles-Joseph Mathon de la Cour, July 9, 1785, BFP. Translation from French by the author.

"*It is right*": Letter to Charles-Joseph Mathon de la Cour, Nov. 18, 1785, BFP.

Only three years: Rose, p. 36.

24   *borne by "citizens"*: Pennsylvania Gazette, Apr. 28, 1790.

with boys bathing: "Pennsylvania Weather Records," pp. 109–121.

25   *looking "sturdy"*: Van Doren, *Benjamin Franklin*, p. 94.

"*rather plain*": Isaacson, p. 43.

"*husky good looks*": Ibid.

"*loud*": Wood, p. 90.

"*untaught*": Van Doren, *Benjamin Franklin*, p. 94.

"*the prospect*": Isaacson, p. 43.

shift of tow: Poor Richard's Almanack, 1733, BFP.

"*A Man*": Reply to a Piece of Advice, Mar. 4, 1735, BFP.

26   "*sufficient tho'*": Franklin, *Autobiography*, p. 94.

"*I Benjamin*": "Power of Attorney to Deborah Franklin," Aug. 30, 1733, BFP.

"*I discovered*": Aldridge, p. 209.

"*Now twelve Years*": "I Sing My Plain Country Joan," c. 1742, BFP.

"*She proved*": Franklin, *Autobiography*, pp. 52–53.

27   "*so verey poor*": Letter from Deborah Franklin, Sept. 22, 1765, BFP.

"*large fine Jugg*": Letter to Deborah Franklin, Feb. 19, 1758, BFP.

"*near 300 miles*": Franklin, *Autobiography*, p. 18.

28   "*generally thought*": Ibid., p. 52.

"*no Credit*": Ibid., p. 33.

"*the shameful place*": Dickens, *Great Expectations,* pp. 165–166. The printshop was on Bartholomew Close. Franklin lodged on the lane called Little Britain. You can still walk the same streets today, though one of the only structures that remains from Franklin's time is St. Bartholomew's Gatehouse.

Pennsylvania law sentenced: Fry, p. 176.

29   *"I took her":* Franklin, *Autobiography,* p. 52.

"*Whereas on Saturday*": *Pennsylvania Gazette,* Nov. 1, 1750.

30   *his penultimate will:* Last Will and Testament, Apr. 28, 1757, BFP.

fear of the ocean: Fry, p. 172.

"*invincible aversion*": Letter to Deborah Franklin, Mar. 5, 1760, BFP.

31   *In a 1759 letter:* Letter from Deborah Franklin, Aug. 9, 1759, BFP.

"*What Room*": Letter to Deborah Franklin, Aug. 1765, BFP.

"*Very busy*": Letter to Deborah Franklin, Apr. 18, 1765, BFP.

"*I love to hear*": Letter from Deborah Franklin, Sept. 22, 1765, BFP.

32   *"Dear Debby":* Letter to Deborah Franklin, Nov. 9, 1765, BFP.

33   *"I have bin":* Letter from Deborah Franklin, Oct. 8, 1765, BFP.

"*I am just now*": Letter to Deborah Franklin, Feb. 22, 1766, BFP.

"*As the Stamp Act*": Letter to Deborah Franklin, Apr. 6, 1766, BFP.

"*We are*": Letter to Deborah Franklin, Dec. 21, 1768–Jan. 26, 1769, BFP.

34   *"distresed att":* Letter from Deborah Franklin, Nov. 20, 1769, BFP.

"*I have not*": Letter from Deborah Franklin, Aug. 31, 1769, BFP.

35   *"The People rave":* Mather, pp. 631–632.

"*Inoculation was*": *Pennsylvania Gazette,* Dec. 30, 1736.

"*and tell him*": Letter from Deborah Franklin, June 13, 1770, BFP.

"*All who have*": Letter to Jane Mecom, Jan. 13, 1772, BFP.

36   *"Don't be surprised":* Abbé Martin Lefebvre de la Roche to C. Pierre Didot, n.d., BFP.

37   *"a total disunion":* Letter to the Massachusetts House of Representatives, May 15, 1771, BFP.

"*I have had*": Letter to Deborah Franklin, July 22, 1774, BFP.

"*Honoured Father*": Letter from William Franklin, Dec. 24, 1774, BFP.

38   *"Our English Enemies":* Letter to Marie-Anne Pierette Paulze Lavoisier, Oct. 23, 1788, BFP.

"*The Body*": Franklin, Epitaph and Adieu, 1728, BFP.

3. Franklin's Inheritors

40   *"badges of mourning":* "From Thomas Jefferson to Benjamin Rush, 4 October 1803," Founders Online, NA.

41   *"fell a Sacrifice at last":* Adams, vol. 3, pp. 417–420.

"Secrecy! Cunning!": "From John Adams to Benjamin Rush, 23 July 1806," Founders Online, NA.

"native genius": Journal of the House of Representatives of the United States, Washington, DC, 1826, vol. 1, p. 198. My account of the government's reaction to Franklin's death is drawn from "Editorial Note: Death of Franklin," Founders Online, NA.

"You will see": "From Thomas Jefferson to William Short, 27 April 1790," Founders Online, NA.

"an Officer": Letter to George Washington, May 29, 1777, BFP.

42   *eight people:* Pulaski died in a charge into British lines in 1779. The half dozen other honorary Americans are Bernardo de Gálvez, William and Hannah Penn, Raoul Wallenberg, Winston Churchill, and Mother Teresa.

"You Have Ennemies": Letter from Lafayette, Feb. 1, 1781, BFP.

"You mention": Letter to Lafayette, Mar. 14, 1781, BFP.

"Many People": Letter from Sarah Bache, Jan. 14, 1781, BFP.

"My fine": The cane had been a gift, Franklin wrote, from "Madame de Forbach, the dowager Duchess of Deux-Ponts."

43   *Louis XVI confessed:* Schiff, p. 397. In the United States, the French king was honored by the settlers who founded Louisville, Kentucky. In 2020, the city's nine-ton marble statue of him was vandalized and removed to storage.

"a Grant": Letter to Charles Thomson, Dec. 29, 1788, BFP.

"But in America": Ibid.

"How I miss you": Letter from Louis-Guillaume Le Veillard, July 22, 1789, BFP.

44   *"a Disposition":* From Benjamin Franklin: Queries and Remarks on "Hints for the Members of Pennsylvania Convention," Nov. 3, 1789, BFP.

45   *"drape arms":* Maclay, p. 246.

"To the town": Massachusetts Centinal, May 5, 1790, p. 1.

46   *pluralistic center:* Baltzell, p. 192.

"Boston was": Ibid., quoting Henry Adams, the great-grandson of John Adams.

its inverse: Wood, p. 219.

"Phyladelphia with all": Diary and Autobiography of John Adams, Oct. 9, 1774, Founders Online, NA.

47   *"a Patent for":* Franklin, *Autobiography,* p. 92.

considered a forefather: DeFeo.

48   *Maryland State House was saved:* Huang, "Saved by the Lightning Rod."

shift his gaze: Letter to George Whatley, May 23, 1785, BFP.

"Reflecting yesterday": Letter to John Franklin, Dec. 8, 1752, BFP.

some two hundred residents: Lemay, vol. 3, p. 629.

Franklin paid the city: Ibid.

Other Philadelphians: Ibid., pp. 629–633.

49   *valued by Rittenhouse:* "Executor's Papers of Benjamin Franklin's Estate," APS.

"A fat Kitchen": Poor Richard Improved, 1758, BFP.

"Life, like": Letter to George Whitefield, July 2, 1756, BFP.

A well-written will: Chaplin, p. 336.

50 *"I hear my":* Jane Mecom to Sarah Bache, Dec. 2, 1790, in Van Doren, *Letters,* p. 343.

"The Public Curiosity": Benjamin Franklin Bache to Margaret H. Markoe, May 2, 1790, APS.

"crossing the Seine": Abbé Martin Lefebvre de la Roche to C. Pierre Didot, n.d., BFP.

"very different": Dorcas Armitage Montgomery to Sarah Franklin Bache, July 26, 1783, APS.

"I learn to Print": Benjamin Franklin Bache to His Papa and Mama, Dec. 27, 1783, APS.

51 *"He is a very sensible":* Letter to Richard Bache, Nov. 11, 1784, BFP.

in a mansion: Le Ray de Chaumont's Hôtel de Valentinois. A plaque at the corner of rue Raynouard and rue Singer marks the spot.

watched demonstrations: Benjamin Franklin Bache to His Papa and Mama, Oct. 30, 1783, APS.

"presented his knuckle": The Kite Experiment: Priestley's Account, BFP.

52 *"I was enable":* William Franklin to Sarah Franklin, Oct. 10, 1761, BFP.

"since it has not": Letter to William Franklin, Feb. 18, 1774, BFP.

"to a Country": Letter from William Franklin, Dec. 24, 1774, BFP.

"I suffer so much": William Franklin to Gov. Jonathan Trumbull, Sept. 15, 1777, *Proceedings of the New Jersey Historical Society,* p. 47.

George Washington denied: "To George Washington from William Franklin, 22 July 1777," Founders Online, NA. William remembered his wife, Elizabeth Downes Franklin, with a plaque at Lower Manhattan's St. Paul's Chapel, where she was buried.

53 *"Free Man":* Letter to William Franklin, Aug. 1, 1774, BFP.

54 *granted by the Crown:* "Privy Council: Order for a Grant of Land for Benjamin Franklin, June 26, 1767," BFP.

William thought: Skemp, p. 273.

"0000": Benjamin Franklin Bache to Margaret H. Markoe, May 2, 1790, APS.

had likely flown the kite: Lemay, vol. 3, p. 108. The land is now bordered by North Tenth Street, Fairmount Avenue, and Parrish Street.

"that fortune-hunter": William Franklin to Jonathan Williams, May 11, 1791, quoted in Skemp, p. 274.

55 *"The Revolution":* Ibid.

"I want Mr. Franklin": William Temple Franklin to Thomas Jefferson, Apr. 27, 1790, BFP.

56 *"never snuffed":* Diller, pp. 22–23.

57 *"good enough":* "From Thomas Jefferson to James Monroe, 5 July 1785," Founders Online, NA.

"If during": William Temple Franklin to John Adams, Oct. 13, 1790, BFP.

"A certain ardor": John Adams to William Temple Franklin, Oct. 16, 1790, BFP.

"No sentiment": "From John Adams to *Boston Patriot*, 8 November 1810," Founders Online, NA.

58   *"A Mob's a Monster"*: *Poor Richard's Almanack,* 1747, BFP.

"Franklin est mort": Aldridge, p. 213.

seconded: Van Doren, *Benjamin Franklin,* p. 781.

59   *"Could I have"*: Aldridge, p. 218. The speaker was Louis-Alexandre La Rochefoucauld, with whom Franklin had translated into French the American state constitutions. During the Reign of Terror, aristocrat-hunters stoned La Rochefoucauld to death and disemboweled him in front of his family.

"One man is dead": Ibid., p. 231. The doctor, Félix Vicq-d'Azyr, was also killed in the Terror.

"Franklin was born": Ibid., pp. 232–233.

"Having been poor": *Poor Richard's Almanack,* 1749, BFP.

was a gift: "Statue of Benj. Franklin to Be Erected in Paris," *New York Journal and Advertiser,* July 26, 1899.

4. The Morals of Chess

60   *"The extracts"*: *Gazette of the United States,* May 29, 1790.

"every step": Boston City Document No. 89, 1866, p. 173, BCA.

"that the Mayor": "Common Council Resolution, July 12, 1790," in "Executor's Papers of Benjamin Franklin's Estate," APS.

61   *"One of the greatest"*: Letter to Jane Mecom, Apr. 19, 1757, BFP.

unknowingly step: Lepore, *Book of Ages,* p. 262.

"My dear brother": Jane Mecom to Sarah Bache, Sept. 6, 1790, in Van Doren, *Letters,* p. 342.

"satisfied with nothing": Defoe, p. 5.

"sincere Thanks": Last Will and Testament, Apr. 28, 1757, BFP.

62   *"Had the Doctor"*: Elias Boudinot to Benjamin Rush, Apr. 28, 1790, BFP.

"undertake the Management": To Samuel Johnson, Aug. 9, 1750, BFP.

"You have never": Letter to John Franklin, Jan. 2, 1753, BFP.

63   *"nobody would"*: Letter from Samuel Johnson, Nov. 1750, BFP.

"Many of the debts": "Pennsylvania Hospital, 13 July, 1790," in "Executor's Papers of Benjamin Franklin's Estate," APS.

"Public Education": From Benjamin Franklin: Tract Relative to the English School in Philadelphia, BFP. Trustee Robert Hare's letter to the executor is dated May 21, 1791. For his response to Franklin, see Letter from Robert Hare, July 14, 1789, BFP.

After raising £2,000: Isaacson, p. 147. In his memoir, Franklin erroneously reported raising £5,000. Franklin, *Autobiography,* p. 92.

65 *"do not enquire":* "Information to Those Who Would Remove to America," Mar. 9, 1784, BFP.

"among the decorated": Abbé Martin Lefebvre de la Roche to C. Pierre Didot, n.d., BFP.

66 *"Among my Books":* Letter to Deborah Franklin, Apr. 29, 1757, BFP.

"Chess is not": "The Morals of Chess," written before June 28, 1779, reprinted from the *Columbian Magazine,* Dec. 1786, BFP.

67 *"We must not":* Letter to Pierre-Samuel du Pont de Nemours, June 9, 1788, BFP.

"You know we have": "Report of George Beckwith, 10 Nov. 1790," in "Editorial Note: Death of Franklin," Founders Online, NA.

"looked over": Maclay, p. 350.

68 *a "coldness":* Ibid., pp. 379–380.

"the memory": Federal Gazette, Mar. 5, 1791.

"It is the first": "Otto to Montmorin, 4 Apr. 1791," in "Editorial Note: Death of Franklin," Founders Online, NA.

69 *"I am of [the] opinion":* "From Thomas Jefferson to Henry Lee, 13 August 1792," Founders Online, NA.

"There is a French interest": "From John Adams to John Trumbull, 31 March 1791," Founders Online, NA.

"I wish you": Letter from Jonathan Trumbull, Apr. 12, 1780, BFP.

70 *"As to you":* Letter from John Trumbull, Nov. 25, 1789, BFP.

"I must beg": Letter from Samuel Johnson, Jan. 1752, BFP.

"totally ignorant": "From John Adams to Thomas Jefferson, February–3 March 1814," Founders Online, NA.

71 *Pennsylvania Assembly:* The colonial body was called the Pennsylvania Provincial Assembly. Since 1776, the state legislature has been called the Pennsylvania General Assembly. Both are referred to simply as the Pennsylvania Assembly in this book.

"I luckily": "From George Washington to Mary Ball Washington, 18 July 1755," Founders Online, NA.

"Those who": "Pennsylvania Assembly: Reply to the Governor," Nov. 11, 1755, BFP.

"always did": Middlekauff, p. 50.

"love your Enemies": Poor Richard Improved, 1756, BFP.

"scribbled himself": Letter to Peter Collinson, Nov. 5, 1756, BFP.

"Smith still": Letter to Peter Collinson, June 15, 1756, BFP.

72 *"I made that Man":* Letter to Mary Stevenson, Mar. 25, 1763, BFP.

"Franklin, though plagued": Middlekauff, p. 97.

was "foul": Ibid., p. 103.

"It is certain": Silence Dogood, No. 7, *New-England Courant,* June 25, 1722, BFP.

73 *"a contemptible"*: Dexter, p. 338.

  "Citizens of Philadelphia!": Smith, *Eulogium on Benjamin Franklin.*

74 *"a habitual drunkard"*: Rush, *Autobiography,* pp. 175–179.

  "I don't think": Lopez and Herbert, p. 311.

75 *The Bank of Massachusetts:* Wallack. Interestingly, Aaron Burr founded the Bank of Manhattan in 1799, upsetting Hamilton's hold on New York finance. Burr's bank eventually merged with Chase to form Chase Manhattan, the predecessor of today's JPMorgan Chase & Co.

76 *most commonly used coin:* Larkin, p. 38.

  "Words": Letter to Mary Stevenson Hewson, May 6, 1786, BFP.

77 *"I begin"*: Letter to Sir Joseph Banks, July 27, 1783. BFP.

5. Dr. Franklin's Legacy

81 *"Dear Sir"*: George E. Kirkpatrick to Samuel McCleary, Oct. 22, 1889, Folder 0100.023, Franklin Fund Records, BCA.

82 *"Philadelphia is most bountifully"*: Dickens, *American Notes,* p. 87.

83 *"Enough has happened"*: Letter to Joseph Priestley, July 7, 1775, BFP.

  "Every mayor": Box 3, Folder 9, McCleary Family Papers, MHS.

  "Wood or other fuel": Box 2, Folder 9, McCleary Family Papers, MHS.

84 *"Is it true"*: Ibid.

  His fellow alumni: Proceedings at the Fiftieth Anniversary of the Graduation of the Class of 1841, p. 8.

86 *Pulling it open revealed:* Box 3, Folder 11, McCleary Family Papers, MHS.

  compiled a report: Boston City Document No. 89, 1866, BCA.

87 *by 1889 Boston's fund:* Franklin Financial Records, vol. 7, p. 4, BCA. The subsequent fund ledger (vol. 8, p. 50) shows a balance of $391,168.68 on the fund's centenary, July 1, 1891.

  Philadelphia's balance: Nineteenth Annual Report of the Board of Directors of City Trusts, Philadelphia, 1889, BCA.

  like money: Chaplin, pp. 110–111.

  as a metric: The website MeasuringWorth.com calculates various equivalencies of money across eras. According to calculations made in August 2021, Franklin's $4,444.44 gift to each city balloons to a value of $15 million in blue-collar wages today.

  broke ground: Indani.

88 *£100 donation:* Bell, *Benjamin Franklin on Philanthropy.*

  Franklin's bill: "Executor's Papers of Benjamin Franklin's Estate," APS.

  an itemized invoice: Ibid. The invoice is dated August 9, 1791. Cemeter-

ies could be a circular industry: After typhus killed Benjamin Rush, he was
interred near his old friend Franklin in the Christ Church Burial Ground.
That night, Rush's colleague—and an example of nominative determinism
—Dr. Physick found a burly man waiting at his door, asking, "Do you want
Dr. Rush?" He offered to dig up the body so Dr. Physick could demonstrate
dissection for his medical students. His price: £4.5. *Transactions of the College of
Physicians*, p. 401.

"*Most People*": *Poor Richard Improved*, 1751, Founder's Online, NA.

89   *Daniel Tuttle*: Franklin Financial Records, vol. 5, BCA.

90   *Samuel Etheridge reappears*: In the ledger, he is applicant number 26 and
46. Etheridge employed the future mayor Samuel Turell Armstrong, elected
in 1836. Etheridge today is recognized for his graphic design. Walsh, pp.
167–168.

His candles: Eighmey, pp. 17–19.

"*It has ever since*": Franklin, *Autobiography*, p. 9.

91   "*cutting Wick*": Ibid., p. 6.

"*I dislik'd*": Ibid., p. 7.

92   *The mayor and aldermen*: Allinson, pp. 59–61.

a patchwork fiefdom: Ibid., p. 83.

John Grant: Dr. Franklin's Legacy Bond Book No. 1, 1792–1828, p. 1, APS.

93   *The preprinted agreements*: Dr. Franklin's Legacy Account Ledger No. 1, 1791–
1870, p. 4, APS. Benny was paid $14.60 to print quires of the agreements.

on the front page: General Advertiser, Aug. 23, 1792.

"*I am sending*": Benjamin Franklin Bache to Louis-Guillaume Le Veillard, Apr.
6, 1792, BFP. Translated from French by the author.

not that unusual: Nash, *First City*, p. 61. Women also ran farms alongside men,
and in at least one instance, they banded together to dispatch their own form
of justice. After a man was found being "unreasonably abusive to his Wife,"
Franklin wrote in his *Pennsylvania Gazette*, "the Women form'd themselves
into a Court, and order'd him to be apprehended by their Officers and
brought to Tryal: being found guilty he was condemn'd to be duck'd 3 times
in a neighbouring Pond, and to have one half cut off, of his Hair and Beard
(which it seems he wore at full length) and the Sentence was accordingly executed, to the great Diversion of the Spectators." *Pennsylvania Gazette*, Apr. 17,
1735.

94   "*I am very busily*": Letter from Sarah Bache, Sept. 9, 1780, BFP.

95   "*often seen drunk*": Franklin, *Autobiography*, p. 48.

which the partner mounted: Ibid., pp. 48–49. The man, Hugh Meredith, tried
homesteading in North Carolina. He would return to Philadelphia by the end
of the decade, borrowing money from Franklin for wedding shoes, a bedstead,
and blankets. Franklin continued to loan him small amounts, noting in 1749
that Meredith was collecting rags for him. He disappeared thereafter. Lemay

notes that Franklin omitted this coda in his memoir, as he "did not want to record distress and failure." Lemay, vol. 1, p. 377.

"TO BE LET": *General Advertiser,* Aug. 23, 1792.

96   "*You know I have*": Letter to Sarah Bache, Nov. 8, 1764, BFP.

98   *their Marylebone town house:* Today the site is the Fitzrovia Hotel, on Bolsover Street.

would have been fashionable: Baetjer, p. 171. The painter was John Hoppner, a leading portraitist of the time.

"*Your sending*": Letter to Sarah Bache, June 3, 1779, BFP.

most read newspaper: Scherr, "Inventing the Patriot President," pp. 369–370.

"*behold papers*": McMaster, p. 227.

"*It is necessary*": L. Peuillet to William Temple Franklin, Jan. 29, 1792, BFP.

99   "*woman possessed*": William Franklin to Jonathan Williams, July 30, 1807, Jonathan Williams Papers, APS.

100   "*I must resign*": William Franklin to Jonathan Williams, Oct. 28, 1811, Jonathan Williams Papers, APS.

one of the city's: Adam Hains. Dr. Franklin's Legacy Account Ledger No. 1, 1791–1870, p. 2, APS.

"*exchange for Groceries*": Minardi.

"*torn off*": "From Thomas Jefferson to Benjamin Franklin Bache, 22 April 1791," Founders Online, NA.

101   "*paper begins*": "From John Adams to Abigail Adams, 2 January 1793," Founders Online, NA.

"*I wish to have*": "From George Washington to Tobias Lear, 12 April 1791," Founders Online, NA.

"*Liberty's Apostle*": *Aurora,* Dec. 29, 1795.

If Americans "have read": Cobbett, p. 294.

"*the son*": Ibid., p. 140.

"*He is an*": Ibid., p. 295.

102   "*We are all*": Benjamin Bache to William Bache, June 16, 1795, APS.

secret government document: Aurora, July 4, 1795.

"*Mr. Washington*": Rosenfeld, p. 238.

"*He that lies*": *Poor Richard's Almanack,* 1733, BFP.

"*This man*": "From George Washington to Jeremiah Wadsworth, 6 March 1797," Founders Online, NA.

103   "*not deign*": Scherr, "Inventing the Patriot President," p. 380.

"*the Duke*": Ibid., p. 390.

"*conjugal character*": "From Abigail Adams to John Fenno, 18 November 1797," Founders Online, NA.

"*particularly named*": "From Thomas Jefferson to James Madison, 26 April 1798," Founders Online, NA.

"*Printers*": Rosenfeld, p. 222.

104   *"one hundred and eleven"*: Ibid.
      "The best skills": Ibid., p. 226.
105   *"the malignant"*: Ibid., p. 228.
      "Benny continues": Ibid., p. 231.
      "to be by her": Benjamin Franklin Bache, Last Will and Testament, APS.
      "Philadelphia at this time": Rosenfeld, p. 232.
      "The printer is dead": Ibid., p. 234.
      "maintaining the republican ascendancy": "From Thomas Jefferson to William Duane, 25 July 1811," Founders Online, NA.
      "I have often heard": "From John Adams to Benjamin Rush, 23 June 1807," Founders Online, NA.
106   "The Freedom": *General Advertiser*, Oct. 2, 1790. Benny inherited his grandfather's propensity for borrowing other writers' words. The *"Bulwark"* line first appeared in section 12 of the Virginia Declaration of Rights (1776), largely penned by George Mason.

6. *"A name that will disappear with him"*

107   *only one American:* Larkin, p. 6.
      nearly 900,000: The 1800 census counted 5,308,483 Americans, including 893,602 slaves and 3,210 residents of the newly created District of Columbia. *Return of the Whole Number of Persons Within the Several Districts of the United States,* https://www2.census.gov/library/publications/decennial/1800/1800-returns.pdf.
      barnyard and privy: Larkin, p. 157.
108   *one large delinquency:* Dr. Franklin's Legacy Account Ledger No. 1, 1791–1870, p. 16, APS.
      bakers and glaziers: Ibid., p. 11.
      "Thomas S. Eayres": "Thomas Stevens Eayres," RootsWeb, http://freepages.rootsweb.com/~silversmiths/genealogy/makers/silversmiths/69553.htm.
      as many hatters: Dr. Franklin's Legacy Account Ledger No. 1, 1791–1870, pp. 26–33, APS.
      producing "superfluities": Letter to Benjamin Vaughan, July 26, 1784, BFP.
      command high prices: See, for example, an 1805 silver teapot on auction for $1,950 on eBay in August 2021, https://www.ebay.com/itm/224415840177, and a teapot and sugar container that sold for $6,900 in 2011, https://www.cottoneauctions.com/lots/4888/liberty-browne-sterling-silver-coffee-pot-sugar-philadelphia-pa-18th-cent.
109   *which with interest:* Dr. Franklin's Legacy Bond Book No. 1, 1792–1828, p. 45, APS.
      the powerful body's president: "Browne, Liberty," A New Nation Votes, https://elections.lib.tufts.edu/catalog/BL0065.

John Clawges Jr.: Dr. Franklin's Legacy Bond Book No. 1, 1792–1828, p. 32, APS.

Charles Wells: Franklin Financial Records, vol. 5, BCA.

one historian recorded: State Street Trust Company, p. 11.

including Tremont: Ibid.

"of the first Magnitude": Letter from John Fitch, Oct. 12, 1785, BFP.

110 *"a description":* "To Thomas Jefferson from Eli Whitney, 15 October 1793," Founders Online, NA.

his cotton gin: "Eli Whitney's Patent for the Cotton Gin," NA, https://www.archives.gov/education/lessons/cotton-gin-patent.

111 *"horsepower":* Lepore, *These Truths,* p. 192.

"I remember": Letter to Jacques Barbeu-Dubourg, Mar. 1773, BFP.

112 *"Be sure you buy":* Lopez, p. 226. Choderlos de Laclos wrote this in 1799. He died in Taranto before seeing his family again. A fort near there, Forte de Laclos, still bears his name.

"a slow coach": Henry Stevens, quoted in Bell, "Henry Stevens," p. 157.

"'Tis hard": Poor Richard Improved, 1758, BFP.

113 *"bear the thoughts":* Quoted in Skemp, p. 275.

"with as much": William Franklin, Last Will and Testament (copy), APS.

114 *Henry Miller:* Dr. Franklin's Legacy Account Ledger No. 1, 1791–1870, p. 38, APS.

"'Tis against": Poor Richard Improved, 1753, Founders Online, NA.

115 *"to the Corporation":* Fox, p. 418.

"A biographer's nightmare": Ibid., p. 416.

Stackhouse defaulted: Dr. Franklin's Legacy Account Ledger No. 1, 1791–1870, p. 95, APS.

Isaac Kite Jr.: Ibid., pp. 134, 154.

added up to: Dr. Franklin's Legacy Account Ledger No. 1, 1791–1870, p. 114, APS.

116 *entries for 1820:* Ibid., p. 139.

"But dost thou": Poor Richard Improved, 1758, BFP.

"a complete history": "From John Adams to *Boston Patriot,* 8 November 1810," Founders Online, NA.

"Nations": Franklin and Franklin, vol. 1, pp. iv–v.

117 *American printing:* Benjamin Franklin and William Temple Franklin, *Memoirs of the Life and Writings of Benjamin Franklin,* 6 vols. (Philadelphia: T. S. Manning, 1818).

"All the bells": Franklin and Franklin, vol. 2, p. 232.

"I am pleased": John Adams to William Temple Franklin, May 5, 1817, quoted in Lopez and Herbert, p. 309.

"all the property": William Temple Franklin, Will and Letters of Administration, Oct. 24, 1814, APS.

Sparks learned: Lepore, *Book of Ages,* pp. 253–255.

118　*Athens of America:* Nash, *First City,* p. 152.

called Brahmins: Oliver Wendell Holmes Sr. coined the term in his 1860 *Atlantic Monthly* article "The Brahmin Caste of New England."

"owned by a Company": Dickens, *American Notes,* p. 58.

annual dividends: Bator and Seely, p. 54.

119　*witnessed McLean's will:* Ibid., p. 88.

120　*"All that can":* Harvard College and Massachusetts General Hospital v. Francis Amory, 26 Mass. (9 Pick.) 446 (1830).

mocked "Parents": Silence Dogood, No. 4, *New-England Courant,* May 14, 1722, BFP.

121　*"Until within":* William Minot to John Thomason, Dec. 23, 1836, William Minot Papers, vol. 9, p. 34, MHS.

7. Boston: Grubby Boys and Angel Fish

122　*word* project: Baker, p. 88.

Ingenious *and* ingenuity: Bunker, p. 9. Franklin scholars seem to have a thing for counting. Many have staked their arguments on his most used words, while Bowen (p. 24) notes one researcher who "counted Franklin's vocabulary and found he had 2,168 nouns, 865 adjectives, 760 verbs, 217 adverbs." She does not say why.

"All the little": Franklin, *Autobiography,* p. 17.

"There was also": Ibid., p. 9.

123　*"Office of Ensurance":* Silence Dogood, No. 10, *New-England Courant,* Aug. 13, 1722, BFP. Franklin's biographers are curiously impassive regarding this plagiarism. See Lemay, vol. 1, p. 166; Van Doren, *Benjamin Franklin,* p. 28; and Isaacson, p. 31.

Its bylaws: Van Doren, *Benjamin Franklin,* pp. 75–76.

"When I was": Letter to Samuel Mather, May 12, 1784, BFP.

124　*"I therefore":* Franklin, *Autobiography,* p. 61.

"This Library": Ibid.

"not as an": Ibid., p. 92.

Franklin learned: Ibid., p. 83.

125　*"Perhaps":* Ibid., p. 19.

"The subscriptions": Ibid., p. 96.

"conceiv'd they might": Ibid., p. 97.

"Don't delight": Letter to Jane Mecom, Sept. 16, 1758, BFP.

"I read": Letter to Abiah Franklin, Apr. 12, 1750, BFP.

126　*about "trifles":* Box 2, Folder 7, McCleary Family Papers, MHS.

127　*"You may give":* Poor Richard's Almanack, 1754, BFP.

"Boston trustees": Curtis, p. 40.

the richer city: Baltzell, p. 211.

128 *A descendant:* "Robert Amory Dies, a Textile Leader," *New York Times,* July 21, 1972.

    One of his sons: "Robert Amory, Jr., 74, Ex-Official of C.I.A. and U.S. Budget Bureau," *New York Times,* Apr. 21, 1989.

    "Boston's First Family": Amory, p. 33.

    controlled more assets: Minot Jr. "held more property in his own office and in his single control than any financial institution in Boston, and equal in amount to a hundredth part of the assessed value of all the property in the city." Minot, *Private Letters,* pp. 10–11.

    building height restriction: Kennedy, pp. 112–113.

    "It was the city": Kay, p. 283.

    Minot's ledger: William Minot Papers, vol. 15, pp. 11–12, MHS.

129 *In his audit:* Boston City Document No. 89, 1866, BCA.

    "The amount": Franklin Fund, Records of the Proceedings of the Trustees, vol. 1, p. 69, BCA.

    "I yesterday": William Minot Papers, vol. 15, p. 361, MHS.

130 *"had a salutary effect":* Boston City Document No. 89, 1866, pp. 23–24, BCA.

    "delinquents of the Fund": Ibid., p. 24.

    "I have frequently": George Richard Minot, Oct. 31, 1797, Diary, Minot Family Papers, MHS.

131 *"President Lincoln assassinated":* William Minot, Apr. 14, 1865, Diaries, 1860–1869, Box 3, William Minot Papers, MHS.

    "I love the enchantment": Louisa Davis Minot, Poetry Book, Box 1, Folder 16, William Minot Papers, MHS.

    "the uniform": William Minot to William and Kate Minot, Jan. 1, 1872, Personal Correspondence, Box 1, William Minot Papers, MHS.

    A receipt: Ibid.

    "to devise": Boston City Document No. 89, 1866, BCA.

    "Men and Melons": Poor Richard's Almanack, 1733, BFP.

    "general happy Mediocrity": "Information to Those Who Would Remove to America," Mar. 9, 1784, BFP.

132 *"in the publick funds":* Hutson, p. 576.

    no "other Security": Ibid., p. 588.

    "Experience keeps": Poor Richard's Almanack, 1743, BFP.

133 *Minot diverted:* Franklin Fund, Records of the Proceedings of the Trustees, vol. 1, p. 75, BCA.

    demanded transparency: Yenawine, pp. 51–52.

    began its turn: Hall, pp. 109–110.

    "The great family trusts": Amory, p. 34.

    "the best institution": White, pp. 199–200, quoting John Lowell to Samuel Appleton, Dec. 26, 1834.

134 *once appeared:* Thornton, p. 245.
"*idle 'prentice*": Quoted in ibid., p. 18.
"*sat as modest*": "Sailors Revere Bowditch," *Boston Globe,* June 5, 1903.
"*We are apt*": "Journal of a Voyage, 1726," Founders Online, NA.

135 "*which I still think*": Letter to Peter Collinson, c. 1752, BFP.
Bowditch spotted: Thornton, p. 64.
"*Diligence*": *Poor Richard's Almanack,* 1736, BFP.
"*ye ship-owners*": Melville, *Moby Dick,* p. 131.

136 *a "long line*": Ibid., p. 93.
"*not received*": "From Henry A. S. Dearborn to Thomas Jefferson, 14 October
1811," Founders Online, NA.
"*Franklinian Democrat*": "From John Adams to Thomas Jefferson, February–3
March 1814," Founders Online, NA.

137 *Bowditch first:* Thornton, p. 155.
His clients: Dalzell, pp. 103–104; White, pp. 27, 39–40.
"*Cash invested*": William Minot Papers, vol. 17, MHS.

138 *positive returns:* White, pp. 25–26.
"*the* grappling-irons": Thornton, p. 177.
"*high minded and independent*": Ibid. I've drawn from Thornton's skillful pars-
ing of public sentiment.
"*quite closely*": Zunz, *Alexis de Tocqueville,* p. 328.

139 "*Real property*": Ibid., p. 247.
"*a species of Savings Bank*": White, p. 34.
Nine out of ten: Lepore, *These Truths,* p. 225.
Bowditch, meanwhile, reported: White, p. 53.
"*Gen. Jackson*": William Minot, Mar. 18, 1837, Diaries, 1837–1850, vol. 2,
William Minot Papers, MHS.

140 "*Nature and Necessity*": A Modest Enquiry into the Nature and Necessity of a
Paper-Currency, BFP.
"*It is an unexpected shock*": William Minot, May 12, 1837, Diaries, 1837–1850,
vol. 2, William Minot Papers, MHS.
"*gold beater*": Loan No. 290, William G. Hersey, Franklin Financial Records,
vol. 6, BCA.
less than 1 percent: The Franklin Foundation v. Attorney General & others, 340
Mass. 197 (1960).

141 "*Our roses*": William Minot Jr., June 20, 1850, Diary, William Minot Jr. Papers, MHS.
"*me, as Treasurer*": William Minot to John Thomason, Dec. 23, 1836, William
Minot Papers, vol. 9, p. 34, MHS.

142 "*skilled artisans*": Yenawine, p. 43.
tradesmen earned: U.S. Bureau of Labor Statistics, *Monthly Labor Review* 30,
no. 1 (1930): 12–14.

"Christopher Minot": Franklin Financial Records, vol. 5, BCA.

143 *"Half the Truth":* Poor Richard's Almanack, 1758, BFP.

"leisure to be ill": Thornton, pp. 239–240.

144 *"Child of this":* Guide Through Mount Auburn, pp. 35–36.

"It seems": William Minot, note, Sept. 21, 1844, Nathaniel Bowditch monument committee records, Boston Athenaeum.

145 *"remain there":* Boston City Document No. 26, Apr. 11, 1853, BCA.

two thousand people: Parton, p. 633.

kept the receipt: Box 2, Folder 3, McCleary Family Papers, MHS.

146 *"Carlyle speaks":* Parton, pp. 635–636.

"arrayed in holiday attire": Shurtleff, pp. 75–76.

"Long life": Parton, p. 638.

"Philadelphia claims": Shurtleff, p. 299.

"earnest student": Ibid., p. 246.

147 *"Behold him!":* Ibid., pp. 265–266.

"Boston kept": Ibid., p. 312.

"Franklin the Boston Boy": Huang, *Benjamin Franklin,* p. 108.

"the satisfaction": "Dedication of the Building for the Public Library of the City of Boston," Jan. 1, 1858, pp. 98–99, BCA.

"inasmuch as": Ibid., pp. 100–101.

148 *"It's very difficult":* Jan. 15, 1858, Diaries, 1848–1859, Box 2, William Minot Papers, MHS.

"My poor dear": Jan. 21, 1858, Diaries, 1848–1859, Box 2, William Minot Papers, MHS.

"her candor": William Minot to Mr. and Mrs. R. H. Gardiner, Jan. 26, 1858, Personal Correspondence, Box 1, William Minot Papers, MHS.

"There seem": Franklin Financial Records, vol. 5, BCA.

national press: "Public Libraries," *New York Times,* Jan. 22, 1858.

lists the names: Franklin Financial Records, vol. 7, BCA.

8. Philadelphia: Anybody Could Have Done It

149 *America's intellectual traditions:* Baltzell, p. 247.

150 *"dark, dusty":* Dr. Franklin's Legacy Bond Book No. 1, 1792–1828, APS.

151 *"Strange":* Poor Richard's Almanack, 1734, BFP.

"a warrant": Yenawine, p. 57.

"corrupt and contented": Steffens, p. 193.

152 *"Our Walnut":* Zunz, *Alexis de Tocqueville,* pp. 248–250.

"I do not": Fitzgerald, "John Neagle," pp. 480–481.

153 *"paughtraits":* "No more paughtraits," Sargent wrote to his longtime friend Ralph Curtis. "I abhor and abjure them and hope never to do another especially of the Upper Classes." Herdrich.

154   *One early paper:* Bache.
       could hardly meet: Sinclair, p. 1.
       resemble the Parthenon: See "Second Bank of the United States," in *The U.S. Constitution: A National Historic Landmark Theme Study,* National Park Service, https://www.nps.gov/parkhistory/online_books/butowsky2/constitution7.htm.
       still sufficient: Laurie, p. 26.
155   *"decided distaste":* Baltzell, p. 374.
       penciled in a balance: Dr. Franklin's Legacy Account Ledger No. 1, 1791–1870, p. 174, APS.
       "Franklin had but little": North American Review and Miscellaneous Journal 7, no. 21 (Sept. 1818): 320.
156   *"Historians relate":* Poor Richard's Almanack, 1739, BFP.
       "Happy Franklin!": Weems, p. 217.
       "I have some": Letter to Ezra Stiles, Mar. 9, 1790, BFP.
       "It was [1827]": Quoted in Huang, *Benjamin Franklin,* p. 46.
157   *"I regard":* Mellon, p. 33.
       "try America": Lepore, *These Truths,* p. 211.
       told Henry Ford: Morris, pp. 622–623.
       "the Late Franklin": Huang, *Benjamin Franklin,* pp. 49–50.
       "closely imitating": Ibid., p. 49.
       "early prostituted": Twain, pp. 56–59.
158   *"liquors and groceries":* "George Washington's Last Will and Testament, 9 July 1799," Founders Online, NA.
       "In the state": Abigail Adams to Mary Adams, Dec. 21, 1800, quoted in "10 Facts About Washington and Slavery," George Washington's Mount Vernon, https://www.mountvernon.org/george-washington/slavery/ten-facts-about-washington-slavery/.
159   *($22,200):* In his will, Washington left the sum of £5,000, which at the exchange rate then of $4.44 to the pound, totaled this amount.
       "an accident": "Last Will and Testament of Alexander Hamilton, 9 July 1804," Founders Online, NA.
       finally awarded her: "Alexander Hamilton's Statement of My Property and Debts," Center for Legislative Archives, NA, https://www.archives.gov/legislative/features/Hamilton.
       Adams's will ensured: "From John Quincy Adams to Executors of John Adams's Estate, 30 September 1826," Founders Online, NA.
160   *supposedly rasped:* "John Adams," *Thomas Jefferson Encyclopedia,* Monticello, https://www.monticello.org/site/research-and-collections/john-adams.
       Great Clock: "To Thomas Jefferson from Henry Remsen, 19 November 1792," Founders Online, NA.
       he had sold: "Sale of Books to the Library of Congress (1815)," Monticello,

https://www.monticello.org/site/research-and-collections/sale-books-library
-congress-1815.

Lewis Descoins Belair: "Thomas Jefferson to Lewis D. Belair, 27 October 1818,"
Founders Online, NA.

$260 Franklin loan: Dr. Franklin's Legacy Account Ledger No. 1, 1791–1870,
p. 86, APS.

Jefferson Benevolent Institution: "Jefferson Benevolent Institution of Pennsylvania to Thomas Jefferson, 21 January 1819," Founders Online, NA.

had negotiated: "Thomas Jefferson and Sally Hemings," Monticello, https://
www.monticello.org/thomas-jefferson/jefferson-slavery/thomas-jefferson-and
-sally-hemings-a-brief-account/.

"humbly and earnestly": "Thomas Jefferson: Will and Codicil, 16–17 Mar.
1826, 16 Mar. 1826," Founders Online, NA.

161 *"careful and extended":* "James Madison, April 15, 1835. Copy of James Madison's Will," Manuscript/Mixed Material, LOC, https://www.loc.gov/item/
mjm022939.

Madison worked: McCoy, p. 15.

"I occasionally": "The Life of Paul Jennings," James Madison's Montpelier,
https://www.montpelier.org/learn/paul-jennings. In 2019, James Madison
University named a new student residence hall in his honor.

"a few Monied Capitalists": Andrew Jackson to Moses Dawson, July 17, 1830,
Andrew Jackson Papers, LOC.

"Our political machine": Zunz, *Alexis de Tocqueville,* p. 265.

162 *"poor white":* "Stephen Girard," p. 484. Girard's first order of business in his
will was to free his slave, a woman named Hannah, and provide her with an
annuity of $200 until her own death.

"most splendid": Dickens, *American Notes,* p. 68.

"derogatory and hostile": Vidal v. Girard's Executors, 43 U.S. 127 (1844).

163 *"every white man":* Douglass, p. 98.

"one or two": Horton, pp. 117–118.

164 *newspaper article: Constitutional Whig* (Richmond, VA), Oct. 1, 1830.

"have paid": Journal of the Common Council of the City of Philadelphia (Philadelphia: Charles Alexander, 1837), p. 46.

165 *"By his statement":* Sparks, pp. 611–612.

"The absent": Poor Richard's Almanack, 1736, BFP.

he purchased: Dr. Franklin's Legacy Account Ledger No. 1, 1791–1870, p. 208,
APS.

1841 ledger shows: Ibid., p. 220.

166 *"a handsome building":* Dickens, *American Notes,* p. 86.

issuing new bonds: Yenawine, pp. 62–63.

167 *"Political caucuses":* McCaffery, p. 21.

"Party is the madness": Poor Richard Improved, 1748, BFP.

"Sell not virtue": *Poor Richard's Almanack*, 1738, BFP.

"So well hidden": *New York Evangelist,* quoted in Dixon.

168   *"The grave"*: *American Presbyterian,* Apr. 12, 1866.

169   *"a railed aperture"*: *Philadelphia Press,* Aug, 26, 1857.

"From present": *Philadelphia Press,* Oct. 29, 1858.

170   *The last time:* In 1826, the fund totaled $19,915. In 1855, nearly all of the money was held in bonds, with entries showing certificates for $9,900, $7,000, and $1,400. Dr. Franklin's Legacy Account Ledger No. 1, 1791–1870, pp. 256–257, APS.

paper reported: Philadelphia Daily Evening Telegraph, May 22, 1866.

"The most distinguished": *Philadelphia Daily Evening Telegraph,* Dec. 4, 1866.

171   *"I owe everything"*: "John Test (1781–1849)," Test Family Genealogy, http://testfamilygenealogy.net/Documents/Newspapers/JudgeJohnTest/Files/JohnTestBiography.html.

he received: Dr. Franklin's Legacy Account Ledger No. 1, 1791–1870, p. 27, APS.

won election to Congress: "Test, John: 1781–1849," Biographical Directory of the United States Congress, https://bioguide.congress.gov/search/bio/T000138.

"the dishonesty": *Philadelphia Inquirer,* Dec. 26, 1870.

"The reasons": *Philadelphia Daily Evening Bulletin,* Feb. 24, 1870.

"Blame-all": *Poor Richard's Almanack,* 1734, BFP.

172   *"to be more impelled"*: Quoted in Yenawine, p. 71.

"There is hardly": Tocqueville, p. 270.

9. They Rowed. And Also They Rowed.

173   *"any information"*: Nineteenth Annual Report of the Board of Directors of City Trusts, Philadelphia, 1889, BCA.

"to serve": *Poor Richard Improved,* 1758, BFP.

"saved the city": Bugbee, p. 260.

174   *the interest on its deposit:* Franklin Financial Records, vol. 7, p. 4, BCA.

"For sixty years": "William Minot," Box 1873, Minot Family Papers, MHS.

for his grandson: At Harvard, Henry Davis Minot became close with Teddy Roosevelt, with whom he shared an interest in birding. Their bond compelled Minot, in a letter addressed "Dearest Ted," to urge the nineteen-year-old Roosevelt to stop his drunken flirting at parties and grow up, "because," as he wrote, "you are capable of filling a high position, and of exerting a high influence." Dec. 1879, Box 1, Henry Davis Minot Papers, MHS. Minot rose to become a director of James J. Hill's Great Northern Railway. As a child, I often walked its tracks, which ran through the cornfields behind my Minnesota home, never suspecting that they would lead here.

175   *"first, go through"*: "In Honor of Franklin," *New York Times,* Jan. 18, 1890.
      "Benjamin Franklin had": *Philadelphia Inquirer,* Apr. 24, 1890.
      also reported: "Forty Hospital Contributors," *Philadelphia Inquirer,* May 6,
      1890.
176   *"Do we"*: A Narrative of the Late Massacres, Jan. 30, 1764, BFP.
      "an Indian War": Letter to John Sevier, June 30, 1787, BFP.
      "During the Course": Letter to John Sevier, Dec. 16, 1787, BFP.
177   *"At the end"*: Turner, p. 38.
      "Yes, you can tell": Standiford, p. 281.
      "our railroads": Minot, *Taxation,* p. 6.
178   *"By no exertion"*: "Wanamaker's Blunder," *New York Times,* Mar. 3, 1890.
      "A SCHOOL": "A School Building to Be Erected with Money Left by Benjamin
      Franklin," *Baltimore Sun,* Sept. 12, 1890.
179   *"POOR RICHARD'S MONEY"*: "Poor Richard's Money," *Philadelphia Inquirer,* Sept.
      30, 1890.
      "BEN FRANKLIN'S HEIRS": "Ben Franklin's Heirs," *Washington Post,* Sept. 30,
      1890.
180   *a featured guest:* "Eulogizing Franklin's Memory," *Philadelphia Inquirer,* Apr. 18,
      1890.
181   *"The Emancipation"*: George Wharton Pepper, "The Emancipation of Married
      Women," speech, June 5, 1889, Box 5, Folder 2, George Wharton Pepper
      Papers, University of Pennsylvania.
      "The heirs": "Benjamin Franklin's Will," *New York Times,* Oct. 9, 1890.
182   *publish an essay:* Green, "The Story."
      "In no other way": Green, *The Inaugural Address.*
      "A large amount": McCleary, p. 10.
183   *"an able"*: Pepper, p. 351.
      "In a way": Ibid.
      Brewster won: Franklin's Administratrix, Elizabeth Duane Gillespie, et al. v.
      City of Philadelphia, 214 Pa.C. 484 (1890).
      "not merely": Franklin's Estate, 9 Pa.C. 484 (1891).
184   *"Not a bit"*: Pepper, p. 351.
      "The [Pennsylvania] Supreme Court": Ibid.
      "was sagacious": Case of Apprentices' Fund, 13 Pa.C. 241 (1893).
      The judge "failed": Pepper, p. 369.
      "I shall never": Ibid., p. 352.
185   *"FRANKLIN'S HEIRS DEFEATED"*: "Franklin's Heirs Defeated," *Washington Post,*
      May 23, 1893.
      "As soon as": McCleary, p. 11.
186   *"A secret ballot"*: Proceedings, Board of Trustees of the Franklin Fund, 1898–
      1902, vol. 1, Nov. 9, 1893, BCA.
      "the erection": Ibid., Jan. 1, 1894.

"Many boys": McCleary, p. 11.

"the junketing": Bugbee, p. 263.

187 *"Under a solemn":* Box 2, Folder 5, McCleary Family Papers, MHS.

"it will at once": Ibid.

"An offer": George E. Kirkpatrick to Samuel F. McCleary, Dec. 30, 1895, Folder 0100.023, Franklin Fund Records, BCA.

188 *finally voted:* Proceedings, Board of Trustees of the Franklin Fund, 1893–1895, vol. 2, pp. 43–44, BCA.

The judge instead: McCleary, p. 14.

"If the social": Boston Journal, July 20, 1896.

189 *"God works wonders": Poor Richard Improved,* 1733, BFP.

"A countryman": Poor Richard Improved, 1737, BFP.

Massachusetts Supreme Judicial Court ruled: Henry L. Higginson & others v. Alfred T. Turner & another, 171 Mass. 586 (1898).

"May we": Letter to Josiah Quincy Sr., Sept. 11, 1783, BFP.

"to make his benefaction": Boston City Document No. 45, pp. 636–638, BCA.

190 "illegal and hostile": Marginalia in Protests of the Lords Against Repeal of the Stamp Act, 1766, BFP.

"If it be": "On the Labouring Poor," Apr. 1768, BFP.

191 *"that it takes":* Boston City Document No. 147, pp. 26–27, BCA.

192 *less than 2 percent:* Sandel.

"RESCINDED": Boston Journal, Dec. 21, 1898.

193 *finally dismissed:* Daniel A. Madden v. City of Boston & trustee, 177 Mass. 530 (1901).

Red Sox: Until 1908, the Red Sox were called the Americans. The team moved to Fenway Park in 1912.

"to testify": Box 3, Folder 9, McCleary Family Papers, MHS.

"one of the very few": Bugbee, p. 263.

voted to lower: "On the Death of City Treasurer Alfred Turner," in *Index to Reports of Proceedings of the City Council of Boston for the Year Commencing January 7, 1901, and ending January 4, 1902,* pp. 395–396, BCA.

a single error: McCleary, p. 13.

194 *also agreed:* Collins and Doyle, pp. 16–17.

city treasurer balked: Ibid., p. 18.

overturning a previous ruling: City of Boston v. James H. Doyle & others, 184 Mass. 373 (1903).

195 *"WITH CLEAN HANDS":* Boston Journal, Nov. 26, 1903, in Scrapbook, Box 3, Folder 10, McCleary Family Papers, MHS.

"could not compel": City of Boston v. James H. Doyle & others, 184 Mass. 373 (1903).

196 *"the practical needs":* Pritchett.

10. "My teacher, Franklin"

199   *"My dear Mr. Carnegie":* Henry S. Pritchett to Andrew Carnegie, Sept. 24, 1904, Box 2, Henry S. Pritchett Papers, LOC.

200   *initially refused:* Wall, p. 816.

     "I'll match Ben Franklin": The Franklin Foundation v. City of Boston & others, 336 Mass. 39 (1957).

     "We are here": Andrew Carnegie to Henry S. Pritchett, Oct. 26, 1904, Box 2, Henry S. Pritchett Papers, LOC.

     had spent $600,000: "The University of Chicago: The Early Years," University of Chicago, https://www.uchicago.edu/about.

     continues to reward: Weaver. By the start of 2020, the fund had awarded a total of 10,135 medals and $41.3 million.

201   *"Say, Schwab":* "Mr. Carnegie's Ambition to Be a Newspaper Man," *New York Dispatch,* Mar. 13, 1904, Box 246, Andrew Carnegie Papers, LOC.

     a casualty: Brands, *American Colossus,* p. 83.

202   *"It was too much":* Carnegie, p. 34.

     "Upon such trifles": Ibid., p. 35.

203   *"The battle":* Ibid., p. 69.

     "The amassing": Ibid., p. xvi.

     "on the very field": Ibid., p. 180.

204   *"Virtue was reckon'd":* A Pocket Almanack for the Year 1744, BFP.

     "There will be": Mitchell.

     "Never before": Bigelow, p. 194.

     "You will": Chernow, p. 674.

205   *Pritchett sent:* Henry S. Pritchett to Andrew Carnegie, Dec. 17, 1904, Box 110, Andrew Carnegie Papers, LOC.

     "It should not": "Dr. Eliot Against Carnegie Gift," *New-York Tribune,* Dec. 21, 1904.

     "I regret": Henry S. Pritchett to Andrew Carnegie, Dec. 23, 1904, Box 2, Henry S. Pritchett Papers, LOC.

     "My Dear President": Andrew Carnegie to Charles Eliot, Dec. 31, 1904, Box 110, Andrew Carnegie Papers, LOC.

206   *after learning:* Zunz, *Philanthropy in America,* p. 24.

     "I hope this fund": Speech Establishing the Pension Fund for University Professors, Apr. 18, 1905, Box 115, Andrew Carnegie Papers, LOC.

     "Saint Andrew": Carnegie, p. 295.

207   *"Our college":* Krass, p. 462.

     Boston's mayor informed: Patrick A. Collins to Andrew Carnegie, July 21, 1905, Box 118, Andrew Carnegie Papers, LOC.

208   *"Nothing further":* Thirty-Sixth Annual Report of the Board of Directors of City Trusts, 1905, p. 34, BCA.

"We can imagine": Andrew Carnegie, speech, Apr. 17, 1906, Box 253, Andrew Carnegie Papers, LOC.

209 *"The educational"*: Andrew Carnegie, speech, Apr. 20, 1906, Box 253, Andrew Carnegie Papers, LOC.

211 *"I have sometimes"*: Letter to John Lathrop, May 31, 1788, BFP.

212 *"Franklin Institute has"*: Andrew Carnegie to Charles Eliot, Dec. 31, 1904, Box 110, Andrew Carnegie Papers, LOC.
"It is inevitable": Fifth Annual Report of the Director of the Franklin Union, May 5, 1913, Box 2, Henry S. Pritchett Papers, LOC.
more than doubled: Boston City Document No. 37, 1913, pp. 56–57, BCA.

213 *"The work"*: Henry L. Higginson to Henry S. Pritchett, May 5, 1913, Box 2, Henry S. Pritchett Papers, LOC.
"He that lives": *Poor Richard's Almanack*, 1736, BFP.
"The fact": Henry S. Pritchett to Walter B. Russell, July 12, 1935, Box 2, Henry S. Pritchett Papers, LOC.

214 *agents told:* Zunz, *Philanthropy in America*, pp. 15–16, 22.

215 *"as a giver"*: Ibid., pp. 172–174.
"The Remissness": Letter to Robert Morris, Dec. 25, 1783, BFP.
"Here lies": "Here Lies a Man Who Knew How to Enlist in His Service Better Men Than Himself," Carnegie Hall, https://www.carnegiehall.org/Blog/2011/08/Here-Lies-a-Man-Who-Knew-How-to-Enlist-in-His-Service-Better-Men-Than-Himself.

216 *"May your son"*: Theodore Roosevelt to Henry S. Pritchett, July 22, 1918, Box 2, Henry S. Pritchett Papers, LOC.
again sued: City of Boston & another v. James M. Curley & others, 276 Mass. 549 (1931).
"I can't help": Walter B. Russell to Henry S. Pritchett, Jan. 6, 1932, Box 2, Henry S. Pritchett Papers, LOC.
"In Rivers": *Poor Richard's Almanack*, 1754, BFP.
"You must have many": B. K. Thorogood to Henry S. Pritchett, July 11, 1938, Box 2, Henry S. Pritchett Papers, LOC.
"I have gone": Henry S. Pritchett to B. K. Thorogood, Aug. 8, 1938, Box 2, Henry S. Pritchett Papers, LOC.

217 *"A penny sav'd"*: Celia Single, *Pennsylvania Gazette*, July 24, 1732.
"The ideal": *New York Times*, May 22, 1938.

218 *"horribly smug"*: Williams, pp. 155–156.
"dry little": Lawrence, pp. 29, 168.
"No interest": Melville, *Israel Potter*, pp. 473–474. In London, Melville lived a few doors down from Franklin's former town house by the Thames. A blue plaque marks the house at 25 Craven Street.
"I do not like him": Lawrence, pp. 16, 19–21.

219 *"study electricity"*: Fitzgerald, *The Great Gatsby*, pp. 173–174.

"The Morning Question": Franklin, *Autobiography*, p. 68.

220   *Franklin's money was offered*: Yenawine, p. 119.

"As I had": Pepper, p. 229.

"The simple fact": Ibid., p. 137.

221   *became the first*: Baltzell, p. 414.

he raised $5.1 million: "Mission and History," Franklin Institute, https://www.fi
.edu/about-us/mission-history.

"Although the architect": Pepper, p. 230.

222   *"all-pervading curiosity"*: Fraser.

"As my life": Pepper, p. 253.

11. Turning the Tap

223   *Historians such as*: "Scotching a Calumny," *New York Times*, Sept. 18, 1938.

224   *"I was the only"*: Walter A. Lyon, interview by Ann Lyon, Feb. 23, 2010, part 1, Highmark Blue Shield Living Legacy Series, Harrisburg, PA.

225   *"'Strike?'"*: Ibid., part 4.

226   *"to suggest"*: Master's Discussion of Testimony, pp. 5–6, Orphans' Court Division, Court of Common Pleas, City of Philadelphia, 1939, PCA. In his memoir, Pepper noted the irony of ruling in behalf of a court that decades earlier had ruled against his petition because it lacked jurisdiction. Pepper, pp. 351–352.

"The City": *Philadelphia Evening Bulletin*, Feb. 28, 1948.

starter home then cost: Yenawine, p. 120.

227   *"a very profitable"*: Franklin, *Autobiography*, p. 50.

His shop became: Arbour, pp. 24–25.

"When you're": *Poor Richard Improved*, 1748, BFP.

personally underwrote: Nolan.

"the beste of the flower": Letter from Deborah Franklin, Nov. 3, 1765, BFP.

228   *"without regard"*: "Franklin Loan Fund Liberalized by Court," *Philadelphia Inquirer*, May 2, 1949.

"The 1950s": Lyon interview, part 7.

Clark demonstrated: "Mayor Clark's Schedule," memo, Dec. 13, 1954, placed inside Dr. Franklin's Legacy Bond-Book No. 1, APS.

candidly admitted: Yenawine, p. 123.

229   *commissioned a study*: Ibid., p. 124.

"one generation": "To James Madison from Thomas Jefferson, 6 September 1789," Founders Online, NA.

The city argued: Girard College Trusteeship, 391 Pa. 434 (1958); Commonwealth of Pennsylvania v. Brown, 270 F. Supp. 782 (E.D. Pa. 1967).

230   *"It may be"*: Hendershot.

231   *"the principal":* The Franklin Foundation v. City of Boston & others, 336 Mass.
      39 (1957).
      ceremoniously planted: "A 250th Birthday for Ben," *Life,* Jan. 9, 1956.
      "a great need": Fenton, "Court Getting Bid on Franklin Will."
      approved an act: Massachusetts Acts and Resolves, 1958, chap. 596.
      "We observe": The Franklin Foundation v. Attorney General & others, 340
      Mass. 197 (1960).

232   *"must be upon the whole":* Letter to Thomas Bond, Feb. 5, 1772, BFP.
      "FRANKLIN'S FUND FREED": Fenton, "Franklin's Fund Freed by Court."
      an interest rate: "Franklin Fund Loans," *New England Journal of Medicine* 267,
      no. 9 (1962): 461–462.
      "he's a Fool": Poor Richard's Almanack, 1733, BFP.

233   *One-quarter:* Yenawine, p. 106.
      "Since it was": Ibid., quoting Records of the Franklin Foundation, Report of
      the Loan Committee, June 12, 1979.
      had approved: The Franklin Foundation v. Collector-Treasurer of Boston &
      others, 344 Mass. 573 (1962).
      "Hopefully": Louis J. Dunham, Annual Report of the Director, Franklin Insti-
      tute of Boston, Oct. 22, 1968.
      "We stand": Quoted in Yenawine, p. 107.
      More acts: Massachusetts House Doc. 5503, 1977.

234   *highest court agreed:* Opinion of the Justices to the House of Representatives,
      374 Mass. 843 (1978).
      "though the wit": Melville, *Moby Dick,* p. 189.
      "Anything related": Lyon interview, part 7.

235   *"FRANKLIN TRUST FUND":* "Franklin Trust Fund $16 Million Short of Ben's
      Vision," *Harrisburg Patriot,* Aug. 22, 1974.
      court-approved adjustments: The adjustments occurred in 1963, 1966, and
      1970.
      "I believe": Assistant Secretary Ruth J. Armour to Alfred Tamerin, Apr. 16,
      1969, APS.
      a little over half: Annual Report of the Benjamin Franklin Fund, 1973, in Wal-
      ter Lyon Papers, PSA.

236   *underwrote first-time buyers:* Ferrick, "Some Fear Franklin's Fund."
      "All of the banks": Author interview with Roy Goodman, Sept. 4, 2014.

237   *"there was doubt":* Wilson Oberdorfer to Walter Lyon, Nov. 14, 1974, Walter
      Lyon Papers, PSA.
      "I am indeed": Walter Lyon to Wilson Oberdorfer, Dec. 26, 1974, Walter Lyon
      Papers, PSA.
      "sensitivity to the problems": Walter Lyon to Howard Scott, July 27, 1979, Wal-
      ter Lyon Papers, PSA.

"non-point": Walter Lyon to Joan Nicholson, Dec. 17, 1979, Walter Lyon Papers, PSA.

238 *"Benjamin Franklin may not":* "Franklin's Gift: What Now?," editorial, *Philadelphia Inquirer,* Nov. 10, 1987.

proposed a bill: Pennsylvania Senate Bill 1135, June 1989, Walter Lyon Papers, PSA.

Lyon sent: Walter Lyon to Terry Fabian, Jan. 26, 1990, Walter Lyon Papers, PSA.

"It does not": Mayor Stephen R. Reed to Hon. John J. Schumaker, Feb. 2, 1990, Walter Lyon Papers, PSA.

239 *supporting Lyon's idea:* Pennsylvania House Bill 2483, Apr. 24, 1990, Walter Lyon Papers, PSA.

"closely aligned": State Representative John H. Broujos, "This week in Harrisburg," June 4, 1990, Walter Lyon Papers, PSA.

"I am dismayed": Walter Lyon to Hon. D. Michael Fisher, Oct. 2, 1990, Walter Lyon Papers, PSA.

12. *"We finally got it away from those bastards"*

240 *"I must admit":* Hon. D. Michael Fisher to Walter Lyon, Oct. 15, 1990, Walter Lyon Papers, PSA.

to sponsor it: Enda.

"FRANKLIN'S WILL SPLITS": Ibid.

241 *"If I were":* Ferrick, "Some Fear Franklin's Fund."

"One, that it": Ibid.

Boston's "1890 distribution": "Franklin's Gift, Compounded," editorial, *New York Times,* Apr. 27, 1990.

"If you'd": Poor Richard Improved, 1754, BFP.

"It's a wonderful": Butterfield.

242 *"go into":* Quoted in Yenawine, p. 136.

"diplomacy and communications": Ferrick, "Ben Franklin's Bequest." The scholar quoted is Whitfield J. Bell.

"As a presiding": Ferrick, "Some Fear Franklin's Fund."

243 *"CITY RETHINKING":* Ferrick, "City Rethinking."

"offer some insight": Quoted in Yenawine, p. 137.

244 *At a public forum:* Ferrick, "A Burst of Ideas."

245 *"It was a pain":* DeLeon.

would raise funds: Ferrick, "Franklin Fund Puts Stock."

"I thought": DeLeon.

"Unless or until": Enda.

246 *"When a broad":* Madison, p. 227.

The resulting bill: Pennsylvania Senate Bill 1135, June 1989 (amended Nov. 1990), Walter Lyon Papers, PSA.

247   *"Labouring and Handicrafts"*: The Nature and Necessity of a Paper Currency, 1729, BFP.

    make annually: Participating counties' community foundations include Beaver, Berks, Chester, Lancaster, Lehigh, and Washington, plus the Greater Harrisburg Foundation.

    "There's a saying": Keefer.

    "If I did it": Charles O'Data, quoted in ibid.

248   *"Lilies that fester":* Shakespeare, Sonnet 94.

249   *"It's fascinating":* Rezendes.

    "MUM'S THE WORD": Lundquist.

    "might be": Aucoin.

250   *"only public institute":* Author interview with Richard D'Onofrio, Aug. 8, 2017.

251   *"I looked at":* Author interview with Richard Allen, Aug. 8, 2017.

252   *"In a decision":* Nealon.

    an appropriations bill: Massachusetts Acts and Resolves, 1993, chap. 495, sect. 127.

253   *"contributions to the community":* "An Order to Distribute Funds Bequeathed to the Disposition of the City of Boston by Benjamin Franklin," memo from Mayor Thomas M. Menino to the Boston City Council, Apr. 4, 1994, Franklin Fund Records, BCA.

    "We finally": D'Onofrio interview.

13. Benjamin Franklin's Return

254   *"drowned in":* Letter to Jacques Barbeu-Dubourg, Apr. 1773, BFP. Translation from French by the author.

255   *employ more people:* Theis.

    1756 tax register: Lemay, vol. 3, p. 629.

    the country's fifty: "The 50 Richest Americans Are Worth as Much as the Poorest 165 Million," *Bloomberg,* https://www.bloomberg.com/news/articles/2020-10-08/top-50-richest-people-in-the-us-are-worth-as-much-as-poorest-165-million.

    "An enormous": "Revisions of the Pennsylvania Declaration of Rights," Founders Online, NA.

256   *half the American workforce:* Noguchi.

    "useful art": "Information to Those Who Would Remove to America," Founders Online, NA.

    credentialism: Sandel. The idea is not new. See Fallows, from thirty-five years earlier.

    "honest job": Smith.

258   *"We educate":* Author interview with Anthony Benoit, Aug. 9, 2017.

    "My favorite": Walker.

259   *"The fundamentals":* Author interview with Anthony Benoit, Feb. 6, 2020.

260   *"This is an area":* Tiernan.
262   *"the apprenticeship model":* Alexander Acosta, quoted in Morath.
      "BEIJING INVESTS": Areddy.
      commissioned a task force: "Inflection Point 2017–18. Supply, Demand and the
      Future of Work in the Pittsburgh Region," Allegheny Conference on Com-
      munity Development, slide show, https://www.alleghenyconference.org/be
      yondinflectionpoint/.
263   *"TIRED OF YOUR CUBICLE?":* Hannon.
265   *"The problem":* Andreessen.
      Connecticut couple: Sullivan.
266   *"He that hath": Poor Richard Improved,* 1758, BFP.
267   *"But another":* Letter to Mary Stevenson Hewson, May 6, 1786, BFP.
268   *"I have some reason":* Letter to George Whatley, May 23, 1785, BFP.

Bibliography

Adams, John. *The Works of John Adams.* 10 vols. Boston: Little and Brown, 1850–1856.

Aldridge, Alfred Owen. *Franklin and His French Contemporaries.* New York: New York University Press, 1957.

Allinson, Edward P., and Boise Penrose. *Philadelphia, 1681–1887.* Baltimore: Johns Hopkins University Press, 1887.

Amory, Cleveland. *The Proper Bostonians.* New York: Dutton, 1955.

Andreessen, Marc. "It's Time to Build." Blog post. Andreessen Horowitz, Apr. 18, 2020, https://a16z.com/2020/04/18/its-time-to-build/.

Arbour, Keith. *Benjamin Franklin's First Government Printing: The Pennsylvania General Loan Office Mortgage Register of 1729, and Subsequent Franklin Mortgage Registers and Bonds.* Transactions of the American Philosophical Society, n.s., 89, no. 5. Philadelphia: American Philosophical Society, 1999.

Areddy, James T. "Beijing Invests in a New Workforce." *Wall Street Journal,* Dec. 5, 2019.

Aucoin, Don. "Ben's Spectacles: For Farsightedness," *Boston Globe,* July 4, 1991.

Bache, A. D. "Attempt to Fix the Date of Dr. Franklin's Observation, in Relation to the North-East Storms of the Atlantic States." *Journal of the Franklin Institute* 16, no. 5 (Nov. 1833): 300–303.

Baetjer, Katharine. "Benjamin Franklin's Daughter." *Metropolitan Museum Journal* 38 (2003).

Baker, Jennifer J. *Securing the Commonwealth.* Baltimore: Johns Hopkins University Press, 2005.

Baltzell, E. Digby. *Puritan Boston and Quaker Philadelphia.* New York: Free Press, 1979.

Bator, Thomas E., and Heidi A. Seely. *The Boston Trustee.* Boston: David R. Godine, 2015.

Bell, Whitfield J. "Henry Stevens, His Uncle Samuel, and the Franklin Papers." *Proceedings of the Massachusetts Historical Society* 72 (Oct. 1957–Dec. 1960): 143–211.

———. *Benjamin Franklin on Philanthropy.* Philadelphia: American Philosophical Society, 2006.

Bigelow, Poultney. *Seventy Summers.* New York: Longmans, Green, 1925.

Bowen, Catherine Drinker. *The Most Dangerous Man in America.* Boston: Little, Brown, 1974.

Brands, H. W. *The First American.* New York: Anchor, 2000.

———. *American Colossus.* New York: Anchor, 2010.

Bremner, Robert H. *Giving.* New Brunswick, NJ: Transaction, 2000.

Bugbee, James M. "Memoir of Samuel Foster McCleary." *Proceedings of the Massachusetts Historical Society* 15 (1901–1902): 255–263.

Bunker, Nick. *Young Benjamin Franklin.* New York: Knopf, 2018.

Butterfield, Fox. "From Ben Franklin, a Gift That's Worth Two Fights." *New York Times,* Apr. 21, 1990.

Callahan, David. *The Givers.* New York: Knopf, 2017.

Carnegie, Andrew. *The Autobiography of Andrew Carnegie.* Boston: Northeastern University Press, 1986.

Chaplin, Joyce E. *The First Scientific American.* New York: Basic Books, 2006.

Chernow, Ron. *Titan: The Life of John D. Rockefeller, Sr.* New York: Vintage, 2004.

Clifford, Catherine. "Bill Gates, Jeff Bezos and Warren Buffett Have More Wealth Than Half the Population of the US Combined." CNBC.com, Nov. 9, 2017.

Cobbett, William. *Porcupine's Works.* Vol. 7. London: Cobbett and Morgan, 1801.

Collins, Patrick A., and James H. Doyle. *History of the Franklin Fund.* Boston: Municipal Printing. Office, 1902.

Curtis, Charles P. "Manners and Customs of the Boston Trustee." *ABA Section Real Property, Probate and Trust Law Proceedings* (1958).

Dalzell, Robert F., Jr. *Enterprising Elite.* New York: Norton, 1993.

DeFeo, Christian. "Benjamin Franklin: The Founding Father of Open Source?," Elsevier.com, Feb. 7, 2017.

Defoe, Daniel. *Robinson Crusoe.* New York: Signet Classics, 2008.

DeLeon, Clark. "Divvying Up Ben: Let's Try for 200 More." *Philadelphia Inquirer,* Feb. 7, 1993.

Dexter, Franklin B., ed. *Literary Diary of Ezra Stiles.* New York: C. Scribner's Sons, 1901.

Dickens, Charles. *Great Expectations.* London: Penguin, 2003.

———. *American Notes.* Mineola, NY: Dover, 2017.

Diller, Theodore, ed. *Franklin's Contribution to Medicine.* New York: Huntington, 1912.

Dixon, Mark. "How Franklin's Grave Became a Monument and Philadelphians Were Persuaded to Like It." Hidden City, Apr. 19, 2017.

Douglass, Frederick. *Life and Times of Frederick Douglass*. Beverly, MA: Voyageur Press, 2016.

Ehrlich, Pamela. "The Royal Academy of Sciences' Bust of Benjamin Franklin." *Antiques and Fine Art*, Sept. 2016.

Eighmey, Rae Katherine. *Stirring the Pot with Benjamin Franklin*. Washington, DC: Smithsonian Books, 2018.

Ellis, Joseph J. *Founding Brothers*. New York: Vintage, 2000.

Enda, Jodi. "Franklin's Will Splits Legislature." *Philadelphia Inquirer*, Oct. 2, 1990.

Fallows, James. "The Case Against Credentialism." *Atlantic Monthly*, Dec. 1985.

Fenton, John H. "Court Getting Bid on Franklin Will." *New York Times*, Feb. 2, 1958.

———. "Franklin's Fund Freed by Court." *New York Times*, Mar. 21, 1962.

Ferrick, Thomas, Jr. "Ben Franklin's Bequest Has Put Two Cities to the Test." *Philadelphia Inquirer*, Oct. 25, 1987.

———. "Some Fear Franklin's Fund Will Be Philadelphia's Folly." *Philadelphia Inquirer*, Jan. 14, 1990.

———. "City Rethinking Its Use of $500,000 Franklin Fund." *Philadelphia Inquirer*, Jan. 18, 1990.

———. "A Burst of Ideas to Make Ben Proud." *Philadelphia Inquirer*, Apr. 3, 1990.

———. "Franklin Fund Puts Stock in Trades." *Philadelphia Inquirer*, Apr. 18, 1990.

Fitzgerald, F. Scott. *The Great Gatsby*. New York: Simon and Schuster, 2003.

Fitzgerald, T. "John Neagle, the Artist." *Lippincott's Magazine of Literature, Science and Education*, May 1868.

Fox, Robert. "The John Scott Medal." *Proceedings of the American Philosophical Society* 112, no. 6 (Dec. 9, 1968).

Franklin, Benjamin. *The Autobiography of Benjamin Franklin*. Mineola, NY: Dover, 1996.

Franklin, Benjamin, and William Temple Franklin. *Memoirs of the Life and Writings of Benjamin Franklin*. 6 vols. London: Printed for H. Colburn, 1818.

Fraser, James Earle. "Franklin's All-Pervading Curiosity." *Dedication of the Benjamin Franklin Memorial*, May 1938.

Fry, Jennifer Reed. "'Extraordinary Freedom and Great Humility': A Reinterpretation of Deborah Franklin." *Pennsylvania Magazine of History and Biography* 127, no. 2 (2003).

Goldstein, Dana. "Seeing Hope for Flagging Economy, West Virginia Revamps Vocational Track." *New York Times*, Aug. 10, 2017.

Goodwin, George. *Benjamin Franklin in London*. New Haven, CT: Yale University Press, 2016.

Green, David B. "This Day in Jewish History: 1788. Benjamin Franklin Helps Save Floundering Philly Synagogue." *Haaretz*, Apr. 30, 2015.

Green, Samuel Abbott. "The Story of a Famous Book." *Atlantic Monthly,* Feb. 1871.

———. *The Inaugural Address of Samuel Abbott Green.* Boston: Rockwell and Churchill, 1882.

Guide Through Mount Auburn: A Hand-Book for Passengers over the Cambridge Railroad; Illustrated with Engravings and a Plan of the Cemetery. Cambridge: Bircher and Russell, 1864.

Hall, P. D. *The Organization of American Culture, 1700–1900.* New York: New York University Press, 1982.

Hannon, Kerry. "Tired of Your Cubicle? Try a Trade." *New York Times,* Apr. 8, 2018.

Hendershot, Ralph. "Franklin Bequest." *New York World-Telegram and Sun,* July 6, 1956.

Herdrich, Stephanie. "No More Paughtraits." Metropolitan Museum of Art blog, Oct. 6, 2015.

Horn, Annika. "Benjamin Franklin Institute Joins Boston Program That Offers Free College Tuition to BPS Grads." *Boston Globe,* Mar. 20, 2019.

Horton, James O., and Lois E. Horton. *In Hope of Liberty.* Oxford: Oxford University Press, 1998.

Houston, Dr. Edwin James. "Benjamin Franklin Trust Funds to the Cities of Boston and Philadelphia." *Journal of the Franklin Institute* 161, no. 5 (May 1906).

Huang, Cindy. "Saved by the Lightning Rod: How a Centuries-Old Invention Showcases American Ingenuity." *Capital Gazette,* July 5, 2016.

Huang, Nian-Sheng. *Benjamin Franklin in American Thought and Culture, 1790–1990.* Philadelphia: American Philosophical Society, 1994.

Hutson, James. "Benjamin Franklin and the Parliamentary Grant of 1758." *William and Mary Quarterly* 23, no. 4 (Oct. 1966): 575–595.

Indani, Esha. "Penn Medicine Announces $1.5 Billion Pavilion, the University's 'Largest Capital Project' in History." *Daily Pennsylvanian,* May 3, 2017.

Isaacson, Walter. *Benjamin Franklin.* New York: Simon and Schuster, 2003.

Kay, Jane Holtz. *Lost Boston.* Amherst: University of Massachusetts Press, 2016.

Keefer, Marsha. "Beaver County Foundation Helps Franklin Pay It Forward." *Times* (Aliquippa, PA), Dec. 18, 2016.

Kennedy, Lawrence W. *Planning the City upon a Hill.* Amherst: University of Massachusetts Press, 1992.

Krass, Peter. *Carnegie.* Hoboken, NJ: John Wiley and Sons, 2002.

Larkin, Jack. *The Reshaping of Everyday Life, 1790–1840.* New York: Harper Perennial, 1988.

Laurie, Bruce. *Working People of Philadelphia, 1800–1850.* Philadelphia: Temple University Press, 1980.

Lawrence, D. H. *Studies in Classic American Literature.* New York: Penguin, 1977.

Lay, Benjamin. *All Slave-Keepers That Keep the Innocent in Bondage, Apostates.* New York: Arno Press, 1969.

Lemay, J. A. Leo. *The Life of Benjamin Franklin.* 3 vols. Philadelphia: University of Pennsylvania Press, 2005–2008.

Lepore, Jill. *Book of Ages.* New York: Knopf, 2014.

———. *These Truths.* New York: Norton, 2018.

Logan, Tim. "Ben Franklin Institute Will Move to Dudley Square." *Boston Globe,* Sept. 30, 2019.

Lopez, Claude-Anne. *My Life with Benjamin Franklin.* New Haven, CT: Yale University Press, 2000.

Lopez, Claude-Anne, and Eugenia W. Herbert. *The Private Franklin.* New York: Norton, 1975.

Lundquist, Carl. "Mum's the Word on Codicil to Ben Franklin's Will." *Boston Globe,* June 23, 1991.

Maclay, Edgar S., ed. *Journal of William Maclay, United States Senator from Pennsylvania, 1789–1791.* New York: D. A. Appleton, 1890.

Madame Tussaud and Sons. *Biographical and Descriptive Sketches.* Bristol, England: J. Bennett, 1823.

Madison, James. *Notes of Debates in the Federal Convention of 1787.* New York: Norton, 1987.

Mather, Cotton. *Diary of Cotton Mather, 1681–1724.* Boston: Massachusetts Historical Society, 1911.

McCaffery, Peter. *When Bosses Ruled Philadelphia.* State College: Penn State University Press, 2010.

McCleary, Samuel F. *A Sketch of the Franklin Fund of the City of Boston.* Cambridge, MA: John Wilson and Son, 1897.

McCoy, Drew R. *The Last of the Fathers.* Cambridge, England: Cambridge University Press, 1989.

McMaster, John Bach. *Benjamin Franklin.* New York: Chelsea House, 1980.

Meacham, John. *American Lion.* New York: Random House, 2008.

Mellon, Thomas. *Thomas Mellon and His Times.* Pittsburgh: University of Pittsburgh Press, 1994.

Melville, Herman. *Israel Potter.* In *Melville.* The Library of America, no. 24. New York: Penguin, 1984.

———. *Moby Dick.* Ware, UK: Wordsworth, 1993.

Middlekauff, Robert. *Benjamin Franklin and His Enemies.* Berkeley: University of California Press, 1998.

Minardi, Lisa. "Adam Hains and the Philadelphia-Reading Connection," *American Furniture,* 2014, www.chipstone.org/article.php/706.

Minot, William, Jr. *Private Letters of William Minot.* Privately printed, 1895.

Minot, William III. *Taxation.* Boston: Alfred Mudge and Son, 1881.

Mitchell, Robert. "Andrew Carnegie Built 1,700 Public Libraries. But Some Towns Refused the Steel Baron's Money." *Washington Post,* Apr. 9, 2018.

Morath, Eric. "Trump Risks Union Wrath on Training." *Wall Street Journal,* Nov. 29, 2019.

Morgan, Edmund S. *Benjamin Franklin.* New Haven, CT: Yale University Press, 2002.

———. *Not Your Usual Founding Father.* New Haven, CT: Yale University Press, 2006.

Morris, Edmund. *Edison.* New York: Random House, 2019.

Nash, Gary B. *Race and Revolution.* Lanham, MD: Rowman and Littlefield, 2001.

———. *First City.* Philadelphia: University of Pennsylvania Press, 2006.

Nealon, Patricia. "Ben Franklin Trust to Go to State, City, Not School, SJC Says." *Boston Globe,* Dec. 7, 1993.

Noguchi, Yuki. "Will Work for No Benefits: The Challenges of Being in the New Contract Workforce." *Morning Edition,* National Public Radio, Jan. 23, 2018.

Nolan, J. Bennett. "Ben Franklin's Mortgage on the Daniel Boone Farm." *Historical Review of Berks County,* July 1945.

Ohline, Howard A. "Slavery, Economics, and Congressional Politics, 1790." *Journal of Southern History* 46, no. 3 (1980): 335–360.

Parton, James. *The Life and Times of Benjamin Franklin.* Vol. 2. New York: Mason Brothers, 1864.

"Pennsylvania Weather Records, 1644–1835." *Pennsylvania Magazine of History and Biography* 15, no. 1 (1891).

Pepper, George Wharton. *Philadelphia Lawyer.* Philadelphia: J. B. Lippincott, 1944.

Price, Richard. "A Translation from the French of the Testament of M. Fortuné Ricard." Appendix to *Observations on the Importance of the American Revolution and the Means of Rendering It a Benefit to the World.* London: Printed for T. Cadell, 1785.

Pritchett, Henry S. *The Story of the Franklin Fund.* Privately published by the Franklin Foundation, 1969.

Proceedings at the Fiftieth Anniversary of the Graduation of the Class of 1841. Boston: Alfred Mudge and Son, 1892.

Proceedings of the New Jersey Historical Society 3 (1918).

Rezendes, Michael. "Franklin's Largesse Has Long Reach." *Boston Globe,* Apr. 17, 1990.

Rose, Hugh James. *A New General Biographical Dictionary.* Vol. 10. London: T. Fellowes, 1857.

Rosenfeld, Richard N. *American Aurora.* New York: Griffin, 1998.

Rush, Benjamin. *Letters of Benjamin Rush.* Vol. 1. Princeton, NJ: Princeton University Press, 1951.

———. *The Autobiography of Benjamin Rush.* New York: Praeger, 1970.

Sandel, Michael J. "Disdain for the Less Educated Is the Last Acceptable Prejudice." *New York Times,* Sept. 2, 2020.

Sappenfield, James A. *A Sweet Instruction.* Carbondale: Southern Illinois University Press, 1973.

Scherr, Arthur. "Inventing the Patriot President: Bache's 'Aurora' and John Adams." *Pennsylvania Magazine of History and Biography* 119, no. 4 (1995): 369–399.

———. "'Vox Populi' Versus the Patriot President: Benjamin Franklin Bache's *Phila-*

delphia Aurora and John Adams (1797)." *Pennsylvania History: A Journal of Mid-At-lantic Studies* 62, no. 4 (1995): 503–531.

Schiff, Stacy. *Benjamin Franklin and the Birth of America*. London: Bloomsbury, 2005.

Scott, Walter. *Guy Mannering*. Vol. 4. Edinburgh: Adam and Charles Black, 1895.

Shurtleff, Nathaniel B. *Memorial of the Inauguration of the Statue of Franklin*. Boston: City Council, 1857.

Sinclair, Bruce. *Philadelphia's Philosopher Mechanics*. Baltimore: Johns Hopkins University Press, 1974.

Skemp, Sheila L. *William Franklin*. Oxford: Oxford University Press, 1990.

Smith, Kyle. "'I Made It All Up': Bruce Springsteen Versus the Cult of Authenticity." *National Review*, Dec. 23, 2018.

Smith, William. *Eulogium on Benjamin Franklin*. Philadelphia: Benjamin Franklin Bache, 1792.

Sparks, Jared. *The Works of Benjamin Franklin*. Vol. 1. Boston: Hilliard, Gray, 1840.

Srinivasan, Bhu. *Americana*. New York: Penguin, 2017.

Standiford, Lee. *Meet You in Hell*. New York: Random House, 2006.

State Street Trust Company. *Mayors of Boston: An Illustrated Epitome of Who the Mayors Have Been and What They Have Done*. Boston: State Street Trust Company, 1914.

Steffens, Lincoln. *The Shame of the Cities*. New York: McClure, Phillips, 1904.

"Stephen Girard, 1750–1831." *Social Service Review* 1, no. 3 (1927): 470–491.

Sullivan, Paul. "When a $1,000 Gift Is Better Than $1 Million." *New York Times*, Aug. 17, 2018.

Tamarin, Alfred. *Benjamin Franklin*. London: Macmillan, 1969.

Taylor, Alan. *American Revolutions*. New York: Norton, 2016.

Theis, Michael. "Nonprofits Now Employ More People Than Manufacturers Do." *Chronicle of Philanthropy*, Sept. 4, 2019.

Thornton, Tamara Plakins. *Nathaniel Bowditch and the Power of Numbers*. Chapel Hill: University of North Carolina Press, 2016.

Tiernan, Erin. "Franklin Institute Move Could Boost Dudley Square." *Boston Herald*, Sept. 30, 2019.

Tocqueville, Alexis de. *Democracy in America*. New York: Doubleday, 1969.

Transactions of the College of Physicians of Philadelphia. Vol. 9. Philadelphia: P. Blakiston, Son, 1887.

Tucker, Tom. *Bolt of Fate*. New York: PublicAffairs, 2003.

Turner, Frederick Jackson. *The Frontier in American History*. Mineola, NY: Dover, 2010.

Twain, Mark. *Essays and Sketches of Mark Twain*. New York: Barnes and Noble, 1995.

Van Doren, Carl. *The Letters of Benjamin Franklin and Jane Mecom*. Princeton, NJ: Princeton University Press, 1950.

———. *Benjamin Franklin*. New York: Penguin, 1991.

Waldstreicher, David. *Runaway America*. New York: Hill and Wang, 2004.

Walker, Adrian. "From Newcomer to Graduation Speaker: An Immigrant's Story." *Boston Globe*, May 19, 2019.

Wall, Joseph Frazier. *Andrew Carnegie.* Pittsburgh: University of Pittsburgh Press, 1989.

Wallack, Todd. "Which Bank Is the Oldest? Accounts Vary." *Boston Globe,* Dec. 20, 2011.

Walsh, Megan. *The Portrait and the Book.* Iowa City: University of Iowa Press, 2017.

Weart, William C. "Franklin's Will Again Modified." *New York Times,* Apr. 21, 1963.

Weaver, Caity. "Profiles in Spontaneous Courage." *New York Times,* Dec. 15, 2019.

Weems, Mason Locke. *The Life of Benjamin Franklin.* Philadelphia: Uriah Hunt's Sons, 1873.

Wertheimer, Eric. *Underwriting.* Stanford, CA: Stanford University Press, 2006.

White, Gerald T. *A History of the Massachusetts Hospital Life Insurance Company.* Cambridge, MA: Harvard University Press, 1955.

Williams, William Carlos. *In the American Grain.* New York: New Directions, 1956.

Wood, Gordon S. *The Americanization of Benjamin Franklin.* New York: Penguin, 2004.

Woolf, Virginia. *The Death of the Moth.* London: Hogarth Press, 1947.

Yenawine, Bruce. *Benjamin Franklin and the Invention of Microfinance.* London: Pickering and Chatto, 2010.

Zunz, Oliver. *Alexis de Tocqueville and Gustave de Beaumont in America: Their Friendship and Their Travels.* Charlottesville: University of Virginia Press, 2010.

———. *Philanthropy in America.* Princeton, NJ: Princeton University Press, 2012.

COURT CASES

Harvard College and Massachusetts General Hospital v. Francis Amory, 26 Mass. (9 Pick.) 446 (1830).

Vidal v. Girard's Executors, 43 U.S. 127 (1844).

Franklin's Administratrix, Elizabeth Duane Gillespie, et al. v. City of Philadelphia, 214 Pa.C. 484 (1890).

Franklin's Estate, 9 Pa.C. 484 (1891).

Benjamin Franklin Estate, Gillespie's Appeal, 150 PA 437 (1892).

Case of Apprentices' Fund, 13 Pa.C. 241 (1893).

Henry L. Higginson & others v. Alfred T. Turner & another, 171 Mass. 586 (1898).

Daniel A. Madden v. City of Boston & trustee, 177 Mass. 530 (1901).

City of Boston v. James H. Doyle & others, 184 Mass. 373 (1903).

City of Boston & another v. James M. Curley & others, 276 Mass. 549 (1931).

The Franklin Foundation v. City of Boston & others, 336 Mass. 39 (1957).

Girard College Trusteeship, 391 Pa. 434 (1958).

The Franklin Foundation v. Attorney General & others, 340 Mass. 197 (1960).

The Franklin Foundation v. Collector-Treasurer of Boston & others, 344 Mass. 573 (1962).

Commonwealth of Pennsylvania v. Brown, 270 F. Supp. 782 (E.D. Pa. 1967).

Opinion of the Justices to the House of Representatives, 374 Mass. 843 (1978).

The Franklin Foundation v. Attorney General & others, 416 Mass. 483 (1993).

NEWSPAPERS

Boston Globe
Boston Journal
Federal Gazette (Philadelphia)
General Advertiser (Philadelphia; later renamed *Aurora)*
Harrisburg Patriot
Massachusetts Centinal
New-England Courant
New York Times
Pennsylvania Gazette
Philadelphia Inquirer
Wall Street Journal

COLLECTIONS

Andrew Carnegie Papers, Library of Congress.
Executor's Papers of Benjamin Franklin's Estate, American Philosophical Society, Philadelphia.
Franklin Fund, Boston City Archives.
George Wharton Pepper Papers, University of Pennsylvania.
Henry S. Pritchett Papers, Library of Congress.
McCleary Family Papers, Massachusetts Historical Society, Boston.
Minot Family Papers, Massachusetts Historical Society, Boston.
Walter Lyon Papers, Environmental Resources, Pennsylvania State Archives, Harrisburg.
William Minot Papers, Massachusetts Historical Society, Boston.

Credits

Index

Page numbers in *italics* indicate illustrations.

... it is my earnest desire to be useful to him even after my departure. I wish indeed that they may both undertake to endeavour the Execution of the Project: because I think that tho' unforeseen Difficulties may arise, expedients will be found to remove them, and the Scheme be found practicable. If one them accepts the Money with the Conditions, and the other refuses; my Will then is that both Sums be given to the Inhabitants of the City accepting the whole; to be applied to the same Purposes and under the same Regulations directed for the separate Parts; and if both refuse, the Money of course remains in the Mass of my Estate and is to be disposed of therewith according to my Will made the seventeenth day of July 1788.

I wish to be buried by the Side of my Wife if it may be, and that a marble Stone, to be made by Chambers, six feet long, four feet wide, plain, with only a small Moulding round the upper Edge, and this Inscription

BENJAMIN AND DEBORAH } FRANKLIN.

178 To be placed over us both.

My fine Crabtree Walking Stick, with a Gold Head curiously wrought in the Form of the Cap of Liberty, I give to my Friend and the Friend of Mankind, General Washington. If it were a Sceptre he has merited it, and would become it. It was a Present to me from that excellent Woman Madame de Forbach, the Dowager Dutchess of Deux Ponts, connected with some Verses which should go with it.

[My] Gold Watch to my Son in Law Richard Bache, and as [a] Gold Watch Chain of the thirteen United States, which I have not yet worn.

My Time Piece that stands in my Library I give to my Grandson William Temple Franklin, I give him also my Chinese Gong.

To my dear old Friend Mrs Mary Hewson I give one of my Silver Tankards marked   for her Use during her Life and after her decease I give it to her Daughter Eliza. I give to her Son William Hewson, who is my Godson, my new Quarto Bible, Oxford Edition, to be for his Family Bible; and also the Botanic Description of the Plants, in the Emperor's Garden at Vienna, in folio, with coloured Cuts. And to her Son Thomas Hewson, I give a Set of Spectators, Tatlers and Guardians handsomely bound.

There is an Error in my Will where the Bond of William Temple Franklin is mentioned as being for four thousand Pounds Sterling, whereas it is but for three thousand five hundred Pounds.

I give to my Executors, to be divided equally among those that act, the Sum of Sixty Pounds Sterling as some compensation for their Trouble in the execution of my Will; And I request my Friend Mr Duffield to accept moreover my French Wayweiser, a piece of Clock Work in Brass to be fixed to the Wheel of any Carriage; And that my Friend Mr Hill may also accept my Silver Cream pot, formerly given to me by the good Dr Fothergill, with the ...